OUTCASTS! *The Lands That Fifa Forgot*
– also by Steve Menary

"Outcasts! is a must-read for all football fans" – *Sporting Life*

"One book that might intrigue the discerning reader this Christmas"
– *Sunday Telegraph*

"Buy this" – *The Times*

"Lively, informative" – *The Independent on Sunday*

"Menary is an enthusiast with a talent for getting the best out of his
interviewees and a keen eye for the encapsulating episode" – *Daily
Telegraph*

"Thought provoking questions about the nature of national identity"
– *Four Four Two*

"Menary is an admirably sure-footed guide ... he never loses sight of
the human stories ... a gentle meditation not merely on the power of
football, but also on what it means to be a country" – *When Saturday
Comes*

"Once in a while a book comes along with an unusual subject matter
that captures the imagination and Menary's Outcasts falls into that
category" – *Yorkshire Post*

"A thoroughly absorbing and entertaining examination of the issues
involved, never threatening to outstay its welcome" – *Isle of Man
Today*

"A fascinating insight" – *Guernsey Press & Star*

"Excellent ... Outcasts is as good as it gets" – *Birmingham Post*

GB
UNITED?

British Olympic football
and the end of the amateur dream

Steve Menary

Published By:
Pitch Publishing (Brighton) Ltd
A2 Yeoman Gate
Yeoman Way
Durrington
BN13 3QZ

Email: info@pitchpublishing.co.uk
Web: www.pitchpublishing.co.uk

First published 2010

ISBN: 9781905411924

Typeset in Adobe Caslon Pro 11pt/14pt

Printed and bound in Great Britain by the CPI Group

FOR MUM AND DAD

CONTENTS

Appendices

ACKNOWLEDGEMENTS

Writing this book would not have been possible without the help of a large number of people. I would like to thank the following in no particular order: David Barber at the FA, Malcolm Brodie, Rob Cavallini, Leigh Edwards, Alun Evans, Blair James, Alan Adamthwaite, Ceri Stennett at the Football Association of Wales, Ian Garland, Peter Holme, Paul Joyce, Peter Lush, Richard McBrearty at the Scottish Football Association museum, Jonny Magee, Steve Marsh, Neil Morrison, Christine Wreford-Brown and Becki Middleton at the British Olympic Association.

Thanks also to the staff at Ringwood Library, and to Gavin Hamilton and Simon Inglis for access to the archives of *World Soccer* and *Charles Buchan's Football Monthly* respectively.

A number of people from outside of the UK also deserve thanking: Roy Hay and Ted Smith (Australia); Borislav Konstantinov (Bulgaria), Vesa Tikander at the Sports Library of Finland; Artemis Pandi and Spyros Chatzigiannis (Greece), Petz Lahure (Luxembourg), Kåre M. Torgrimsen (Norway), Remco van Dam (the Netherlands), Dariusz Kurowski (Poland) and Martin Alsiö and Tommy Wahlsten (Sweden).

I am again grateful to Jennifer Tennant for her translation, Andy Stevens, Oli Munson and Randall Northam for their editorial input and in particular to Paul Camillin and everyone at Pitch for publishing the book.

Most of all, I would like to thank all the Olympic players and their families who took time to talk over the phone or, more often, to meet in person to share their memories and make this book possible.

FOREWORD

Before London was awarded the 2012 Games, most people had forgotten we ever had an Olympic football team, and I was pleasantly surprised – and proud – to find out on reading this book that I had scored more goals than anyone else and jointly made the most appearances for the team.

Plenty of players that played for the Olympic team also won full international caps, like Vivian Woodward and Bernard Joy. During World War Two, my father, who everyone knew as Big Jim (I was of course Little Jim), also won a cap for England, but the days when amateurs could still play for the full England team were over when I began playing.

The year that I came back from India after finishing my national service, London hosted the 1948 Olympic Games. Football was tied by the maximum wage then. Becoming a professional did not seem so attractive to everyone and there was still something special about being an amateur, particularly as that offered a chance to go to the Olympics.

I was fortunate enough to get a good job with Thermos and played amateur football at Walthamstowe Avenue, where my father had also played. For all of the amateurs like me, the Olympic Games was a peak, something that we all aspired to be part of.

I was too young to get into Matt Busby's squad in 1948 but four years later I was called up by Walter Winterbottom for the Olympics in Helsinki.

I went on to play in the finals of three successive Olympic Games and although I later played for Chelsea, where I was part of the team that won the first division title in 1954/55, I was still able to play for the Great Britain team as I remained an amateur.

Playing for the British team was something special. I visited places few people of my age got to travel to such as Australia and Bulgaria, which was then a country that no one really knew anything about. At those Olympics we also got to mix with real sporting legends like Emil Zatopek and Muhammad Ali.

All the adventures that I had with the team, the games (good and bad) are all in this book, which brought back very many great memories for me, both of playing for the Olympic team and the players I played with.

In London in 2012 there will be an Olympic team again, and just as when I played, I am sure that all of those players who take part will have one of the greatest experiences of their lives.

Jim Lewis

AUTHOR'S NOTE

The team that this book is about has at times represented England, Great Britain and even, on occasions, the whole of the United Kingdom of Great Britain and Northern Ireland. The United Kingdom of Great Britain and Northern Ireland is a clumsy title for a book and even the acronym UKGB&NI does not bear much repetition.

Where the British team playing at the Olympics was put forward solely by the FA and only Englishmen were considered, the team is described as England. Where the side is drawn from the United Kingdom of Great Britain and Northern Ireland, for clarity's sake, the team is referred to simply as GB.

This book features many abbreviations that are spelt out on first use and listed opposite as reference.

ABBREVIATIONS

The FA – The Football Association latterly representing England

The SFA – The Scottish Football Association

The FAW – The Football Association of Wales

The IFA – The Irish Football Association representing football in the whole of Ireland until the creation of the Republic of Ireland in 1921, and the game in Northern Ireland afterwards

IFAB – International Football Association Board set up by the Home Nations to agree on rules for the game and still dominated today by the UK

Fifa – *Fédération Internationale de Football Association,* football's world body

IOC – International Olympic Committee

BOA – British Olympic Association, previously the British Olympic Committee

AFA – Amateur Football Association, later the Amateur Football Alliance, a break-away faction set up by purists in reaction to professionalism in 1907

PFA – Professional Footballers Association, trade union for professional players

Gentleman – a footballer who plays the game solely for love and *never* for money

Player – a footballer who plays the game for money

Shamateur – a footballer who plays the game as an amateur but takes secret payments for playing

POMO – Position of Maximum Opportunity, a football tactic involving the most direct route to goal

INTRODUCTION

"It would be great if our country could have a football team in the Olympics. To perform at the Olympics would be special for a lot of players. I might come out of retirement – if I'm retired by then!"

David Beckham, 2005

ON 6 JULY 2005, BRITAIN WAS ALIVE WITH NEWS THAT THE world's biggest sporting event was coming. The International Olympic Committee (IOC) had decided that in 2012, the Olympic Games would return to London, bringing the best athletes from virtually every sport on the planet, including one that few in Britain associate with the modern Olympiad – football.

Of all the Olympic sports, football today seems most out of kilter with the original Olympic spirit. A game obsessed with money. Wages, debts, transfer fees all seemingly inflated beyond belief. But football was not always like that. Just like the Olympics, football's origins lay in playing the game for sport, for fun. Most people still play football that way today; the tackling rougher, the passes less accurate, but for no reward other than simply playing the game of football.

Britain's last involvement with Olympic football had petered out more than three decades before London won the rights to host the 2012 Games and the prospect of a home team drew great interest.

"It would be great if our country could have a football team in the

Olympics," said England star David Beckham after London won the bid in 2005. "To perform at the Olympics would be special for a lot of players. I might come out of retirement – if I'm retired by then!"

But not long after those initial heady days, the squabbling over international football's greatest anomaly began. In the Olympics, the United Kingdom of Great Britain and Northern Ireland is represented by one team in all sports. In football, the independence of the four Home Nations dates back to the game's origins. No one was giving up their autonomy.

"The FAW will not undertake anything that would jeopardise its position as a separate nation within Fifa and Uefa," said Football Association of Wales (FAW) secretary general David Collins. "Wales doesn't want to compromise its position as a separate nation within Fifa and Uefa. It wants to continue playing football internationally as Wales. And I must say that everything I've heard from the Welsh media and the supporters in Wales fully endorses the [FAW] council's decision."

Fifa's statutes included a special, longstanding rule permitting the independence of the four Home Nations. In 2004, these statutes were revised as part of a centenary project. Fifa's executive committee discussed the "British statute" but its continuing role was not even put to a vote. Any of Fifa's 208 members can question the statute. A change would require support from three-quarters of Fifa's members but no challenges ever emerged because for many years there was little justification. London 2012 changed all that.

By late 2005, the Scotland Football Association (SFA) and the FAW had insisted that unless Fifa president Sepp Blatter back up in writing his verbal assurances that taking part in the Olympics would not damage their independence, they would not take part in 2012.

With the Irish Football Association (IFA) representing Northern Ireland sitting warily on the fence, but then Prime Minister Gordon Brown advocating a united team – and Sir Alex Ferguson as manager – England's Football Association (FA) were in a politically impossible position. When David Will, a Scottish lawyer and former Fifa vice president, warned in October 2007 that Blatter's verbal assurances could not be relied on, a united team was all but finished. Will told the BBC:

> "There's nothing to stop an association saying 'the four
> British associations have played together at an Olympics

so they can do at a World Cup as well'. We should not take the chance of joining a British team. I'm sure Sepp Blatter means what he says but why should the associations take that chance? I have never accepted that we should take such a risk. It is more important to be in the World Cup as independent associations than in the Olympics as one. For many years there were threats to the independence [of the Home Nations] and those could surface again."

Blatter subsequently shifted his position in March 2008. To end British bickering over the issue, he suggested that a team comprised solely of English players play in London.

In early 2009, the Northern Irish, Scots and Welsh wrote a joint letter to the FA opposing the whole concept of a GB Olympic XI and refusing to discuss the idea ever again. Secretly, however, all four associations were thrashing out a deal. The Irish, Scots and Welsh agreed to let the FA take sole charge and only Englishmen would be British Olympic footballers in 2012.

The pact took the international game in Britain back more than a century, when football and the Olympics combined to produce the sport's first real world championship. Then, only Englishmen represented Great Britain too – and everyone played for free.

Few players desire international football for the money but appearance fees are paid, although not disclosed by the likes of the FA. In the Olympics, commercial opportunities abound and few athletes in any discipline could be described as true amateurs, but no one gets appearance money.

That ethos was the one so loved by the public schools and their alumni that developed and codified football. These were gentlemen bred to uphold the British Empire and often lead battles. A Corinthian ideal on how to play the game emerged long before Baron Pierre de Coubertin began to put his dream of reviving the Olympics into play. In the British Isles, solidarity was prised with matches played to the highest standards of sportsmanship. Should an opponent lose a player to injury, good form insisted that the other side simply take a man off to even up the sides. Matches were not to be played for trophies and leagues were not tolerated.

A Victorian trend for codification saw rules of the game formalised in 1863 and the FA was formed in London to agree regulations. The FA's founders, those who set themselves up to run the game, came from southern England, the universities and the public schools. The FA's first meeting in the evening of 26 October 1863 at the Freemason's Tavern on Lincoln's Inn Fields in central London included representatives from prestigious public schools like Blackheath Proprietary, Charterhouse and Kensington. Those few clubs present, like Crusaders or the No Names XI, were all southern.

Their organisation was not the English FA but *the* FA, still to this day the only one set up with no geographical boundaries. The game was more developed in Britain than anywhere else in the world and England's pioneers were all amateurs, gentlemen of the sport, purists. Men who believed in that Olympian ideal of sport for sport's sake and neither wanted nor needed money to compete.

"You see, it is not worth the while of a university or public school man to run the risk of accepting payment for his services on the football field," said Charles Wreford-Brown, England's captain in the mid-1890s. "Taking wages and presents, a good pro makes about £5 a week all the year round but just think what a public school or university man, or anybody of social position, would lose if he were discovered taking money secretly."

Born in Bristol in 1866, Charles Wreford-Brown is the epitome of the footballing gentleman. A fine all-round sportsman, who later played county cricket for Gloucestershire and chess for Britain, his football career started out in goal before the burly Wreford-Brown moved to centre-half. His skills won him five full England caps and his wit a footnote in the game's history.

After leaving Charterhouse, Wreford-Brown went to Oriel College, Oxford. On leaving his digs one day with his sports kit a passing friend stopped Wreford-Brown. Public schoolboys of the day often added "er" to the end of words. Wreford-Brown was asked if he was playing "rugger" as rugby union was then known. Football was "association" or "soc" and, with a touch of wit, Wreford-Brown added the obligatory "er" and replied that "no," he was off to play "soccer". Football suddenly had a new name. It stuck.

Wreford-Brown loved football and the Corinthian spirit mirrored in de Coubertin's new Olympic movement. Over the years, Wreford-Brown would lead efforts to keep these values untainted, reacting against increasing commercialisation that would prompt many of his peers to turn their backs on soccer.

When the FA Cup had been set up in 1871, the competition was dominated by Wreford-Brown's social elite and their Old Boys' clubs. Winners in the first decade included grand old names such as Old Etonians and Old Carthusians, a club for ex-Charterhouse students such as Wreford-Brown.

Football was also well established in Scotland, driven partly by the foundation in 1867 of gentlemen's side Queen's Park in Glasgow. Internationals between England and Scotland began in 1872. The Scottish FA (SFA) was created the following year – the first of many dividing lines in the history of British football.

The game changed rapidly as more people began to benefit from stopping work halfway through a Saturday. Working men now had time to play and watch this sport that the gentlemen loved.

When organised football under the auspices of the FA had begun, all players were amateurs but secret payments quickly started. By the 1870s, football was a popular spectator sport and clubs such as Aston Villa began taking gate money. Players in turn asked for travel expenses. The sport was drifting towards professionalism in both England and Scotland, where young Scotsmen were being lured south by better pay. The SFA responded by barring these exiles from their national team.

In 1882 the English FA ruled that a player receiving "remuneration or consideration of any sort above his actual expenses and any wages actually lost" would be banned for an indefinite period. Clubs immediately looked for ways round this rule. Ruses ranged from duplicate sets of accounts to paying players for non-existent jobs outside football.

To many of the gentlemen, money was perverting their sporting idyll. Nothing symbolised this ague more than Scotland routinely gaining the upper hand over England in the annual fixture. For ferocious English gentlemen such as NL "Pa" Jackson, this was simply untenable. A response was needed to combat money and the Scots. The answer was the formation of a private members' club for university graduates and ex-public schoolboys to play together regularly and strengthen the England side.

Corinthian FC was created in the 1882/83 season to play friendly matches against the public schools and top professional sides. The aim of these matches was to instruct the opponents in how to play the game and also boost England. Over the next seven seasons, 88 England caps were awarded for the matches against Scotland – 52 went to Corinthian players.

The gentlemen had briefly re-established themselves but nothing could stop the juggernaut of professionalism. Underhand payments were rife. On 20 July 1885, the FA accepted that the situation was uncontrollable. Professionalism was ushered in. Earnings varied from 30 shillings a week at Sunderland to players taking a cut of the gate receipts at Birmingham.

To uncompromising Corinthian idealists like Jackson, these professionals were known as players. Anyone who played for free was a gentleman. In match programmes, professionals were listed solely by their surnames but amateurs' initials were included as a prefix, so everyone knew who took money and who did not.

Jackson even preferred to separate gentlemen from players wherever possible outside of matches. When England sent a squad on tour to Germany in 1909, Jackson was reported as being "astounded" that amateurs and professionals in the team not only travelled in the same train carriages but ate and went to concerts together.

Not everyone was as obdurate as Jackson. Steve Bloomer, a leading professional with Derby County, recalled playing an international match against Scotland, when Wreford-Brown was his captain. The moustachioed Wreford-Brown played in long shorts with side pockets full of money. After each professional scored a goal, the patrician Wreford-Brown pressed a coin into the palm of the scorer's hand.

The social divides were not as extreme as cricket, where gentlemen would often insist on separate dressing rooms from the professional players, but as football clubs in the Midlands and the North embraced professionalism and recruited working-class players, the isolation of the southern gentlemen amateurs increased.

The people that created the distinction between "association football" and "rugby football" and set down the rules were losing their grip, but chances to retain their status were there.

When the Football League was set up in 1888, one early plan included seven professional clubs from the Midlands and the North and one from the South – the gentlemen amateurs of Old Carthusians – but to the league's founders, like the Birmingham shopkeeper William McGregor, there was no place in his competition for these dinosaurs. Football's history played out very differently.

The idea of an amateur club playing in the English professional league would linger for decades but the days of gentlemen winning the FA Cup were gone. In 1894, to sate the demands of ambitious gentlemen who wanted a competition that they could win, the FA set up the Amateur Cup. PA Jackson was chairman of the FA Amateur Cup Sub-Committee, who spent £30 on a splendid trophy. To put that sum in context, a farm labourer could expect £25 for a year's work tilling fields.

That first tournament featured a host of clubs well established in the professional elite today, including Tottenham Hotspur, Middlesbrough, Ipswich Town and Reading. The first champions in 1894, however, were Old Carthusians, with Wreford-Brown dominant at centre-half. He missed the next year's final, when Old Carthusians lost to Middlesbrough but returned in 1887 to claim another winners' medal.

Corinthians sat out the competition, thinking it beneath them, but the Casuals, another amateur club set up for Old Boys from Charterhouse, Eton and Westminster, soon took part. The two clubs were always close (and shortly before World War Two would merge) and an early pact saw Corinth – as Corinthians were often known – standing aside to allow Casuals a clear run at the Amateur Cup, but the Old Boys' clubs soon lost interest in the trophy. Old Carthusians did not even bother to defend the trophy they had won in 1897.

Many of these gentlemen's clubs existed in a sporting nether world, oblivious to changes in the sport, notably the introduction of the penalty kick in 1891, which was deemed unsporting and often simply ignored. "Penalties are an unpleasant indication that our conduct and honesty is not all it should be," an Old Carthusians official told *The Times* after a debate between the club and Casuals before the 1894 Amateur Cup final in Richmond.

When the Arthur Dunn Cup for public schools later began in 1902/03, many of the Old Boys' clubs quit the Amateur Cup for their own exclusive competition, away from the established amateur game, now often full of working-class amateur teams.

Seeing their peers sidelined on the pitch, gentlemen like Pa Jackson and Wreford-Brown, who loathed gambling on sport, saw money streaming through the game and instead looked to influence the running of the game.

In 1886, the FA introduced match fees for internationals of 10 shillings a game. Amateurs playing for England took nothing. In 1891, the Football League first tried to regulate wages. This was partly to pacify the avarice of club owners but also underpinned the amateur game by making professionalism unpopular in terms of earnings for any gentlemen tempted to go pro. Initially, players could earn no more than £10 a week. This was a maximum not an average, and for the next 70 years footballers would struggle to free themselves from this yoke.

In 1901, the clubs tightened their grip. A maximum wage of £4 a week was put in place. That wage was twice what a works foreman earned and four times a farm labourer's take-home pay. Only the very top players received such a sum, while a works foreman and farm labourer generally had better terms and conditions than a footballer. The game also developed the invidious retain-and-transfer system, where players were kept at clubs after their contract expired. Unless transferred or agreeing to a new club-proposed contract, players had to stay with the club – usually unpaid.

A fledgling players' union foundered in 1901 but six years later the Association of Football Players and Trainers Union (the forerunner of the PFA) was formed. Negotiations with the Football League produced a rise in 1910, taking the maximum wage to £5 – on the proviso this was paid in two rises of 10 shillings apiece after two and four years of service respectively.

When World War One broke out, wages were cut until after the war. The union protested and a rise to £9 a week was secured in 1920. International match fees, last increased in 1908 to £4 a game, went up to £6 a game. For non-international players, this settlement was not great. Players new to the league started on £5 a week and the new rise came in increments of an extra £1 per week each year. To reach the top of the pay scale was a lengthy business. The union protested, asking for £10 a week, but membership was weak. In 1922, the league draconically cut the maximum wage to £8 in the playing season and £6 in the 15-week summer break.

The PFA agitated but the limit stayed right up until 1945, when the close-season rate went up to £7 a week. By comparison, average manual workers then were earning about £24 a week. Little wonder that playing football was seen as unattractive.

A handful of talented amateurs with sufficient time to train played in the Football League but with many eschewing the professional game altogether, a flourishing amateur scene developed around northern England and the London area.

Gentlemen such as Wreford-Brown had mostly vanished from the pitch but their influence within the FA produced legislation to protect their credo. An amateur who tried but failed to break into the professional game faced an uncertain future. Players needed to seek reinstatement as an amateur from the FA. This was possible but far from certain. Former Olympian Hugh Lindsay, widely regarded as one of the most talented amateurs never to turn professional, explains that:

> "If you didn't make it as a pro you couldn't even play on a Sunday. All you could do was go into the Southern league with the other old pros. In some ways, the professional game was a bit of a closed shop, them and us between the amateurs and the professionals. If you went in as a mature person, you were looked on as an amateur because most of the lads had been apprentices and cleaned the boots. If you waltzed in at 20 or 21, you weren't always looked on that favourably."

The maximum wage continued to make the professional game unattractive for anyone with aspirations of a decent wage but in 1947 the PFA achieved its biggest breakthrough by forcing the introduction of minimum pay levels. At the bottom, a professional aged between 17 and 18 would be paid at least £3 a week. For players aged 20 and over, the base rate was £7 a week in the season and £5 in the break. These negotiations, which involved a National Arbitration Tribunal, set the maximum wage at £12 a week in the season and £10 a week in the summer. This ruling applied to England, Scotland, Northern Ireland and the Republic of Ireland.

Another raise was secured in 1951 – to £14 a week – and the next year, playing internationals became even more attractive when appearance fees surged 50 per cent to £30 a game. As the austerity of the 1950s passed, earnings were gradually pushed up to a playing season maximum of £20 with a floor for players aged over 20 of £8 a week. Most players outside the top flight, however, still earned less than the maximum set by the Football League right back in 1891, but the restrictions put on the game were slowly unravelling.

Entertainment tax had been introduced during World War One, but in 1957 activities such as football and theatre were exempted. This freed up more money and the players knew it. In 1960, when the average manual worker's wage was £56 a week, Jimmy Hill's PFA made further wage demands that were backed up by a strike threat. The following year the league caved in. The maximum wage was finally abolished.

Football became even more of a free-for-all as amateur clubs used money from the entertainment tax exemption to fuel higher secret payments to players. This had always gone on but shamateurism as the practice became known was rampant by the 1960s. The FA again tried to legislate with rules, such as banning players from signing for clubs more than 50 miles from home. This was aimed at stopping teams that flagrantly attracted the best players with big enough secret payments to make lengthy trips worthwhile, but the amateur ideal was in its dog days; nowhere more so than at the Olympics.

The amateur code had supported British footballing efforts at the Olympics, which ranged over six decades from glorious success to failures that were sometimes pitiful, sometimes valiant.

For the amateur players, the Olympics was the peak of their ambition, offering an often once-in-a-lifetime experience rarely available to their peers, an opportunity to mix with the world's greatest athletes in all disciplines, a chance to travel to places that so many people could only dream of. This is their story.

CHAPTER ONE: ORIGINS

"The most important thing in the Olympic Games is not
to win but to take part just as the most important thing
in life is not the triumph but the struggle. The essential
thing is not to have conquered but to have fought well."

The Olympic Creed

THE PERIOD WHEN THE TOP LEVEL OF FOOTBALL WAS A
game for a game's sake was all too brief, a halcyon hiatus in the sport's
development. The power of money was already sewn deep into the fabric
of the British game when the grandly moustachioed French Baron Pierre
de Coubertin decided to revive the Olympic Games and its great ethos of
amateur competitors competing for the love of sport in the 1890s.

His vision of countries competing together came from continental
Europe, where the development of football was in its infancy. As de
Coubertin's Olympic ideas began to gestate, British football had already
divided. After the foundation of the English and Scottish associations, the
Football Association of Wales (FAW) was set up in 1876 and the Irish
Football Association (IFA) – then responsible for football in all of Ireland
– was formed in 1880.

Regular friendlies between the teams were formalised as the British
Home Championship in 1881. The International Football Association
Board was founded in 1886 to represent all four associations overseas and
formalise the game's rules – a role that the IFAB still carries out today.

The concept of playing international matches between the four Home Nations was firmly entrenched in the British Isles long before a modern Games was held, immediately compromising the idea of football at the Olympics for the British. Put simply, four national teams would not fit into one, but a year before the game in Britain embraced professionalism in 1885, an incident occurred that could have wiped out international football's greatest glitch at a stroke and made sending a British representative football side to de Coubertin's Olympics a far simpler proposition.

After Preston North End had beaten Upton Park in that season's FA Cup, their opponents, a strictly amateur team from east London, complained to the FA that the Lancashire side were professionals. Preston's manager William Sudell, a bullish local factory owner, was nonplussed. Sudell had been recruiting and paying players from across England and Scotland to improve his side for some time. This was, he insisted, common practice. The southern gentlemen of the FA disagreed. Sudell's Preston were thrown out.

Having spent significant amounts of money strengthening North End, the heavily bearded Sudell was infuriated. Fired up with resentment at these high-handed southern amateurs, he rounded up forty or so other leading, mostly northern, clubs that also paid players, such as Villa and Sunderland, and threatened to form a breakaway British Football Association (BFA). The FA's response was one loved by politicians everywhere throughout the ages. A sub-committee was formed.

As the FA's mandarins arched their eyebrows and tacitly looked into professionalism, Sudell's threat was neutered and his idea of a British Football Association dissipated.

The world game's governing body, Fifa, did not then exist and William Sudell's attempts to form a British FA had come to nothing. By 1894, the year that de Coubertin held his first meeting about reviving the Olympics, Preston's former manager Sudell was jailed for embezzling £5,000 from his employers. The British and the FA in particular reigned seemingly unchallenged.

As Sudell was getting used to his reduced circumstances, de Coubertin drew together nearly 80 people from a handful of countries at the Sorbonne University in Paris to discuss his proposal. A modern Olympics had been staged in the Shropshire town of Much Wenlock in 1850 but the behemoth that de Coubertin would create was born in the Sorbonne. In the French university, a decision was taken by the delegates to host a modern Games in the land of the original Olympiad. Handily, Greece was also the home of Dimitrios Vikelas, the president of the *Comité International des Jeux Olympiques* – the forerunner of the International Olympic Committee (IOC).

At that meeting in Paris, delegates also discussed which sports to include and football was on the agenda. In Britain, nets may have only been introduced three years earlier but the British game was on a different plane to most countries represented in the Sorbonne. Delegates agreed to go home and find out whether raising a national football team was feasible. As many of these countries did not have a national association, let alone a team, football was quickly forgotten, although some records suggest a small exhibition match may have been played. With rowing called off due to bad weather, Athens 1896 officially staged just nine sports. Football was not one of them.

Four years later, the Games moved on to Paris, which was hosting the World Fair at the same time. Although 1,500 athletes from 23 countries competed in the same number of disciplines, Parisians generally saw the Olympics as a sideshow to the larger World Fair. This time de Coubertin made great efforts to stir up interest in football and the sport appeared for the first time as a demonstration event – but even in 1900 the game was an oddity for many Europeans. One correspondent remarked that football was even more curious than fishing in the River Seine, which was also an Olympic event in Paris!

European countries were slowly forming national associations – the Danish and Dutch were the first outside of Britain in 1889 and the Belgians followed in 1895 – but the concept of national teams had still not been grasped completely.

The British Olympic Association (BOA) did enter a side but as the IOC only recognised Great Britain and not England or Scotland, the English FA bullishly assumed responsibility for sending a team. The England side was increasingly dominated by professionals, so the FA sent a club side – not out of high-handedness but because no other countries would send national teams.

One of the first attempts to stage a world championship of football was reduced to a farce. The Games organisers then tried to get national club champions to take part, but in France there was not even a national association and the *Union des Societes Francaises de Sports Athletiques*

(USFSA), a general sports club, were overseeing development of the sport. French champions Havre Athletic Club were asked to play in the Olympics but refused. Runners-up Club Français de Paris took their place and were joined by three other Parisian players to play as USFSA.

The other entrants were Belgium, whose efforts to drum up a side resembled a pub team. Top Belgian side Racing Club de Bruxelles had been asked to represent Belgium but declined. The Belgian FA then asked Frank König, a popular forward and all-round sportsman, to find a team. But he failed, so the Belgians tried to find some students, who surely had sufficient spare time for a trip to Paris. Apparently not, so the Belgians resorted to newspaper adverts and finally corralled students from Brussels sides, Léopold Club, Racing Club and Skill Club, and the provincial clubs, FC Liégeois, SC Louvain and Spa FC. Finding 11 Belgians proved impossible though. The ten players that the Belgians eventually sent to Paris included Dutchman Henk van Heuckelum and Englishman, Eric Thornton. Arriving in Paris, this polyglot selection co-opted another player already there, Eugène Neefs, to bring their number up to the necessary XI.

The British efforts were better organised but distinctly low-key. As all Olympians had to be amateurs, no sides from the professional first and second divisions could play. Old Etonians had won the FA Cup in 1882 but that was the gentlemen's last hurrah. Finding a suitable team meant turning to the FA Amateur Cup, but even here a tectonic shift had taken place. Old Carthusians won the competition a second time in 1897 but working-class amateur sides, often from the North, now dominated. Early northern winners included Middlesbrough, Stockton, Bishop Auckland and Crook Town. These teams trained and played in a similar style to professionals instead of trying to emulate the likes of Corinthians, who arrived at the ground still dressed in their top hats and carrying their canes.

The professional game was providing salutary lessons, where clubs found that expenditure did not always match income. The Birmingham and District League lost two professional clubs within a matter of weeks in 1900. Both Worcester Rovers and Wellington St Georges disbanded after being unable to sustain professional football. Wellington folded with debts of £50. In contrast, rich, well resourced and well supported professional clubs prospered.

Within the FA, this helped foment a rebellion among a faction of southern amateur clubs and county associations that goes some way to explaining the choice of side sent to Paris for the Olympics. Upton Park were one of 15 sides to take part in the first ever FA Cup in 1871/72, but their playing record over the next 40 years was undistinguished to say the least. The club won the inaugural London Senior Cup in 1882/83 only to fold four years later. After reforming, Upton Park failed to even reach the semi-finals of the Amateur Cup in the seven years before the Paris Olympics. Exactly why the FA chose the club to go to Paris remains a mystery, but secret payments to supposed amateurs were becoming rife, even in southern England. Upton Park's position as avowed amateurs from the ruling gentlemen's southern backyard would certainly have counted in their favour.

Every county association had formed Amateur Status Committees to battle the invasion of money. These committees continually investigated clubs finances for evidence of under-the-table payments to players, which became known as shamateurism. The gentlemen of southern England would not stand for such a slur on their sport. By 1900, these investigations were constant, particularly among southern clubs, and their findings ruled out many sides. Shepherds Bush FC, West Hampstead, Clapton Orient and West Norwood were all investigated as part of one large probe early that year, when the FA went through 66 balance sheets. No wrongdoing was found but even the investigations proved too much for some of these sporting auditors. The *Sportsman* newspaper reported in early January 1900 that after investigations into London Welsh AFC, "some members of the Amateur Status Committee of the [London] FA have had quite enough of their unpleasant duties." Upton Park would certainly have been probed by the Amateur Status Committee at some stage and a clean set of accounts would have counted in their favour. Another clue to the selection of Upton Park for Paris lies in records describing the team as the first to agree to go to France, not the first approached.

Upton Park, who only played friendlies and cup matches and shunned leagues, did not start their Olympic year in much style. A 2-2 draw was scrambled with the Royal Veterinary College in early January 1900. Two weeks later, Upton Park visited Chelmsford for their annual match, only to be demolished 7-1 despite scoring first. Going to the Olympics held some allure though. Arthur Turner, an outside-right with Crouch End Vampires, joined Upton Park just to be able to play in the Games.

Upton Park's secretary was their Camberwell-born goalkeeper, J.H. Jones, who was well aware that he needed to strengthen his side. Jones witnessed the forward play of Chelmsford's William Gosling at first hand earlier that year and was impressed. Gosling played cricket and football at Eton before taking a commission in the Scots Guards in 1888 and serving in the Boer War. Gosling played for Chelmsford on leave, when Jones persuaded him to sign up for the Paris jamboree.

At 31, Gosling was among the older players in the party – only Jim Zealley, at 32, was older – but the team's younger players were the strongest part of the side. Alfred Chalk was only 23 and a pacey right-half, who played for Ilford. Many of the gentlemen then had time and money to play more than one sport to a good standard and Upton Park's most noted sportsman was Claude Percival Buckenham. A tall, gangling man from Herne Hill with a toothcomb moustache, Buckenham was only 22 but was an accomplished fast bowler and lower order batsman with Essex County Cricket Club and on the verge of an England cricket call-up.

Upton Park's captain, A. Haslam, led these five players plus F.G. Spackman, J. Nicholas, T.E. Burridge – spelt Barridge in some records – and William Quash out for their match with the hosts' representatives to find that just 500 spectators had turned up. The French wore white jerseys sporting the five Olympic rings, while Upton Park played in their scarlet and black strip in a 2-3-5 formation. The home side provided the referee, a Monsieur Moignard. Upton Park were 2-0 up at half-time and ran out 4-0 winners with a brace from Nicholas and goals from Zealey and Turner.

The French made amends in their second match by thrashing the mostly Belgian side 6-2 in front of 1,500 people at the same venue. By the bizarre logic that would govern many future Olympic football tournaments, Upton Park were declared champions as they had beaten the French, who beat the Belgians. No gold medals were awarded in Paris, although one was subsequently awarded many years later by the IOC.

BY 1911 UPTON PARK HAD FOLDED AGAIN, THIS TIME FOR good. Their existence would have been forgotten but for the footnote to history they provided in Paris in 1900. Arthur Turner had quit the club immediately after returning from Paris and re-signed for Crouch End Vampires. William Gosling, the club's other new signing for the Games, was the brother of the England international Robert Gosling, but William never emulated this feat. William served in World War One with the Scots Guards then took over the family seat at Hassiobury near Bishop's Stortford after Robert's death in 1922. William was appointed High Sheriff of Essex five years later and died in 1952.

Only Claude Buckenham's sporting career really took off – just not at football. He played four cricket tests on England's 1909/10 tour of South Africa and played for Essex until 1914, when he served with the Royal Garrison Artillery in World War One. After the war, Buckenham joined Forfarshire cricket club in Scotland as a club professional and died at Dundee in 1937.

After Paris, the Olympic bandwagon was due to roll into the American city of Chicago in 1904 but after a dispute with the IOC, US president Theodore Roosevelt intervened and the venue was switched to St Louis. The Games were mostly contested by Americans – Britain and France did not send a single competitor – but football did appear again, albeit in an even more bizarre tournament than previously. The Games were staged in July but, five months later, three teams visited St Louis for an Olympic football tournament in the freezing American winter. Two Canadian sides were due to compete but the University of Toronto pulled out shortly before their XI were due to leave for St Louis after losing to fellow Canadians, Galt FC, who would also go to the Olympics.

The matches played in St Louis were only 30 minutes each way and Galt FC started the tournament by thrashing the local Christian Brother College 7-0 and then beat the other US side, St Rose School, 4-0. The two US sides then played each other three times between 20 and 23 November but neither team could manage a single goal in 180 minutes of Olympian football. Galt were the champions.

The next Olympics was due in 1908 but the four-year cycle of the Games had not been firmly established. After 1896, the Greeks tried to persuade the IOC to hold the Games permanently in Athens and lobbied for an interim Olympiad two years later. This was dismissed but an interim Games was staged in Athens in 1906 and football again returned. Fifa was formed as the game's nascent world governing body in 1904 but was a weak, fragile grouping and had no part in a tournament that was becoming increasingly arbitrary.

By 1906 there was a rigid distinction between the amateur and professional codes in Britain. After the 1884 Reform Act gave voting rights to all males, the massive increase in football's popularity made the game a great platform for the personally and politically ambitious elite. William Sudell was out of prison and moved to South Africa and into journalism, but there were plenty of others like him; businessmen using football as a vehicle to establish themselves as patrons and benefactors to the masses. This patronage could only extend so far and the Football League brought in the maximum wage in 1901 at £4 per week. For future Olympic football sides, the maximum wage would provide a form of automatic self-selection, putting off more financially ambitious or career-minded players.

At the turn of the century, money from football was often more of a supplement to a working wage than a primary source of income. Gentlemen with talent for football and independent means could play on their terms and not sign a contract. They were the lucky ones, the educated and ambitious, who did not need football for money. They were not so different from the athletes focused on the interim Olympiad in Athens.

Opposition to football's increasingly close relationship with money grew in Britain – especially in southern England. The problem was not working men playing for money, but club owners exploiting the game they loved for fiscal benefit. The elite southern grouping last supplied an Amateur Cup winner in 1902, when Old Malvernians triumphed. Most of the Old Boys' sides played together in their own newly formed exclusive tournament, the Arthur Dunn Cup. Some purists preferred to be locked away in their own sporting limbo but, for the gentlemen administrators at the FA, there was no getting away from money's ability to change everything. Shamateurism was so rife that when, in 1903, the Middlesex FA investigated allegations that Clapton Orient – now Leyton Orient – were not a bona fide amateur club the supposed amateurs simply turned professional.

The Middlesex FA had been among the first county associations to establish an amateur status committee and, along with Corinthians, were behind the drawing of yet another line: separating gentlemen and players into different national sides. For the gentlemen, the initial problem was that there was no one to play against. So in 1906, prompted by Corinthians' new secretary Bill Timmis, his counterpart at Middlesex FA, R.L. Holland, travelled to Ireland and persuaded the Irish FA to challenge their English counterparts to an international solely for amateurs.

The IFA started out strictly amateur. One of the seven IFA founder clubs were the staunch amateurs of Cliftonville, Belfast's equivalent of Scotland's Queen's Park. Irish football had close ties to the Scots, who invited the Irish to attend a conference in Liverpool during the 1885/86 season to debate professionalism. When the English declined to attend, the Irish pulled out too and professionalism was not introduced in Ireland until 1894. Gradually, a system evolved that saw amateurs and professionals (often semi-professionals, in reality) playing together with just Cliftonville clinging on to the all-amateur ideal.

The idea of splitting gentlemen and players came from the English but the Irish agreed. The concept of amateur internationals gradually spread with the English preaching this gospel and finding willing – although not always able – converts. In an early amateur game with France, England romped home 15-0 with four goals scored by a young man called Vivian Woodward, who was one of a dwindling number of gentlemen amateurs who also played for the full side.

When the interim Olympiad came round, the idea of an amateur-only national team had progressed from an idle gentleman's pipe dream put together over afternoon tea within the oak-panelled confines of a London gentlemen's club to a reality. Great Britain, or more likely England, entered a football team in the 1906 Games but were among many countries that did not agree with the concept of interim Games.

So the British footballers withdrew their entry along with Austria, France, Germany and the Netherlands. All that remained was a team from the hosts, Denmark, and sides from Salonika and Smyrna (now Izmir), which were then part of the Ottoman Empire and had separate Olympic committees. Both entered teams even though football was barely established in either country. The British introduced the game to Smyrna with matches at Kadköy and Moda. The first inter-city football played in what is now Turkey was between Smyrna and Istanbul with games played in 1897, but it featured solely expats, many from Britain. The first Turk – Selim Tarcan – did not get a game until 1898 and the locals remained a minority for some time.

With few native players to call on, the Smyrna team was made up of foreign nationals. This included a Frenchman, an Armenian defender (Zaren Kuyumdzian), and five players from one British expatriate family, the Whittalls.

Albert, Godfrey, Herbert and Edward were joined by Donald, an outside-right, who also took part in the rowing. The Whittalls had become one of the richest merchant families in the region after brothers Charlton and James moved to Smyrna and established the British Levant Trading Company in 1812. The Whittalls lived in grand Levantine mansions around Bornova from 1906. Most were born in Turkey but considered themselves British. Other players from the team, including Charnaud, Giraud, Joly and de la Fontain, are also believed to be of English extraction despite their surnames.

Apart from a strong Danish side, the other teams also included players from other wealthy merchant families. Salonika was represented by an art group, Omilos Filomouson Thessalonike, and featured another Englishman, John Abbot. He could do little to prevent a 5-0 thrashing by club side Ethnikos Syllogos, representing Greece. The games were all played in the Podilatodromio, a velodrome with a specially constructed bicycle track now known as the Karaiskaki Stadium.

The mostly British Smyrnans were then thumped 5-1 by Denmark, who advanced to the final. In the final, the Danes were 9-0 up at half-time. Not confident of scoring ten in the second half, the Greeks, in rather un-Olympic fashion, locked themselves in their changing room at half-time and refused to come out. The Greeks were later asked to contest a play-off with Smyrna for the silver medal but refused to play anyone again. Denmark were awarded a gold medal; the two Ottoman sides played off for the silver medal with the Whittall brothers among the scorers in a 12-0 stroll for Smyrna.

The IOC never recognised the interim Olympics of 1906 but considers the other football tournaments official events and later awarded retrospective medals. Fifa on the other hand does not recognise any of these tournaments. In Fifa's records, football only started at the 1908 Olympics, when the Games came to London for the first time.

Great Britain was already in the thrall of professional football – the 1901 FA Cup Final at Crystal Palace was watched by an unprecedented 110,000 people – and the increasingly popular Home Internationals. However, the country's cursory involvement in the early Olympic football tournaments had barely registered. Apart from the likes of the *East Ham Gazette*, few newspapers bothered covering Upton Park's contribution. In 1908, Olympic football would move into the British consciousness, when a real national team representing Great Britain would take the field.

CHAPTER TWO: LONDON 1908 AND FOOTBALL'S GREAT GENTLEMAN

"Amateur sport should not be controlled or adminis-
tered by those whose chief aim and interest is to engage
the services of the most skilful players with the sole ob-
jective of obtaining the most lucrative gates."

Corinthians' statement before the Great Split of 1907

Bobby Moore is sealed in the memory of England fans as the only
Englishman to have led his country to World Cup glory, on home soil in
1966. But lost in football's hurtle towards the future is another man who
arguably achieved even more. Back when Fifa's World Cup did not exist,
when the Olympic football tournament was the only world championship,
a dashing young amateur set the standard for Moore, and then did it again.
A young man in love with sport for sport's sake, who inspired his country to
beat the best in the world: Vivian John Woodward.

Epithets attached to Woodward ranged from all-rounder to prodigy,
perhaps even a touch of the playboy, but the most celebrated and talented
English footballer never to turn professional is best remembered as the game's
greatest gentleman. Not only because Woodward would never accept money
but because he was a true gentleman in the wider sense of the word.

The seventh of eight children, Woodward was born in Kennington near
the Oval cricket ground in south London, in 1879. His parents had regularly
visited Clacton-on-Sea, a new, small town with no rail links and then only

accessible by steam ships crawling along the Essex coast. Enjoying the beach, Vivian's parents leased a house and moved to Clacton. During the week, Vivian's father remained in London, where he worked as an architect during the week in Lambeth.

Young Vivian's sporting talent was prodigious at an early age. At 12, he played cricket with boys four or five years older for the school team at Ascham College, where he also began playing football – the sport that would prove to be his true calling. At 16, Woodward made his debut for Clacton Town reserves and within months was a first-team regular. In 1901, aged 22, he had a trial at Tottenham Hotspur, then in the Western League. Cups remained the prestige events and Spurs had reached that season's FA Cup semi-final, where they faced West Bromwich Albion. A number of first-team players were rested for the preceding league game and Woodward made his Spurs first-team debut. He played no part in Spurs' FA Cup win that season but continued to feature in the league.

The next season, Vivian, who followed his father into architecture, played regularly for Spurs and was a big hit. However, he still found time to show his commitment to the amateur game. As Clacton Town had temporarily folded, he turned out instead for Chelmsford. Switching between a big professional side like Spurs and the amateur game did not deter the selectors from calling Woodward up to the full England team. In 1903, Vivian made his international debut against Ireland in an England team that also featured his brother, Alex.

The next year, Woodward went on the first trip by a British football side to North America. The tour by a side known as the Pilgrims, featuring England's top amateur players, included a game against then Olympic champions, Galt, in front of 4,000 people in Ontario. The game was billed as a world championship but there was no winner, the game finishing 3-3.

Football, particularly in England, was a tough game. Hacking and charging were part of most matches and a slight, talented player like Woodward was often upended by brutal defenders. He rarely took umbrage. In 1905, an injudicious tackle kept Woodward out for some time. When he finally returned to playing at Craven Cottage the following year, he was set upon by two rough Fulham defenders, Ross and Morrison. Three days later, ignoring his injuries, he played in an England amateur game against France. Records of the scorers of the 15 goals vary, with Woodward credited with eight goals in *The Times* and four according to Fifa.

Over the next two years, Woodward continued to combine playing regularly for both England sides and Spurs as his legend grew. Cigarette cards were a popular collector's item and no card was more popular than that of the greatest amateur of them all, the enigmatic Vivian Woodward. In 1908 Woodward was 29, and his footballing career would have been drawing to a close, but the arrival of the Olympic Games provided him with an opportunity to test himself against the best in the world.

Whether Woodward or a football team representing Great Britain would have travelled to Italy in 1908 will never be known as London was not the original choice for that year's Olympics. The IOC and de Coubertin initially chose Rome but Italy's preparations proved slow and when Mount Vesuvius erupted in 1906, Italy admitted they could not cope. With just two years' notice, the British Olympic Council (BOC) – as the BOA was then known – agreed to take over. As part of the preparations, a stadium would be built that years later would become a home for itinerant British amateur sides including the nomadic, unloved Olympic football team.

The 90,000 capacity stadium for the 1908 Games was built in a year at Shepherd's Bush in west London, where a Franco–British exhibition was also being staged. The stadium included a cinder running track and a central arena for field events, rugby union, lacrosse and hockey. A number of white buildings for the exhibition were already built and the site soon became known as White City. The organisers wanted to spend no more than £40,000 on the stadium but final cost estimates range from £60,000 to £85,000, some at nearly £200,000.

Most of the stadium costs were stumped up by the exhibition organisers, who also used the arena, but money to stage the actual Games was provided by the BOC. Two months before the Games were due to start, the £15,000 target for the budget was still short by £7,000. A public appeal began and the FA sent a £250 cheque. For the FA that was money well spent as the Games represented a chance to reassert itself over the English game after a challenging 12 months.

In 1907 the rebellious southern gentlemen had mutinied, taking their boots and balls and leaving, seemingly for good. What started as a local issue at the Middlesex FA escalated into a conflict with the FA Council that would weaken the challenge for the following year's Olympic title.

The row focused not so much on the increasingly rampant shamateurism but on the admission of professional clubs to county associations. A faction of southern gentlemen formed the Amateur Football Defence Council to scrutinise the professional clubs applying for admission to the county FAs. The professional clubs resented this interference and the thwarted gentlemen went off and formed rival county FAs in Middlesex, Surrey, Essex, Kent and Suffolk. The amateurs were not against the admission of professional clubs per se but against those who sought to make money controlling football, the club owners.

At the head of this rebellion was Wreford-Brown, who had joined the FA as Old Carthusians' representative 15 years earlier in 1892, aged just 26, and went on to become Oxford University's representative within the organisation – a role he would keep until his death in 1951.

On 8 July 1907 Wreford-Brown was at a meeting at the Holborn Restaurant in London, where his old side Corinthian stated their position on the divide between amateurs and professionals, between gentlemen and players. That view summed up what most gentlemen thought:

> "Amateurs have no objection to professional clubs or professional players as such and indeed are quite ready to play with or against them but they do claim that amateur sport should not be controlled or administered by those whose chief aim and interest is to engage the services of the most skilful players with the sole objective of obtaining the most lucrative gates."

After that meeting, the ex-public school and varsity men of Corinthian seceded from the FA to form the Amateur Football Association (AFA). The AFA took with them a handful of breakaway county FAs, minor associations such as the City of London FA and the London Banks FA, clubs like Crouch End Vampires and Richmond Idlers, and a number of sides from the Isthmian League, which had been founded in 1905 to provide regular league games for clubs of southern gentlemen not averse to a league such as the Casuals, Civil Service and Ealing. Just six clubs initially joined this league, whose motto, *honour sufficit*, summed up their concession to the new order. There would be no prizes awarded for winning this league, honour would suffice. The rebels were not against the idea of regular games and founded the Southern Amateur League, where honour would again have to suffice. With this split, all rebel players removed themselves from the reckoning for the following year's Olympics.

The FA had felt that their own arrangements, such as using money from the professional game to stage the Amateur Cup, allowing amateur clubs into the FA Cup and an amateur international side, would be enough to keep the gentlemen amateurs happy. The FA ruled that their members could not play against AFA teams and a great schism developed. The rebellion was confined to southern England where not all the amateur clubs followed the pied pipers of Corinthian. Dulwich Hamlet were not even at the Holborn Restaurant for that fateful meeting and stayed with the FA, along with many other amateur sides. The Army Football Association also sided with the FA but with 100 or so member clubs, the AFA removed a large swathe of players from the amateur game. Tellingly, Vivian Woodward sided not with the gentlemen but the FA.

The FA looked for support from the Scots but found none. Scottish football had developed differently to English and there was no clique of southern gentlemen trying to hold on to their doctrine. A Scottish Amateur Cup started in 1910 and the first winners were a school's Old Boys' team, but the gentlemen's game did not have the wide base that was found in England. The Scots' junior leagues developed as a semi-professional alternative for players outside the league system but just like the Southern league in England, teams would become dominated by hardened ex-professionals, who made young players run hard and tackled them even harder.

This focus for the Scots' amateurs, as in Ireland, revolved mainly around one club. Professionals usually wore shirts tucked into their shorts but Queen's Park thought of themselves as gentlemen and did the opposite, playing with their distinctive striped jerseys flapping outside to indicate to opponents that they were amateurs. Just like the English gentlemen, Queen's Park – who had been major players in the formation of the Scottish FA in 1873 – initially eschewed the new league; they did not join the Scottish Football League until 1900, a decade after its inception.

By the time that the FA wrote to the SFA in 1907 asking for the Scots to bar members from playing AFA clubs, Queen's Park were established members of the Scottish League, and the SFA refused to take sides. The SFA said it was "essential for the sake of the sport that the area of the dispute should not be widened [outside of southern England] unless for solid reasons."

In Scotland, the game had prospered during Glasgow's industrial boom in the 1860s. Clubs grew out of social clubs held to honor the Scots' poet Robbie Burns or Caledonian Clubs aimed at uniting Scotsmen. Queen's Park represented the amateur ethos but economics still ruled. The Spiders quit the FA Cup after being unable to afford to travel to London in 1872 for a replay with The Wanderers. The game in Scotland went professional in 1893 in recognition of players drifting south to play the game for money in England. Another three years would pass before the SFA allowed English-based Scotsmen into their national team. Few Scottish clubs would have sided with the AFA but the SFA's letter to the FA in 1907 warned of creating "resentment" should any of its clubs be barred from playing profitable friendlies against the likes of Corinthians, who were still a big draw. The Corinthians did not play a single match in Scotland during the period of the split, but the SFA's decision hardly encouraged good relations with the English.

In Wales and Ireland, the game had not developed at the same pace. Five of Wales' players in their first international were born outside of the Principality. Simply living in Wales was sometimes qualification enough. Scottish doctor Daniel Grey set up practice in Ruabon and was soon capped by his new homeland. By 1890, 37 of the 125 players capped by Wales were born outside the Principality and professionalism soon intruded on the FAW's amateur idyll. In 1882, the FAW had warned that "the hydra headed monster [of professionalism] has shown itself in private clubs as well as in the ranks of the association ... Let pastimes, be pastimes, and not degraded into a medium for pocketing a few shillings, or it may be pounds."

Five years before this ominous warning, the first Welsh Cup was staged, but keeping out the English was just as difficult as rooting out the professionals. The competition included sides from the bordering English counties of Shropshire and Cheshire. A Welsh league was set up around Wrexham in 1890 but folded nine years later after members quit for the Combination in England. For the amateurs, the Welsh Junior Cup was changed in 1902 to an amateur competition, which immediately led to chaos. Barely a round could be completed without teams being cited then ejected for fielding professionals.

By the turn of the century, amateurs like the Morgan-Owen brothers still played for the full Welsh side, but the landed gentry and upper-classes were more dispersed than in southern England and the AFA's breakaway had little impact in Wales. The split seemed to have occurred in a prism outside of Welsh footballing life – as did the 1908 Olympics, which was barely even mentioned at the FAW.

The FA and professional English clubs had more money through greater support but gradually the other three Home Nations' associations asserted their independence more forcefully. This was done mostly through the Home Internationals but the Scots had their own, increasingly powerful league. The Irish league was less strong and although the formation of a Welsh league started in 1912, the competition was based in the south and the Principality's strongest clubs preferred English competitions.

Within the UK, the four Home Nations had established themselves as separate sporting nations but not initially outside the British Isles, where the concept of four teams in one country remained confusing. At a Fifa congress in 1908, Scotland and Ireland were proposed as members by the English – but were rejected on grounds that each of the 26 Austrian and 12 German confederate states would have to be admitted. This strengthened the position of the FA, which was struggling to balance the idealism of die-hard gentlemen with bullish owners of professional clubs and increasingly militant players.

In the same year as the Great Split, the FA had finally deigned to allow the players to form a union – a breakthrough that had been brewing since 1898 and was accelerated by the manacle of the maximum wage.

Faced with these torturous divisions at home, the FA had tried to embrace the international game by joining Fifa in 1905. The next year, Blackburn man Daniel Burley Woolfall became Fifa's second president but attempts to organise a World Cup in Switzerland faltered. In 1907, the AFA tried to join Fifa but were rejected. The new world order ultimately admitted the SFA and FAW in 1910 and the IFA a year later but when de Coubertin's Olympians arrived in London, who would represent the host nation was a fait accompli. Fifa was organising the football tournament and only one association from the British Isles was a member – the FA.

In August 1907 the FA proposed that England enter an amateur team and that the other three Home Nations do the same after Fifa had agreed to let each of the Home Nations play independently in the Olympics. The Irish and Welsh associations declined this offer. Scotland's response is unknown but money was undoubtedly part of the reason as Ireland, Scotland and Wales would have to attend at their own cost.

For the Scots there was also another concern. Shortly after the 1908 Games finished, an article in *The Sportsman* newspaper told of SFA plans for a friendly against Denmark. As the Scots, unlike their opponents, were not in Fifa, the article suggested that their team would have to be picked by the only British team in the world body – the English. This is likely to have also been the case for the London Olympics. The minute books of the Scottish FA from 1908 to 1912 are missing but the chances of the Scots paying to send a side south then letting the English choose the starting XI are as unlikely then as now.

Fifa had asked every national football association to send their national team to London – providing, of course, that they were amateurs. With football in its infancy, countries such as Poland and Portugal did not even have national associations let alone teams. Only seven countries entered but the 1908 Olympic event could reasonably lay claim to being the first world championship and Vivian Woodward would be its undoubted star.

WITH WORLD WAR ONE ONLY SIX YEARS AWAY, POLITICAL tension plagued Europe and ate away at the tournament. Hungary were a strong side but part of the Austro-Hungarian empire, who favoured Austria. The Austrians chose not to enter and as a result the Hungarians were told to stay at home too, although the official reason was "financial considerations".

Bohemia also stayed away for far different reasons. Since the Great Split, the AFA had been busy. A pact was forged with the USFSA and the Bohemians for a rival world order. The AFA would send an "England" team to Prague for an international match on 7 November. A tour by Corinthians would follow in Easter 1909 and amateur internationals between the AFA and a French "national" side organised by the USFSA would be played in Paris. This left Bohemia little choice but to stay out of the Olympics, leaving only Denmark, the Netherlands, a rival France side and Sweden. The tournament was in danger of becoming nonsense again.

Whether the French would participate was in question up to the start of the Olympics as an internecine struggle gripped the French game. The USFSA joined Fifa then quit shortly before the 1908 Olympics and were in the process of being replaced by the Comité Français Interfédéral (CIF).

Amidst all this upheaval, the French held trials for 41 players but could not make a decision. In a Gallic fudge, the French offered to bring two teams to London. That offer met with few complaints among the beleaguered organisers.

With only Englishmen to be considered, the powerful, shadowy selectors who then chose national teams were focused on the new amateur side, who would remain unbeaten for 20 matches up to 1910. The Scots did not start playing the English at amateur international level until 1926 but that early unbeaten run from England included matches against the best of Ireland and Wales. As the FA was rather sniffy about standards in Europe, the full professional side was saved for the Home Nations and only the gentlemen sent abroad to play the Europeans. With Vivian Woodward holding sway, most of these matches were won easily.

In early 1908 England's amateurs toured central Europe, thrashing Belgium 8-2 and Germany 5-1. That summer the team visited Gothenburg and trounced Sweden 6-1. Woodward played against the Belgians and Germans but wisely sat out the Swedish trip, when the team's boat home limped into Grimsby 17 hours late with most of the players violently seasick.

As the greatest of all the amateurs – though he would have shunned the title himself – Woodward could afford to miss games should his work commitments take over. In the run-up to the Olympics Woodward did not even focus solely on football. He played as many sports as possible, purely for fun. That summer he played cricket, was a regular billiards player and won the Spencer Club Lawn Tennis Championship in south-west London. Woodward even found time to take up the then new craze of roller skating. Woodward could do almost anything and was a certainty among 33 players named by the FA in an initial Olympic squad in 1908.

Woodward was joined by a number of other gentlemen playing with professionals. The squad included players from Liverpool, Everton, Blackburn Rovers and Nottingham Forest, who had refused to side with the AFA to play to as high a standard as possible.

For players like Birmingham's Walter Corbett, social change, not just the vote but opportunities to join the professional classes, meant that the often dangerous world of football would only ever be a part of their lives. With the legal hacking and charging common, football then was a rough game. With no welfare system in place, players that were forced to miss work because of injuries sustained playing football simply did not get paid.

Known commonly as Watty, Corbett was the third child of a Shropshire printer and as a child moved with his family to Birmingham, where he went to King Edward VI Grammar School in 1891 and excelled at sport. Aston Villa offered him a trial but he finished his schooling before accepting. After games for Villa's reserves, he made his first-team debut in 1905 against Middlesbrough, but subsequent appearances were sporadic. This was partly because Corbett was cover for regular full-back Howard Spencer but was also because he devoted much time to his work at an export house. "He plays football as an artist and loves the game for the joy," the *Sports Argus* of 22 December 1906 said of Corbett.

Corbett was a clever, cultured player – and fearsome tackler – who played in an England trial between the gentlemen and players in Sheffield in 1905. His performance then secured a regular place when the amateur team was formed the following year. Though Corbett was a committed gentleman, like many of the amateurs playing in the Football League he was not opposed to professionalism.

When Villa offered him professional terms, Corbett reluctantly left, but not for an AFA club. He preferred to play among the professionals and joined local rivals Birmingham. His appearances remained intermittent due to work but Corbett went on the England amateurs' central European tour in early 1908 and was named in a slimmed down 18-man Olympic squad after a meeting at High Holborn, the gentlemen's favourite corner of London, on October 2 1908.

Corbett, who lived to the grand old age of 80, played little more than 100 games in his entire life. For players with the prospect of a long-term job elsewhere, a job for life perhaps, playing football was a risk. No one would exemplify that risk better than goalkeeper Ron Brebner.

From Darlington, Brebner played for Northern Nomads – Manchester's version of the Corinthians, a roaming team with no home ground that refused to play in a league – and Stockton. He then went to Edinburgh University to train to be a dentist. On graduating, he moved back to the English capital and signed for London Caledonians, a club founded in 1886 to provide a game for the Scots' diaspora in England. Only players born in Scotland or with Scots parentage could play but Brebner's Scottish university links gained the Darlington dentist entry. Over the coming years, he would also play for Chelsea and Queens Park Rangers and play in two Olympic squads as he roamed across the UK. In 1914, Brebner pitched up at Leicester Fosse, the forerunners of Leicester City, and was badly injured during a Football League game. Ten months later, as a result of those injuries, he died. Ron Brebner never took a penny for playing football but the game cost him his life.

In 1908 Brebner would cede the keeper's jersey to a man he later replaced at club and international level. Unlike Brebner, who never progressed beyond a trial for the full England team, Horace Bailey managed five caps but never gave up his job as a ratings official with the Midland Railway in Derby. Bailey knew that the Midland Railway would provide longer-term employment than football ever would. Still, he risked injuring himself to play the game he loved, first for Derby County, then Ripley Athletic and Leicester Imperial before moving to the city's Football League side, Fosse, where he became the first player from the club to make the full England side. With Fosse winning promotion to the first division in the 1907/08 season, Bailey would be the Olympic number one.

The rough and tumble nature of the football even at the top level is best epitomised by a player from the 1908 team, who was always a gentleman, later a member of the clergy, an FA Cup winner and one of the most infamous chargers the game ever saw.

Kenneth Reginald Gunnery Hunt was the grandson of a Christian missionary to North America and his own father Robert had been a priest for eight years by the time the future Olympian was born in Oxford in 1884. The Hunts moved to Wolverhampton in 1889 and sent their son to the local boys' grammar school. By 1900, Kenneth was captain of the school team and described as "A very promising half, playing with more head than some of his seniors. Kicks and tackles well, sticks to his man."

The school report did not mention his charging but after attending Trent College in Derbyshire, where he captained the football and cricket XIs, Hunt developed a talent for the good old shoulder charge, which was then an accepted part of the game. A strong runner and shot for the school's rifle club, he went up to Queen's College Oxford and played in the varsity football match against Cambridge four times and later featured for Pa Jackson's Corinthians. In 1906, the moustachioed Hunt signed as an amateur for Wolverhampton Wanderers and became a player to be feared. In his autobiography, former Arsenal and Sunderland player Charlie Buchan recalled: "The big, strong cleric was noted for his vigorous charging. He delighted in an honest shoulder charge, delivered with all the might of his powerful frame. He was an opponent, not to be feared – as he never did an unfair thing in his life – but to be avoided if possible."

In 1907 he won his first cap for the England amateur team against Wales and in the year of the Olympics, when he graduated from Oxford, the man who became known as the "Footballing Parson" had the most memorable season of his sporting life.

Bogged down in one of the many financial crises that were then a common feature at Wolves, the club were keen to sign the very affordable Hunt, who would only cost them travelling expenses rather than a playing wage. Wolves then were a mundane second division side unlikely to emulate their only previous FA Cup win in 1893. Kenneth Hunt had other ideas. In an early tie against Swindon, Hunt came in for injured skipper Woolridge and was knocked unconscious – twice. Each time, Hunt got back up, played on and eventually managed to turn the course of the tie. His bravery on the pitch endeared Hunt to the fans but his team arrived at Crystal Palace for the FA Cup Final with Newcastle as total underdogs. Wolves had scored seven goals on the way to the final; their opponents – losing finalists in 1905 and 1906 – racked up 18 scores.

Watched by 75,000 fans, the final was goalless heading into half-time when Hunt intercepted a defensive clearance. Forty yards from goal, he looked up briefly then sent the ball thundering into the back of the net. Another Wolves goal followed before half-time. The intimidating Hunt helped maintain pressure on Newcastle and Wolves secured a famous 3-1 win as the Footballing Parson made himself a certainty for the Olympics.

He was joined in the squad by a player that could not have been more unlike the avuncular, muscular Hunt. That Harold Hardman played football at all was a surprise to his games master at Blackpool High School, who thought his pupil far too puny for any kind of sport. Hardman defied his games master and learnt to use his slim physique to good effect as a speedy outside-left. After leaving Blackpool HS, he played for Northern Nomads then signed for Everton in 1903 as an amateur, while he trained to be a solicitor.

In 1906, Hardman joined Kenneth Hunt as one of only three amateurs in the twentieth century to claim an FA Cup winners' medal as Everton beat Newcastle. The year before the Olympics Hardman appeared in the final again but Everton lost to Sheffield Wednesday. In the run-up to the Olympics he also made four appearances and scored one goal for the full England team and was an automatic choice for the Games.

For clubs like Everton and Wolves the gentlemen provided a saving on the wage bill. One club would utilise this source of "free" players to provide a Football League haven for many amateurs. Glossop North End were a tiny Derbyshire club whose fortunes soared after ambitious chairman Sir Samuel Hill-Wood gained control. The side were founded in 1886 and turned professional four years later on, joining the North Cheshire League. Two years later, Glossop NE were elected to the second division of the Football League, securing a place in history – and many pub quizzes – as Glossop's then population of 18,000 made the town the smallest to ever provide a Football League club. Hill-Wood, who later held the same position at Arsenal, invested heavily. Glossop were promoted to the first division in their first season but income and expenditure did not stack up. For Hill-Wood, there was a chance to try and balance his books by signing some of the scattering of amateurs in the top flight.

Harry Stapley was a small, slight schoolteacher from Tunbridge Wells, whose first love was football. He roamed England, joining schools only after finding a nearby club to play for. In 1904, Stapley left Reading Collegiate School for Woodford Town, where he was made captain, and worked at Woodford College. Halfway through the 1905/06 season Stapley was snapped up by West Ham and he went on to rattle in 41 goals in 75 league and cup matches in two and a half seasons before Hill-Wood swooped. Stapley was taken on by Hill-Wood as a private football and cricket tutor for his three sons and signed for Glossop with his brother Will. Both Stapleys remained amateurs and Harry would go to the Olympics.

With Corinthians siding with the AFA, none of their players could be considered. What effect this had on the squad is hard to gauge. Corinthians' star was slowly waning but they could field a formidable side on occasions. Before the Great Split, Corinthians would take on many of the big professional teams and often won. In 1904, Corinthians had thrashed FA Cup holders Bury 10-3, but those scorelines were gradually becoming an exception even before the split.

The Old Boys' teams were no longer a match for amateur teams composed of working-class players – even in their heartland, where southern English clubs like Oxford City and Clapton won the FA Amateur Cup in the seasons before the Olympics. For the Games, Clapton supplied Clyde Honeysett Purnell, a 31-year-old from the Isle of Wight and living in London's Muswell Hill, and Oxford City sent Herbert Smith, a left-back from Witney with four full England caps.

Some players quit AFA clubs in reaction to the split, such as Frederick Chapman, who was with Notts Magdala FC when the club quit the FA for the breakaway grouping. So Chapman left the club for Oxford City, where he was made captain, mixing playing there with occasional performances for Nottingham Forest at full-back or centre-half. By the time the Olympics came round, Chapman played mostly for amateurs South Nottingham.

Another Olympian from outside the elite was Bob Hawkes of Luton Town, then in the Southern league. Born in Breachwood Green in 1880 and educated at Luton Higher Grade School, Hawkes joined Luton Town in 1901. A frail-looking left-half and a poor header of the ball, excellent judgment and skilful ball-play more than compensated and he became Luton's captain.

Some players only took up football relatively late in life, such as the Liverpudlian Arthur Berry, who played rugby at Denstone College then switched to football after going up to Wadham College at Oxford University. An outside-right, he won his Blue in 1908 and with the varsity match watched by the Olympic selectors, Berry made the final squad.

Whether Vivian Woodward was present when the Bishop of Pennsylvania, Ethelbert Talbot, gave his speech that inspired the Olympic creed, no one knows, but he would surely have agreed with the gist. "The important thing in these Olympics is not so much winning as taking part," Talbot told the fifth conference of Anglican bishops in London in 1908. Hearing this, de Coubertin later came up with the creed above the Olympic scoreboard at every Games.

For the most prodigiously talented English amateur footballer of all time, the Games would be the biggest challenge of his career so far but, with the Olympics at hand, the players were still turning out in Football League matches. Woodward featured for Spurs in a 0-0 draw with Derby and Stapley netted Glossop's two goals in a 2-1 win over Clapton Orient. Poor Horace Bailey turned in a man-of-the-match performance for Leicester Fosse but was still on the end of a 5-0 drubbing from Manchester City.

The tournament draw was made on 2 October, before Bohemia and Hungary withdrew, so the Dutch and French were handed a bye to the semi-finals. The first match was on 19 October with the Danes taking on the French second string. The Danes would be the biggest challengers to the hosts but only arrived at their base, the Osborne Hotel in Holborn, a few days before kick-off. Their side was drawn solely from Copenhagen, many from university. The Danish team included Professor Harald Bohr, younger brother of Nobel Prize winner Niels Bohr, and two of the three Middelboe brothers. All three brothers played in the strictly amateur Danish league at Kjøbenhavns Boldklub but Einar did not travel to London with Kristian and the team's star, Nils.

Nils Middelboe had much in common with his opposite number in the English team. He was the Danish team's lynchpin and another great sporting all-rounder. A Danish triple-jump champion and 4 x 100 metre relay champion, Nils Middelboe also set national records in the 800 metres and the triple jump. A relative giant at six foot two inches, Middelboe was a lawyer and played centre-half, which in 1908 was usually a position just behind the forwards instead of in defence. In the Danes' opener, Middelboe scored twice in a 9-0 rout of France's B team. The Frenchmen's short passing was totally inadequate against the Danes on a White City pitch already ominously cutting up rough with so many different sports played on the surface in such a short period of time.

A day later, England would make their debut with five players – Bailey, Hardman, Hawkes, Smith and Woodward – from the full England team. In those days, committee men held sway and chose the team but the side had a coach in former Everton and England international Edgar Chadwick. The manager was Alfred Davis. The English team was based at the Inns of Court Hotel in Holborn, near to the venue of that AFA meeting where the Great Split had gained such momentum.

Their opponents seemed to have thrown in the towel before kick-off if a letter sent by J.S. Ekstrom, the honorary secretary of the Swedish Olympic Committee, to FA secretary F.J. Wall is anything to go by. The draw had not been kind to the Swedes and Ekstrom wrote: "We might fight the superior English team and know that we will be beaten but we must go to the large expense and send a team just to show our good feeling and get up good sport. We are very pleased to hear that you are arranging consolation games and hope to have better success there." And that was before a ball had even been kicked.

20 October 1908
White City Stadium, London. England vs Sweden
On the day of the match, a mere 2,000 fans, many paying the minimum ticket price of just sixpence, turned up to watch. Their number included a Japanese doctor sitting in what one newspaper described as "oriental stillness and stoicism", taking notes throughout. What he saw was not a great advert for the English game. Maybe England had been listening to the gloomy Swedish administrators and felt little effort was needed. *The Times* later rather stiffly described England's showing as "not … a good display". *The Sportsman* was more damning, saying the team "failed to realise expectations" and described Horace Bailey as "unconvincing".

Early on and with the game goalless, Sweden's Almkvist from the Uppsala club hit the bar, but the English soon began to score. Goals often came from poor clearances from the Swedes' last-ditch defending. At half-time, the score was 7-0. Purnell and Woodward each scored twice. For the first 20 minutes of the second half, Sweden kept their opponents out before another brace from Purnell, two from Hawkes and a second from Stapley took the total to a dozen.

Despite the scoreline, Sweden played well in parts, picking up a goal from a Bergstroem effort that Chapman deflected into his own net past Bailey. In front of goal, the underconfident Swedes often shot wildly. With more poise and confidence, the Swedes might have scored more than one. "This excitement was doubtless due to a want of experience and nothing but time can cure it," says the official report. Four decades later, the Swedes would return to London and demonstrate to the home of football just what the passage of time could achieve by winning the gold medal at football.

22 October 1908
White City Stadium, London. England vs the Netherlands
A crowd of 6,000 indicated growing interest in the tournament but the semi-final hardly tested the stadium's capacity. There were no Corinthians in the England team and had there been, the hosts' opening goal would have horrified those purists, who saw themselves as the guardians of football's

true spirit. English referee John Howcroft failed to notice the Dutch centre-half lying injured and Stapley easily scored. Despite the set back, the Dutch had more self-belief than the timorous Swedes. Their players created openings but the forwards could not take their chances. After half-time Stapley added two more by running unopposed down the centre of the pitch and added his fourth by heading home a Hardman cross. The Dutch played better than the score suggested and beat Sweden 2-0 to take the bronze. According to *The Times*, the Dutch "showed far better form than any of the other continental teams" and their quick touches made the game hard for England, whose defenders "could have been sounder". *The Sportsman* agreed, citing the slippery pitch and "dreadful cold" for denying the Dutchmen a goal. On the same day, what was supposedly the French first team played their only match in the other semi-final. Their selectors' inability to decide on their top side was painfully obvious. The French dwelt too long on the ball, were easily dispossessed and their defenders took to standing off the bow-legged Dane Sophus Nielsen, a part-time blacksmith, who plundered ten goals in a 17-1 rout.

22 October 1908
White City Stadium, London. England vs Denmark
The English team arrived in the final after two performances that belied the scorelines to face a buoyant Danish side, who – if the interim Games were taken into account – were the holders. A cool, damp October had not helped the pitch, which had deteriorated rapidly. To make matters worse, the kick-off was put back to accommodate the lacrosse final between Britain and Canada.

The 8,000 crowd for the football final was swelled by the FA's committeemen, including the heavily bearded Lord Kinnaird, who had played in England's second ever international in 1873. A strong proponent of the very un-Olympic tactic of hacking players down with a kick to their shins, as head of the FA Kinnaird was the bête noire of the AFA. Kinnaird took his seat at White City amid London's high society, including Lord and Lady Desborough, Sir George Truscott and his wife, and the Sheriff of London. Foreign royalty included Count Brunetta d'Usscaux of Italy and Baron and Baroness de Tuyll of the Netherlands. Was Wreford-Brown present? No one knows.

The game finally kicked off at 3.30pm and the home side's forwards immediately pressed. After eight minutes, Purnell shot and Danish keeper Ludwig Drescher spilled the ball, which dropped to Chapman to open the scoring. Led by Nils Middelboe, the Danish response was immediate and for the next 50 minutes, the English amateurs played the hardest game they ever experienced. The Danes tried to mark Vivian Woodward out of the game and captain Kristian Middelboe at the heart of the Danish defence proved impossible to beat.

As the game progressed, the sun retreated. The October gloom was advancing by half-time and the break between halves was short. On the restart, the English still struggled. The crowd gasped as Bailey nearly fluffed two consecutive shots that skidded up from the greasy surface. Fifteen minutes after the restart England were still on the back foot and in desperate need of inspiration. The source was obvious. Vivian Woodward sent a fine, low left-foot shot crashing past Drescher.

The Danes responded by creating half a dozen chances and were on top for the last 30 minutes. England clung on with good saves from Bailey, including one from Wolffhagen, who ran the length of the pitch before shooting. The Danes lacked concentration in front of goal and a dearth of competition from their first two matches proved telling. Middelboe created chances but they were passed up due to errors from the Danish forwards, who swung at the ball in the gathering dusk. Both teams had a couple more shots but neither could score, hindered by clear sight of the goal amidst the advancing twilight. Bailey would keep his clean sheet and Woodward's team were Olympic champions.

AFTER THE FINAL WHISTLE, THE LORD MAYOR DISHED out medals to the players as the elegant Lord Desborough remarked on all the fair play through the tournament. He had, perhaps, not seen Stapley's breakthrough goal against the Netherlands when the home referee did not see – or ignored – an injured Dutch defender. The media were less kind. *The Times* wrote: "The Danes made them look a very ordinary eleven. In pace, dash and kicking the Danes quite held their own, comparing most favourably with their opponents, and in their methods they were at no disadvantage. Since the split, the Football Association apparently cannot find an eleven capable of doing England's amateurs justice."

Some Olympic football matches were played on a green adjacent to White City and attendances for the overall tournament averaged just 3,300. Given how many people regularly attended professional games, the crowds were paltry. Perhaps there was no appetite for Englishmen representing Britain but Woodward's side had done all they could by winning. At 29 in 1908, Woodward might not have been expected to lead the holders' defence four years later but would do so.

By 1912 his winning team-mates were no longer at the same level or in some cases even in the amateur game. A year after winning Olympic gold, Clyde Purnell lifted another trophy, scoring in Clapton's 6-0 win over Eston United in the final of the FA Amateur Cup, but he would not go to Stockholm, the venue for the next Olympics in 1912.

Some players joined the professionals, like Bob Hawkes, who made 22 appearances for England's amateur team and then turned professional with Luton in 1911. Hawkes would play five times for the full England team and played for Luton until the end of the 1919/20 season, when after a few matches for Bedford Town he retired to his business as a straw-hat manufacturer. He died in Luton on September 12 1945.

Often the players who remained gentlemen would feel a source of responsibility to the game and, like Wreford-Brown, went into administration roles. Harold Hardman and Herbert Smith were cut from this mould. After five seasons and 156 appearances for Everton, Hardman joined Manchester United. He later played for Bradford City in the first division and Stoke City but, after retiring, returned to Old Trafford as an administrator and was elected a director in 1912 – a post that Hardman, who was a solicitor, held for the rest of his life. He died in Sale in 1965, aged 83.

Oxford City's Herbert Smith played in all three Olympic Games and went on to win 17 caps for the England amateur side up to 1910. He was later registered with many teams, including Derby County, Stoke City and Reading, where he was captain. In 1910, he joined the Oxfordshire FA council and was elected president seven years later – a post he held until his death in 1951, aged 71.

Frederick Chapman also moved into administration and helped found the English Wanderers, a touring side restricted solely to players with amateur international honours. Chapman, who had won 16 amateur caps, was joint secretary and he persuaded Woodward to captain the team. In World

War Two, Chapman served in the Royal Horse Artillery and as a major commanded a section of the Notts Battery in Mesopotamia. After the war, Chapman was a director at Nottingham-based ladies' clothing manufacturer, Lord & Chapman. He passed away in September 1951, aged 68.

Harry Stapley was first and foremost a player and Glossop's leading scorer every season between 1908 and 1912, banging in 89 goals in 189 appearances but clearly had talents as a coach. All three sons of his employer Samuel Hill-Wood later won a Blue for cricket at Oxford or Cambridge. Hill-Wood was later elected a Member of Parliament for the High Peak constituency and Stapley remained in his employ, dying on his 54th birthday in 1937.

Of the other victorious British Olympians, Kenneth Hunt would eventually return to the team but not in Stockholm, where Vivian Woodward, Arthur Berry, Horace Bailey and his great rival for the keeper's jersey, Ron Brebner, would travel in four years' time to again face their great protagonist in the London final, Nils Middelboe.

CHAPTER THREE: STOCKHOLM 1912 AND WOODWARD SIGNS OFF IN STYLE

"Thanks King."

GB Olympian Harold Walden on receiving
his medal from the King of Sweden

A TOP-CLASS FOOTBALLER QUITTING AT THE PEAK OF HIS game is not unheard of but few share Vivian Woodward's reasons for leaving Spurs. He had work to do. Football was a rough game, certainly, but at the end of the 1908/09 season Woodward quit Spurs to concentrate on his architectural practice. He loved football too much to stop playing though and, amazingly, quit Spurs and the Football League – for Chelmsford.

Woodward did not play his first game for Chelmsford until 12 October but 1,300 people turned up to see one of English football's greatest players in a league fixture against Barking. He might have been playing non-league, but he was still a star whose face adorned many of the then increasingly popular cigarette cards. Woodward carried on playing for England's amateurs but could not stay away from top level football for long. In November that season, Woodward stunned the football world by returning to the Football League – with Chelsea.

Crippled by injuries, Chelsea were going through a bad run and Woodward's signing was the cause for much celebration. Stories circulated that Woodward had fallen out with Spurs but he insisted not, saying:

"Mr Kirby, the chairman of Chelsea, wrote to me a few days ago pointing out [the club's injury list] and explained how difficult his club found it to complete a side, especially in attack. He reminded me in his letter that three seasons ago, I promised that if ever I was free-lance I would come to Chelsea if they thought I could be any service to them. When I received Mr Kirby's letter, I immediately recalled my promise. I replied that if a place was found for me, I would endeavour to do my best to fill it."

No wonder that Chelsea's directors and fans were happy: the club secured the signature of one of England's top international footballers without paying a transfer fee. To top that, he did not even want paying. For Vivian Woodward, honouring a three-year-old promise was more important than being paid a penny by relegation-threatened Chelsea.

On 27 November 1909, Woodward, who had been a full England international for six years, finally made his Chelsea debut in a league game at Sheffield Wednesday. But even Woodward could not prevent Chelsea losing 4-1, their seventh defeat in eight games. On his home debut on 4 December, the Woodward effect thundered around a packed Stamford Bridge. The great man delivered, scoring twice in a 4-1 win over Bristol City. Woodward continued to play full and amateur internationals for England and his absences for internationals undermined Chelsea's revival: the club was relegated.

Woodward stayed on but with his business commitments increasing, something had to give. He was not about to break his promise to Claude Kirby and so, incredibly, he gave up playing full internationals. In typical Woodward style, he signed off with two goals against Wales in 1911. In 23 full England internationals – and 13 as captain – Vivian Woodward had scored 29 goals.

A gentleman to the last, he continued to play amateur internationals. When his beloved Clacton reformed, he even managed to turn out in a cup match for his home town team. Unsurprisingly, he scored both goals in a 2-1 win. Woodward's Chelsea games became more sporadic due to work but with promotion in sight, he promised to play the last three matches.

Chelsea subsequently won promotion back to the top flight. When the 1912 Olympics in Stockholm rolled into view, Woodward had belied his age – he was 33 at the time – and status as an amateur by playing at the top level of the English game and would lead England's crusade to hold onto their Olympic title.

Through hosting and winning the 1908 Olympics football tournament, England finally embraced the rest of the world – or at least those European countries that could seemingly rustle up a team. After 1908, the England team tentatively began to take on opponents outside Britain with the full side playing the likes of Austria and Hungary. Vivian Woodward was then playing for both the full and amateur XI who became more adventurous with matches against teams such as Switzerland and Belgium. Most of these games were won by huge margins, reinforcing the British game's sense of superiority and a need for separate national teams to provide some decent competition for the Europeans.

Despite seemingly embracing the world, England and the British did so on their own terms. In 1909 England were invited to play in a tournament staged in Italy by millionaire industrialist and philanthropist Sir Thomas Lipton. The FA would have nothing to do with the competition, so Lipton invited West Auckland Town, an amateur team comprised mostly of Durham coalminers.

The Sir Thomas Lipton Trophy featured the best clubs from Italy (Turin), Germany (Stuttgart) and Switzerland (Winterthur) but West Auckland won without conceding a goal. Two years later, the tournament was held again. Still the FA refused to get involved. West Auckland's gentlemen won again, this time letting in just one goal in two matches, which came in a 6-1 pasting of Juventus.

For the British associations and the FA in particular, the development of the game was moving at a rapid pace and signs of *entente cordial* in the divisive split with the AFA finally emerged before the Stockholm Olympics. The AFA had played that "international" in Prague against Bohemia in November 1908, winning 2-0. A breakaway federation was formed the following year featuring the AFA, the USFSA, which opposed both the professionalism in the English game and the spread of the English language, and the Bohemians.

As part of the Austro-Hungarian Empire, the Bohemians had been rejected by Fifa on the same grounds as the Scots and the Irish. Then and against its own statutes, Fifa ushered in Scotland and Wales in 1910, and Ireland in 1911. This effectively neutralised any possible new converts to the AFA's international regime, although in reality the rebellious southern gentlemen had few allies outside of England.

By the 1910/11 season the AFA's potential was reached. Before the split the gentlemen amateurs and Old Boys played regularly against professional sides. The professionals had been sending second-string sides for some time but gates held up. After the split AFA clubs could only play each other and gates slumped. In the five years after the split, gate receipts at AFA member Cambridge University halved. Tours by British sides were increasingly popular, particularly gentlemen amateur sides from England, who strove to popularise the game outside of Britain, but AFA clubs struggled to find fixtures in countries that had joined Fifa.

With big amateur clubs suffering, Thanet's Member of Parliament Norman Craig even raised the issue of the split in Parliament in 1910, but no state intervention was needed. The pressure on the AFA told and the breakaway bloc splintered. Attempts to lure in the likes of the Sevenoaks League failed. Competitions like the Thanet Thursday League quit the AFA and returned to the official Kent County FA. A stalemate simmered in southern England that helped no one.

Increasingly hemmed, the gentlemen of Corinthians made the first overture for reconciliation in 1912. A proposal at the AFA's annual general meeting to open negotiations with the FA was heard but proved too late for that year's Olympics.

The AFA was unrecognised by anyone and their players faced exclusion from the Olympic side. In September 1911, *The Times* published a letter from a group of leading gentlemen asking for AFA players to be considered for Sweden that hysterically described this situation as "evil".

How many AFA players would have been selected remains hard to measure but the gentlemen's clubs within the FA were firmly outstripped in the Amateur Cup by working-class amateur sides. Only military sides provided success for the gentlemanly elite with the Royal Engineers and Gosport RMLI – a team drawn from the Royal Marines – winning in 1908 and 1910 respectively. Shortly before the 1912 Olympics, the FA tried a last-ditch attempt to forge a truce. Secretary Frederick Wall wrote to his

AFA counterpart, Henry Hughes-Onslow, a ferocious gentleman amateur and Old Etonian, but no agreement could be reached. The AFA arrogantly decided to sit out another Olympics, with the top players playing under their banner the real losers.

British representation at the 1912 Olympics looked likely to become even more fractured after a Fifa congress in the German city of Dresden in June 1911. The FA attended along with Germany, Denmark, Hungary, France, Austria, Switzerland, Holland, Belgium, Sweden and Norway. At the meeting the results of a recent IOC meeting in Budapest were disclosed. A new regulation had been drawn up allowing each national FA in Fifa to send a team to Stockholm – meaning the British IOC could have sent four teams. This was solely for the benefit of the four Home Nations. Fifa quickly discouraged multiple entries from other Fifa members. In Stockholm, Fifa also laid down clear rules as to what constituted an amateur: no expenses bar hotel and travel bills, never teaching football for "pecuniary gain", which would have ruled out Harry Stapley, never playing professionally and never pawning prizes won in football for money. For once everyone seemingly agreed. Stockholm would be the last Olympics where money would not be a major issue in the football tournament.

With the AFA in self-imposed exile, the Swedish Olympic Committee should have had a simple task, but rival British sports bodies were myriad. In athletics, the Amateur Athletic Association (AAA) ran parallel with the breakaway National Athletic Association; many cyclists left the AAA for the National Cyclists' Union, while rowers were split between the Amateur Rowing Association and National Amateur Rowing Association. In football, some French clubs still existed outside of the new French FA that had replaced the USFSA. In the midst of this chaos, a window that had temporarily opened for the Scots, Welsh and Irish footballers quietly closed. In Stockholm, only the English would be British at football. In Stockholm, there would seemingly be no professionals, no Scots, no Irish, no Welsh, and no AFA.

AS REQUIRED BY IOC RULES, THE FA ASSEMBLED ANOTHER mammoth 33-man squad after a selectors' meeting at Russell Square in London, which was then slimmed down to 18 players to travel to Stockholm. The team was all English but again contained players with Scottish connections. Ron Brebner had returned and would this time be preferred to Horace Bailey in goal. The squad also included Douglas McWhirter, an Amateur Cup winner in 1911 with Bromley, who despite a Scottish surname, was born in Erith in 1886. Another player with Scottish heritage was Thomas Burn, who was born at Berwick-upon-Tweed in Northumberland in 1888. Like Brebner, Burn played for London Caledonians and won the Isthmian League with the club in the season before the 1912 Olympics.

Vivian Woodward's selection as captain was inevitable and he was given the honour of holding the British standard for the entire BOA squad at the opening ceremony. The new faces accompanying Woodward again included some full England internationals such as Ted Wright from Earlsfield Green in Surrey. An Oxbridge man, Wright went to Cambridge and, before graduating, played for England against Wales in 1906. He played for Worthing, Reigate Priory, Leyton and Hull City, where he would be captain for seven seasons. With 15 England appearances in the four years leading up to the 1912 Games, Wright was an obvious choice for Stockholm.

Harry Stapley's best was behind him but Glossop remained a popular club with amateurs like Henry Littlewort, a 29-year-old defender originally from Ipswich. Another Glossop player who would travel to Stockholm was Gordon Rahere Hoare. Born in 1884 in Blackheath, the heartland of southern amateur football, Hoare started out with West Norwood, a big amateur club shunned by the exclusive AFA, then signed for Woolwich Arsenal in 1907.

He made his debut on the last day of the 1907/08 season against Sheffield Wednesday in a first division match. The next season, staying amateur, he scored 5 goals in 11 games for the Gunners and made the England amateur team. Unhappy at a lack of first-team football, Hoare switched to Glossop in December 1909 only to return to Arsenal a year later. Unable to shift regular starters John Chalmers and Charles Randall, Hoare quit Arsenal yet again and returned once more to Glossop in February 1912.

Ivor Sharpe also played for Glossop but left for Leeds United and then moved to Derby, where the high scoring outside-left established himself in the England amateur team in the run-up to Stockholm. The number of amateurs, like Sharpe, who were playing in the Football League was dwindling, but gentlemen often played for professional clubs outside the two division structure – players like Reading centre-half Ted Hanney and

Portsmouth's Arthur Egerton Knight, who went to Stockholm for the first of his two Olympics.

The university's influence had waned but Cambridge's captain Leonard Dawe, a hard-shooting centre forward described as "a scientific and energetic player with a thorough knowledge of the game … responsible for two thirds of the goals scored", was selected. But this son of a life assurance manager from Southsea, who usually played with spectacles on, had also been playing in the Southern league for Southampton.

With the Old Boys of the AFA out of the reckoning, there was space for players from outside the elite environs of the public schools like Arthur Egerton Knight, a talented all-round sportsman born in Godalming in 1887. Known more commonly as AE, Knight did not go to university but left school and took a job with an insurance company. At 17 he was sent to work in Portsmouth and signed for Pompey. After a season in the reserves, his solid tackling and ability in the air secured him a place in the first team and many England amateur appearances.

Teaching offered players like Joe Dines the flexibility to play at a high level. Born at King's Lynn in 1886, he went to Peterborough Teacher Training College then returned home to take a schoolmaster's post but later taught in Essex, where he joined Ilford and played occasionally for another ambitious professional side, Millwall.

In the Olympic year, the Amateur Cup was lifted by Stockton. Harold Stamper, Stockton's dominating centre-half known as Collie, was selected but representation for the thriving northern amateur community was paltry. Amateur clubs whose players could find the time to train and play in a manner not dissimilar to professionals were clearly viewed in a dim light by the FA's southern traditionalist administrators, who suspected secret payments.

Quite what the FA made of Harry Walden is hard to imagine but he was probably not bothered either way. As the laconic Mancunian showed in his post-Olympic life, he certainly did not lack confidence and Walden probably caused his fair share of muttering in the oak-panelled rooms of the FA and the private members' clubs. Harry Walden was a Victorian adventure seeker who at 14 lied about his age to get into the Cheshire Regiment and was sent to India for two and a half years.

When the Cheshires returned home to England, Walden began playing football seriously for the first time. The Cheshires were soon posted to Belfast, where Walden, now a corporal despite his youth, played for the Army and Linfield. Back in England for the 1909/10 and 1910/11 seasons, he signed for Bradford City. Walden failed to make the first XI and briefly left for Halifax but returned to Bradford and the first XI and was playing in the Football League in 1912, when he was picked for the Olympics.

The team was again chosen by the amateur selection committee but Crystal Palace trainer Adrian Birch – often known by the odd nickname of "Shy" – was the team's trainer. Birch had joined Palace from Middlesbrough on the south London club's formation in 1905 and was recruited by the FA to work with representative teams, including the amateur international tour in 1911/12. In charge of the party was George Wagstaffe Simmons, a well-known referee and official from the Hertfordshire FA, who four years previously helped form St Albans City.

Although 1908 had provided an official Olympic football tournament for the first time, there was no guarantee of a repeat four years later. The Swedish organisers were concerned that the game was not sufficiently popular around the world to merit inclusion. After a long debate, football was featured and 11 entries received – all from Europe. Bohemia entered again but were still not in Fifa and were therefore rejected. The French pulled out because a number of their players could not get time off. When the Belgians then withdrew, the competition was reduced to just eight teams.

On 29 June, the tournament started with the Dutch edging out the hosts 4-3 in Stockholm's main Olympic Stadium. The Swedes had been concerned about the game's popularity but 14,000 people turned up. The same day, a mere 2,000 watched Austria thrash Germany 5-1 at the Rasunda Stadium, also in the capital. With Stockholm sweltering in the Swedish summer and 90-degree temperatures, the heat was a deterrent for everyone.

In the run-up to their opening match, the English amateurs joined their German and Hungarian counterparts and attended a reception hosted by the Crown Prince at Drottingholm. Each day the players trained for just one hour at Östermalms Idrottsplats, a sandy patch near the Olympic Stadium, finishing off each session with a single lap of the field. Among the locals, Vivian Woodward proved the biggest draw. Quizzed by the local media, the calm, serious Chelsea player revealed only that he liked salmon fishing when not playing football.

Wagstaffe-Simmons proved less staid, often joking with the locals, but he was taking the tournament seriously. "In my opinion, this will be the most severe test the England amateur team has ever been called upon to face," he warned. "This will be an exceedingly tough match. The Hungarians can play dashing, scientific football."

30 June 1912
Stockholm Olympic Stadium. England vs Hungary

When Vivian Woodward led his team out, he was pleasantly surprised to see virtually as many fans as had watched the 1908 final filling the stands for the holders' match with Hungary. In January of that year, Hungary's top club side Ferencvaros had played the Wanderers at Chelsea and Woodward was reacquainted with many of the players from that game.

The heat in Stockholm was getting more oppressive, dragging the players down, who were relieved to find that the organisers had left buckets of water on the touchlines. England again started slowly and nearly fell behind early on when Burn fouled Borbas and Brebner had to make a spectacular save to deny Bodner from the penalty spot.

England recovered and Walden sent a shot rocketing past the Hungarian keeper Domonkos from 20 yards. Two minutes later, Walden added a second after the referee failed to spot what seemed to be a handball by the Bradford player.

The match was interrupted on half a dozen occasions as English players struggled with injuries. Hanney was hurt in a collision and left the field for ten minutes. Clearly in great pain, Hanney returned but at half-time accepted that he couldn't go on and left the field for good. With no substitutions then allowed, England were reduced to ten men. When the half-time whistle went, Hanney's sweltering team-mates trooped past the buckets of water into the changing rooms, where they stripped off and jumped into a cold bath to cool down. "The weather was so hot that it was impossible to sit on the pitch for more than a few moments," recalled Ivan Sharpe years later.

With Hanney out, Littlewort went to centre-half and Gordon Hoare, who was also suffering, moved to right-half, leaving Sharpe alone on the left wing. Harry Walden was also suffering from an injury but the cold bath proved restorative for the ten Englishmen. When an early Hoare shot struck a post, Woodward pounced on the rebound.

The self-assured Walden then plundered another four goals, one a fine header, to take his tally to six and the score to 7-0. Perhaps understandably given the conditions and their heavy cloth kit, England were not at their best. The match was described as being of a "scrambling nature" by *The Times*, whose correspondent noted that the English played better a man down. Despite the scoreline, Hungary had been no walkover. Only some dazzling forward play from Woodward to play in Walden had inflated the score. The official report later remarked: "If the Hungarian forwards had been a little cooler in front of goal and had calculated their chances better, the result might have been altogether different." As Hungary were supposedly superior to Austria, the victory made England favourites to retain their title. The only real challenge was expected to come from Nils Middelboe's Denmark, who had thrashed Norway 7-0 in their first match.

2 July 1912
Stockholm Olympic Stadium. England vs Finland

For their semi-final, Woodward's team returned to the Olympic Stadium, where the deathly heat had been replaced by driving rain. A light drizzle that morning had turned into a downpour and only a few hundred spectators had gathered for the kick-off. For England, Harold Stamper replaced the injured Hanney and Ted Wright replaced Berry, who was suffering from a sore ankle. After being crushed 7-1 by a Swedish reserve team in a warm-up, the Finns proved the surprise of the tournament, beating Italy 3-2 and Russia 2-1, but were still not expected to provide a match for the revered holders. This was seemingly confirmed in the first minute, when a clearance by a Finnish defender deflected off Sharpe to put England ahead. Five minutes later a decent move was finished off by Walden slotting home.

The Finns charged into attack but were ineffectual in front of Brebner's goal, failing to muster a shot on target for the first 20 minutes. The game was played mostly in Finland's half. Only the slippery conditions and a conservative approach from the Englishmen, who knocked the ball about in their own half at length, kept the score down. This Corinthian approach to avoid humbling their opponents culminated in a fine slice of idealism that typified their captain. A penalty was awarded by the Swedish referee Ruben Gelbord against the Finns after 15 minutes but the English, to a man, disagreed with the decision. No one, least of all Woodward, could stomach scoring in such fashion. A.E. Knight placed the ball on the penalty spot, paused to wipe sweat from his brow, took a couple of steps back – and promptly sent the ball flying over the crossbar to the surprise of the bemused Finnish keeper.

In the second half, the Finns showed how they had managed to win two matches, playing far better, strengthened perhaps by travelling fans shouting, "We want more goals". Brebner was forced into action and the Finns would have been on top but for Woodward, who relentlessly broke up their attacks. Half an hour into the second half, Walden added a third and then Woodward himself rounded off a 4-0 victory. The rain had eased throughout the game and the crowd swelled to 4,000 fans by the finish. In the final, England's opponents, almost inevitably, were Denmark, who beat the hosts 4-1 in an exciting game.

4 July 1912
Stockholm Olympic Stadium. England vs Denmark
With two days' rest, England's amateurs reassembled for the final, which proved a real draw, confounding the organisers' initial concerns. Crowd estimates range from 15,000 at kick-off to 25,000 by the close, fans flocking to see if Nils Middelboe could claim a trophy that had seemed to be within his grasp four years previously.

For England, after playing right-half in the first two games, Henry Littlewort moved to centre-half and Arthur Berry returned. The Danes were weakened by injuries and despite winning the toss were soon on the back foot as Berry pushed England forward. The Danes responded, exposing Knight and Burn, but Walden opened the scoring on 12 minutes by firing home a Sharpe centre.

The Danes rallied and Brebner was nearly caught out by a dipping shot that he just pushed over the bar. The game pulsed from end to end and Hoare added a second, catching Danish keeper Sophus Hansen wrong-footed on 22 minutes.

The reply was sudden. Just four minutes later and from point blank range, Anton Olsen smashed a shot which Brebner, although he got a hand to the ball, could not keep out. Some British reports suggest that Olsen was offside but the referee disagreed. The Danes flooded forward only for defender Charles Buchwald to come off second best in a tackle with Woodward. The Dane left the field with a suspected broken arm. As the Danes reshuffled, the Swedish Crown Prince left his box to go and visit the injured Buchwald, whose absence proved disruptive. Ten minutes later Hoare headed in a centre from Berry. Just before half-time, Berry demonstrated his brilliant dribbling by taking the ball round Hansen in the Denmark goal for a fourth.

At half-time, the Crown Prince of Sweden descended from his royal box to mix with the players and introduce himself. Such a gregarious show from a royal was unheard of back home and Britons in the crowd broke into a rousing chant of "For He's a Jolly Good Fellow", which the prince clearly enjoyed. After the restart, Nils Middelboe switched places with Anton Olsen, who quickly reduced the deficit with a second goal that bounced off Knight's leg into the net. Under pressure, Brebner was forced into clearing the ball upfield on occasions as Denmark's ten players dominated. But even the Danish maestro could not alter the score. With eight minutes left, Berry created a chance for Woodward but Hansen saved. Woodward, his signature knee-length shorts flapping in the wind, pounced on the rebound and shot again. Hansen again saved. Woodward picked up on two more rebounds to shoot from point blank range but each time Hansen kept him out. Soon after, Hoare hit the post and the ball bounced out of play. The game was over. England had won again.

A VISIBLY PROUD WOODWARD LED HIS TEAM UP TO RECEIVE their trophy and medals. As Swedish King Gustav V handed over a medal to Harry Walden, aware that royals in Sweden might appreciate a bit of familiarity, Walden simply replied: "Thanks King."

The presentations over, the Swedish Crown Prince again paid a visit to the Danish dressing room to commiserate with the injured Buchwald over his injured arm.

For the hosts the tournament was a massive success off the pitch with the games attracting bumper crowds and generating sufficient money for the Swedish FA to take over the national league, the Allsevenskan, which had previously operated as a private competition.

On the field, the tournament was a disaster. In years to come, Sweden would dazzle in the Olympics under an English coach but in 1912 the supervision of Charlie Bunyan, a rumbustious former goalkeeper, seemingly did little to help the Swedes.

In football's early days, goalkeepers could handle the ball anywhere inside their own half. The colourful Bunyan could regularly be found leading attacks only to berate his defenders if a goal was conceded. In 1887 Bunyan conceded a record 26 goals for Hyde United in an FA Cup match with William Sudell's Preston North End. After various run-ins with the football authorities, Bunyan quit England in 1909, first for Belgium then Sweden, where he managed Gothenburg-based Örgryte IS.

In the run-up to the 1912 Olympics, Bunyan was working in Stockholm. Having also been involved with the clubs in Gothenburg, Bunyan had knowledge of the best players in Sweden but rows between the clubs in Sweden's two main cities dogged his selection plans. A final line-up was not decided until the night before the Swedes' opener with the Dutch, which saw the hosts crash out 4-3 after extra time. Bunyan returned to Belgium soon after.

Apart from the desultory performance of the Swedes, most British correspondents noted the vast improvement in the playing standards of the continentals. Some carped that playing gentlemen who played regularly with professionals was not fair on the Europeans but the holders had simply played within the rules. The tournament featured a consolation event for teams knocked out in the first round. The Russians probably found little consolation though. Hungary beat Austria 3-0 in the final but the Russians were crushed 16-0 in their first game by Germany and reports say the Tzar refused to pay for the players' journey home.

That consolation tournament would not occur at the next Olympics, which instead of taking place in Berlin's Grunwald Stadium in 1916 would be eight years off in a different country altogether. The shadow of the Great War fell across Europe and the players that had played in Stockholm.

Many of the 1912 winners were involved in WWI, but some did not emerge. Joe Dines volunteered for service with his two brothers, and the Olympian was made a second lieutenant and served in the Ordnance Corps, the Middlesex Regiment, the Machine Gun Corps and the Tank Corps, where he was based in Liverpool. The winner of 24 England amateur caps, Dines played a single wartime match for Liverpool – a 2-1 win over Chelsea at Stamford Bridge – shortly before being sent to France with the 17th Service Battalion of the Middlesex Regiment, which was raised from footballers. Just 11 days after Dines arrived in France he was cut down by machine gun fire on 27 September 1918 at Ribecourt, leading his platoon in an attack on enemy lines. His battalion took 600 prisoners but lost 125 men and six officers, including Dines, who is buried at Grand Ravine British Cemetery in Harvincourt.

Arthur Berry survived the war but never added to his only full England cap. After playing for Everton, Fulham, Liverpool, Northern Nomads and Wrexham, Berry was playing for Oxford City in 1913, when he was called up to the Bar. Berry played for Oxford City in that year's Amateur Cup final, then retired to concentrate on his career. After serving in the war, Berry joined the family law firm run by his father Edwin, who was Liverpool's chairman from 1908 to 1912. Berry passed away in March 1953 in his native Liverpool.

Harold Walden served in the West Yorkshire Regiment during the war, rising to the rank of captain. Afterwards he returned to football and Bradford City. He was poached by Arsenal but Walden had his sights on another career before he even moved to Highbury. While at Bradford, Walden had made his stage debut at the city's Alhambra Theatre, singing in a show to raise money for a lifeboat appeal. Impresario Francis Laidler had been so struck with Walden's turn that he booked him for a week on a variety bill. The lure of the stage gripped Walden. After just two games and one goal for Arsenal, Walden returned to Bradford and hung up his boots for a new career.

He was initially booked as a singer but during one variety show in Bradford a comedian was taken ill and the supremely self-possessed Walden grabbed the microphone. When he played football Walden's hair was combed back, but for the stage he effected a new style, combing his hair onto his face for a kiss-curl. At one show, Walden borrowed a straw hat from a bookmaker in the audience – his new image was complete, although his old Bradford number nine shirt would sometimes surface during performances. Walden later toured the Australian outback in a covered wagon and nearly died after a paraffin lamp was knocked over, starting a blaze. Everything was lost in the fire, including the party's water supply. The resilient Walden returned from the outback on top of an open railway truck laden with pit props.

He cut at least one record, a 78 RPM for Imperial with "Ronnie the Robin" on the A-side and "And Only Me Knows Why" on the B-side. In 1920 Walden appeared in a film adaptation of the Harold Brighouse play

The Game. For the screen, the story was re-titled *The Winning Goal*, which Walden scored.

Walden later joined the Ernest Binns Follies on Morecambe Pier for holidaymakers, many of whom were from Bradford. Asked why he quit football for the stage, Walden said: "With football it's 45 minutes each half, rain or snow, with a ten minute interval and a raspberry from the crowd if you don't score. On the Halls, it's ten minutes each show, with twice nightly and a two-hour interval in-between; and there's a benefit at the end of each week whether you score or not."

Walden performed with Big Bill's Rocky Mountain Singers during World War Two. A trouper to the end, he continued performing until 1955, when he made one of his last performances in a show to raise money for the annual Christmas appeal from the *Yorkshire Evening News*. Two weeks later on 2 December, he died of a heart attack at Leeds railway station, aged 66. Boy soldier, Olympian, singer comedian: a life lived in full.

Few of his team-mates could match Walden's story but Leonard Dawe, despite not featuring in any of the matches, would etch a place in the history books, when he nearly upset the entire Allied plan for D-Day. Dawe served in Mesopotamia in WWI with the Hampshire Regiment before moving into teaching and in 1926 took a job at London's Strand School – a year after he had begun compiling crosswords for the *Daily Telegraph*. In the spring of 1944 the words Juno, Gold, Sword and Utah all appeared as solutions in Dawe's crossword puzzles.

When Omaha, Overlord, Mulberry and then Neptune appeared, MI5 swooped on the unsuspecting bespectacled headmaster at his home in Leatherhead. Dawe was at a loss to explain how he had managed to publish eight codewords for forthcoming D-Day landings for everyone to read in the *Daily Telegraph*.

In the 1980s, nearly two decades after Dawe died, one of his pupils, Ronald French, came forward with an explanation. Dawe occasionally let some of his pupils fill in the blank spaces in his putative puzzles. French had heard the words used by American and Canadian soldiers staying near the Strand, which relocated to Effingham in Surrey for the duration of the war. Unaware that the words were top secret, French had scribbled them onto Dawe's blank puzzle then kept it secret for nearly forty years.

Thomas Burn returned to London Caledonians and was selected for

71

an FA tour of South Africa in 1920, from where he sent reports on to *Athletic News*. Ivor Sharpe also worked for the papers, becoming a respected journalist after making his own minor piece of history by becoming one of only a handful of players to represent Leeds United and Leeds City. Before World War One, City were the biggest professional club in Leeds only to be expelled from the second division after running into financial problems. Sharpe scored 17 goals in 65 appearances for Leeds City but left in 1915. In 1920 Sharpe signed for Leeds United and spent two and a half years with the club but only made one appearance. He never went professional, though, and often turned out for Yorkshire Amateurs, the county's leading amateur side.

A number of Olympians would turn to journalism over the years. Henry Littlewort was one of the first. He was invited to play for Essex County Cricket Club – an invitation he rejected due to injury – but played football for Crystal Palace, Spurs and Fulham. He retired from football to become a journalist for the *News Chronicle*. On his way from his home in Edmonton, North London, to cover a match between Spurs and West Bromwich Albion, Littlewort was taken ill. He died a week later on 21 November 1934, aged just 52.

For some players, Stockholm was the end. Horace Bailey never added to his five full England caps or resumed his Football League career after returning from the Olympics. Others, like Gordon Hoare, carried on playing for Football League clubs. Hoare joined Glossop for a second spell and then played for Queens Park Rangers and Fulham before retiring in 1920. Douglas McWhirter went professional but found that once he crossed this line there was no way back. After signing professional forms for Leicester Fosse, he tried to return to the amateur game in 1921 but the FA refused to issue him a permit, reinstating him as a gentleman. When he died at Plumstead in 1966, he was buried not as a gentleman, but as a player.

Ted Hanney also turned professional, signing for Manchester City for £1,250 – then a considerable amount of money – immediately after returning from Stockholm. His career was abbreviated by the Great War, where he too served with the 17th Middlesex. Sergeant Ted Hanney was hit in the face and neck by shrapnel but survived. He later played for Coventry, Reading and Northfleet before coaching in Stuttgart and Italy before returning home to run a pub in Reading.

Hanney's captain, the man who led England to Olympic glory not once but twice, travelled back to Sweden for his final two matches for the England amateur side. Vivian Woodward signed off in style, scoring one goal in a 5-1 win over the hosts then a brace in a 5-0 win two days later.

When World War One broke out, Woodward immediately applied for a temporary commission in the regular army and joined the 17th Middlesex in 1915 as a second lieutenant. After a spell on Salisbury Plain he left for France. In 1916 Woodward, now a captain, was wounded in the leg by a rifle grenade during a skirmish with the Germans. Returning home, the dashing former Olympic captain was found to have scabies. Woodward did not return to the trenches for eight months. When he did it was immediately to a salvo of heavy shelling from the German artillery.

Woodward survived and, his fitness regained, was made captain of the British Army football team for a game against their Belgian counterparts in 1919. During the war Woodward had turned out for Chelsea on a couple of occasions. He returned to some adulation to Stamford Bridge in May 1919, typically scoring in a 3-2 win for the Army over the French Army.

After being demobilised, Woodward finally decided enough was enough. His boots would be hung up but saying goodbye proved hard. He returned to his much-loved Clacton, where he agreed to play one final competitive game against the First Battalion of the Cheshire Regiment. The match was in Colchester but more than 500 people from Clacton piled into charabancs and travelled up to see the game. Woodward had a number of opportunities to score but passed on each occasion to a team-mate as Clacton ran home 3-0 winners. His last appearance was for Chelsea against an Army XI in a fund-raiser for ex-servicemen. Chelsea won 2-0 and, at 41, Woodward scored one of the goals.

Woodward did not marry, but loved to play games with his nephews and nieces – never to teach them but purely for the love of playing games. In his forties, Woodward concentrated on his farm at Weeley Heath near Clacton and gave up his architectural practice, although one of his designs is believed to have been used for the main stand at the 1920 Olympics in Antwerp.

Woodward shunned the limelight, running his farm and a dairy business along the Essex coast in nearby Frinton. He spent his spare time taking photographs, fishing and breeding pigeons. In 1922, football came calling and Woodward was asked to become a director at Chelsea. He accepted, staying until 1930. When World War Two broke out Woodward was too old to serve, but immediately signed up as an air raid warden. After the war, he returned to his farm but was diagnosed with nervous exhaustion. Unmarried and childless, Woodward was forced to quit the Essex coast he so loved. He returned to London and an Ealing nursing home. Woodward's fragile health took another blow when a visiting FA representative, Andrew Walston, died at his bedside.

In 1953, the sports journalist Bruce Harris went to see Vivian Woodward. Harris found the man who could play mostly every sport, from billiards to cricket, and who took up roller skating only months before he was due to captain England in the 1908 Olympic Games, bedridden at 74. His two former football clubs and the FA helped him financially. His relatives, including the nieces and nephews he had played sport with as children, all visited often. But according to *Vivian Woodward – Football's Gentleman* (Norman Jacob's account of the great player's life) Woodward told Harris: "No one who used to be with me in football has been to see me for two years. They never come. I wish they would."

The life had been sucked out of the vibrant young man who had set two Olympics alight, but his affection for football was undimmed. He missed the camaraderie of the dressing room, the action and excitement of a game he loved more than any other.

In response to Harris's article, the FA sent Woodward, who could by this time barely read, a television set. On 1 February 1954, not long after Harris's account was published, one of English football's greatest players and certainly one of its greatest gentlemen, who would rather stick a dubious penalty over the bar than score and who would brook no payment for playing any sport, died. He was still England's leading goalscorer at the time.

CHAPTER FOUR: ANTWERP 1920 AND A SHOCK TO THE SYSTEM

"We are not likely to have it all our own way in Antwerp."

FA secretary Frederick Wall on arriving at the 1920 Olympics

AS THE WORLD RECOVERED FROM THE MASS SLAUGHTER of the Great War that had left Joe Dines buried in a foreign field and Vivian Woodward traumatised, sport was seen for what it was; a frivolous pastime. Between 1915 and 1919, football in Great Britain was put on hold and the game languished.

One Olympic winner that did not have to fight was Kenneth Hunt, though he undoubtedly felt the pain of the war spiritually. After winning the FA Cup and Olympic gold, Hunt became a celebrity. Few clergymen played football to such a standard. Fewer still would be described as "hard as teak" in the popular collectable footballing cards of the time.

In 1908 Hunt took a job as games master at the prestigious Highgate School in North London. He was ordained the following year but preferred teaching to preaching. Hunt left Wolves and signed for Leyton Orient before moving on to Oxford City, where he seemed to have enjoyed his last brush with glory after reaching the 1913 FA Amateur Cup final. In the run-up to the outbreak of war, Hunt was made a lieutenant to the school's officer training corps, which was attached to the 3rd Volunteer Battalion of the Middlesex Regiment. Many of the pupils commanded in the school battalion left for the real thing. Many did not return home. Kenneth Hunt, young enough to fight but a man of the cloth, stayed at home.

After the war, Highgate saw a surge in boarders enrolling. A new house, Grindal, was instituted in 1920. Hunt was made housemaster but memories of playing at Wolves' Molineux Stadium stayed with him. Hunt returned there on occasions and was due to play a couple of games in the spring of 1920. One game was missed after his uncle passed away so the Footballing Parson's comeback was restricted to just one game. The fans had not forgotten him and 15,000 turned up to see Hunt play in a 4-0 win over Stoke City.

Hunt had generally preferred to play with professionals but had quiet, unspoken sympathies with the AFA and the likes of Wreford-Brown, who had lost a younger brother in the war. The post-war period was a time for the previously exiled gentlemen to re-establish themselves within the hallowed walls of the FA after the AFA agreed a return in 1914. In return for ending their own separatist ambitions, Onslow-Hughes and the AFA were given representation within the FA that would soon become evident. AFA men could sit on the FA's crucial International Selection and the Amateur Cup committees. The former allowed the southern gentlemen to lobby for inclusion in the England team of the diminishing number of their brethren playing at the top of the game, while a place on the latter committee would see a continuation of the corrosive division within the amateur game, between privileged southerners and working-class northerners.

With playing rosters decimated by the war, experienced amateurs were hard to come by. As the AFA were back within the halls of the FA, their influence over selection soon became evident. After the war England began playing sporadic amateur internationals and the selectors surprisingly chose the veteran Hunt, who played in a 5-0 thrashing of France in Rouen in April 1920. This gave him the distinction of being the oldest man to represent England at amateur international level and he would make a shock return to the Olympics that same year.

With international football slowly creaking back into life, victory matches were played between the four Home Nations' professional sides in 1919/20 with Wales coming out on top. Later that season England sent their full squad on a tour of South Africa. A lengthy trip culminated in the tourists crushing their hosts 9-1 in Cape Town – evidence that the British game was seemingly dominant. Outside of Britain, however, the rest of the world was slowly catching up.

The sport in Denmark, Norway and Sweden benefited from a neutral political position in the Great War. Football there was not disrupted and promising players not sent to their deaths. Outside of Europe, Fifa's attempts to organise a world cup, first mooted in 1906, were still no closer. At a Fifa congress in 1912 that all started to change. Argentina quit and others followed. With the FA too busy reconciling themselves with the AFA in their boardroom, the world order started to change, but the Olympics were still the closest there was to a real world football championship.

Getting all of Fifa's growing membership to enter again proved impossible. The Great War fractured sporting relations and England's Fifa man, Daniel Woolfall, had died. The Home Nations retreated behind political lines. No British national team would play against their foes from the battlefield of the Great War. The Central Powers of Austria, Germany and Hungary could not be entertained in any form. That was perhaps understandable but, led by the FA, the Home Nations also refused to play any other team that entertained the Central Powers, like the neutral Scandinavians. At a Fifa conference in Brussels in 1919, France, Belgium and Luxembourg sided with the Home Nations. Another divide was struck.

Regular international contact was essential for associations where the game was less developed than in the Home Nations. Those associations slowly crept over to the side of the Scandinavians. In May 1920, the fragile alliance split. The Home Nations were isolated and quit Fifa. The Belgians tried hard to win over the Home Nations and arranged a Fifa meeting during the 1920 Olympics in Antwerp to build bridges. Before relations with Fifa had completely soured, the FA promised to send a side to Antwerp to defend their trophy. That promise could not be broken, but the holders would be left wishing they had stayed at home. On and off the field, the hubris of the gentlemen was to be punctured, provoking a damaging retreat for the British game.

The other three Home Nations had made no such pledge to Fifa. Nor had they been involved in either of the earlier tournaments. None of this trio would be going to Antwerp and the 1920 Olympics are barely mentioned in the annals of the Scottish FA. With the Austrians, Germans and Hungarians all pariahs, Fifa scraped together a mere 14 teams for the Antwerp Games. Just one, Egypt, came from outside of Europe.

As the tournament loomed, English preparations were lax. With the AFA faction back in the fold, the pursuit and eradication of money's influence was more of a priority than emulating pre-war Olympic success. Probes into clubs' finances remained common. Shortly before the 1920 Olympics, the FA was tied up in a major investigation at Weymouth. The Dorset club had "flagrantly broken and evaded" FA regulations on finances. Four Weymouth men were named and shamed in the media and banned from football for life.

The scandal was well covered in the media in contrast to England's forthcoming defence of their title. England's opener in the 1920 Olympics was on the day after the first games of the 1920/21 football season. *The Sportsman* detailed every fixture – except the reigning Olympic football champions' first-round game against Norway. England, Britain even, had forgotten they were world champions. *The Sportsman* devoted as much coverage to the start of the shooting season as the entire Olympics.

BASED IN ENGLAND, *THE SPORTSMAN* HAD BACKED THE AFA to such a point that one editorial in 1907 urged readers to buy the first AFA annual. Not surprisingly, *The Sportsman* described the footballers in Antwerp as Britishers. To be English was to be British, yet even papers outside England seemed happy to let the footballers represent them. In reports on the 1920 Games, *The Scotsman* routinely described the team as British.

In Antwerp, the team would include a player with stronger Scots connections than the deceased Ron Brebner or Tom Burn. London Caledonians lost players to virtually every Highland regiment in WWI. Only four of the pre-war team were available when the club started the 1919/20 season but Caley – as London Caledonians were known – quickly rebuilt to become a force in London amateur football. One of the new recruits, back Basil Gates, who had a Scottish mother and played for Caleys with his brother Eric, was called up for Antwerp.

Wales were also represented at the Olympics – albeit off the pitch – and ironically, by a professional. The team would be managed by George Latham, the winner of a dozen full caps for Wales and a professional for Wrexham, Liverpool and Southport. After Southport, Latham had joined Cardiff and took over as coach in 1911.

Latham's employment in the professional game may not have been viewed favourably by some of the purists but this was offset by his military record. A veteran of the Boer War in South Africa, in World War One Latham was commissioned into the Royal Welch Fusiliers and made a lieutenant in 1916. A year later, he was leading a small platoon in Gaza that had taken a swathe of territory despite strong Turkish opposition. When news filtered down that 7,000 Turkish troops were on their way, Latham was ordered to retreat and abandon the ground made up. He did so – but only briefly. Leading the Fusiliers back into action, all the lost ground was reclaimed and Latham was awarded the Military Cross. The Bar followed in 1918. On demob, Latham returned to his dug-out at Cardiff City and in 1920 his team were invited into the Football League as the old top division of the Southern league was transformed into Division Three South of the pro game.

Some records suggest one of the 1920 Olympic players was also Welsh but Fred Nicholas was actually born in Malaya. On returning to England, he went to Oxford and gained a Blue in cricket, later sprinting for Great Britain and playing county cricket for Essex as a wicketkeeper and lower-order batsman.

The number of gentlemen playing at the highest level was dropping off and just six players came from clubs recognisable as Football League sides today. Millwall supplied H.S. Buck, Bury sent F. Heap, Reading supplied half-back Charlie Harbridge and two players, Jack Brennan and Max Woosnam, came from Manchester City.

Max Woosnam was probably the most talented amateur footballer of his day and an obvious choice for captain. Another World War One veteran, he had been born to a wealthy Liverpool family but was raised mostly at Aberhafesp in Mid Wales. Another fine all-round sportsman, Woosnam played squash, captained the golf and cricket teams at Winchester College and once scored 144 for a Public School XI against the MCC at Lord's. In 1911 he went to Cambridge University.

Woosnam, a centre-half, had played a handful of matches for Chelsea but mostly turned out for Corinth before the war, when he fought alongside famous poet Siegfried Sassoon on the western front and in Gallipoli. Surviving, Woosnam resumed his varied sporting career, playing tennis at Wimbledon. To the privileged Woosnam, turning professional in any sport was simply "vulgar". A complicated character, Woosnam drove a bus out of a sense of public responsibility in the 1926 General Strike and once beat actor Charlie Chaplin at table tennis – using a butter knife instead of a bat.

Even in the 1920s, Max Woosnam was already something of a throw-back. The era when the best gentlemen could play with the professionals was ending but Woosnam had not noticed. After moving to Manchester, he signed for City as an amateur and such was his ability that he was made club captain; a gentleman in charge of players. He was called up to the England amateur team and asked to captain the Olympic side in Antwerp, but Woosnam had already been asked to play tennis at the Games, which, he told the FA, was what he'd rather play.

After Woosnam's decision to focus on tennis, the most talented and experienced player in the squad was the other 1912 winner, A.E. Knight. Before the war, Knight occasionally played cricket for Hampshire. After the ceasefire Knight returned to the wicket and in the winter turned out for Portsmouth Football Club. In the year of the Olympics he won a cap for England's professional football side and captained Pompey to the 1920 Southern League championship. A devoted amateur, he was an obvious choice to replace Woosnam.

The Great War and an eight-year gap since the last Olympics meant few players from the 1912 Olympics were still in the running for a place. Only Kenneth Hunt would join Knight from previous Olympics. Probably the 1920 squad's strongest player was the Corinthian Kenneth Hegan, who had played in the England amateur game in Rouen with Kenneth Hunt, earlier that year. Born in Coventry, Hegan – generally known as Jackie – attended Bablake School and then went to the Royal Military College and onto the First Dublin Fusiliers. A professional soldier, Hegan only made his debut for Corinthians in December 1919 in a 7-2 win over the Army because Corinthians were three players short, but he would stay with the club for the rest of his playing days.

The Amateur Cup had resumed in 1920 and was won by the staunchly amateur Dulwich Hamlet, who provided goalkeeper EH Coleman to the Olympic team as reserve to Manchester University goalkeeper James Mitchell. Runners-up Tufnell Park provided half-back W.H. Swayne but the return of the AFA to the FA saw many players from the more prominent amateur clubs left out.

Selection worked on a system of lobbying from senior committee men and county associations that would remain in place for years. With the reconciliation, the AFA's gentlemen could make their voices heard over the "evil" inflicted on them in 1908 and 1912. In the initial 33-man squad, there were four Corinthians, another from that other bastion of southern gentlemen, the Casuals, plus a total of eight from the Oxbridge set, including Humphrey Ward, whose cousin was the Oxford University president, and Cambridge student Wesley Harding, who despite being shot through the heart in WWI recovered sufficiently to warrant a place in Antwerp. There would have been no room on the steamer from Harwich for the likes of Harry Walden.

The North was the other stronghold of the English amateur game but was poorly represented. Bishop Auckland played in two Amateur Cup finals before the competition was suspended at the end of the 1914/15 season. The club would win the competition at the end of the 1920/21 season but southern prejudices prevailed. Bishop's only player in Antwerp was England amateur international, George Atkinson.

Suspicions that the England amateur team and the Olympic side were the preserve of players from the Old Boys' clubs and public schools were hard to shake off. Given the people and clubs behind the split and the formation of the amateur team, those suspicions were well-founded and would gain great credence later in the decade with a massive purge of supposed shamateurs in the North East.

Certainly the man put in charge by the FA as the official leader of the footballing contingent going to Antwerp was wholly representative of the southern traditionalists. Charles Wreford-Brown had always been a hard-working administrator. The return of the AFA saw him to the fore in the Olympic effort, influencing not just selection but the whole trip. His final full England appearance had been in 1898 and the last of his 161 starts for Corinthians in the 1902/03 season, but Wreford-Brown loved the game too much to quit playing altogether. Corinthians' first three games after the war were only "A" team matches against three public schools. One was against Charterhouse and Wreford-Brown, then in his early fifties, pulled on his boots against his old school.

The grand Old Carthusian joined the party that left Harwich on 26 August by steamer for Antwerp. A number of players had dropped out due to injuries, such as reserve keeper Coleman, and a handful of replacements were called up. For the second consecutive Olympic football tournament, a Bunyan would also be involved.

Charlie Bunyan had left Sweden and moved to Belgium, where he managed Standard Liege and the national team. His sons were also now playing and one, Maurice, was the top scorer in the Belgian first division in the two years before World War One broke out, scoring 33 and 28 goals respectively for Racing Club.

When Germany invaded Belgium in 1914, the Bunyans immediately fled. Disguising himself and his family as refugees, they quickly escaped to England. Within 30 hours of landing, Maurice and his two brothers, Ernest and Cyril, had signed up and joined the 17th Middlesex. The following year, their father Charlie cut eight years off his age and told the authorities that he was only 38 in order to join his sons in the same regiment, only to be discharged in 1916.

In 1917 Maurice managed a few games for Chelsea, including one – a 0-0 draw with Spurs – that saw Bunyan junior line up alongside the Great Dane himself, Nils Middelboe. After the war the Bunyans returned to Belgium, but in 1919 Maurice had been in Croydon, where he got married, and the following summer he was called up as a late addition for the holders' trip to Antwerp.

The war was over but a military presence remained in the squad. Apart from Hegan, forward Bert Prince was still in the Royal Medical Corps and Freddie Willie Herbert Nicholas was in the Bedfords. A holder of the Military Cross, Nicholas was another sporting all-rounder. He was a fine sprinter, opened and kept wicket for Essex County Cricket Club, captained the MCC on tour to the West Indies and was even a talented piano player. In addition to these talents, he also played football and captained the Army, but would never have turned professional. "A public schoolboy then would never have been a professional in those days," says his daughter-in-law, the mother of cricketer and TV presenter Mark Nicholas.

Another Army man, Colonel R.J. Kentish, was put in charge of the overall BOA party, which was again mired in money problems. The cost of sending the entire Olympic party to Antwerp was £5,000 but a fortnight before leaving, the BOA was still £1,500 short. Fundraising continued after the party arrived in Antwerp and the footballers were not booked into accommodation in the Belgian port but the Hotel de Negociants in Brussels. As the FA party disembarked, secretary F.J. Wall, walking down the gantry to shore, remarked to a reporter, "We are not likely to have it all our own way in Antwerp."

Wall was referring to the progress made by the Swedes and Dutch rather than England's first-round opponents in a tournament that was again a knock-out competition. The holders' first round opponents, Norway, only formed a national association in 1902. The Norwegians joined Fifa six years later but did not enter the 1908 Games. Their only Olympic experience was a 7-0 pasting by Nils Middelboe's Denmark in the first round in 1912, but the 1920 vintage had far more experience than the defending champions.

Of the England team from Rouen, Knight, Hunt, Atkinson, Harbridge, Nicholas, Harold Hardinge, Jackie Hegan and Dick Sloley of Corinthians all started in Antwerp, but they were short on experience. Knight had 20 amateur caps. Hunt had 16 caps but no other player had made more than three appearances for the England amateur side. Keeper Mitchell, who occasionally wore spectacles in matches, had just a single cap to his name, while Maurice Bunyan, one of the leading goalscorers in early Belgian football, was not even picked.

The Norwegian Olympic association would only send athletes or teams they felt would make the top six in their event to Antwerp. Ominously for GB, the Norges Fotballforbund were happy to send their footballers. Their team had played together regularly since spring 1918, beating Denmark and Sweden for the first time. Those first victories were on sand but in 1919 Norway began playing on grass and repeated the feat to win that year's Nordic championship. The 5-1 win in Gothenburg remains Norway's biggest win over Sweden.

The experienced Norwegian side had a tight defence, excellent half-backs and forwards who could score. In their 1919 game with Denmark the lead changed hands three times but the Norwegians were strong enough to come back and claim victory. In Antwerp, the experienced Kaare Engebretsen was lost to injury. His replacement Einar Wilhelms only had two caps. The rest of the Norway side were vastly more experienced. Captain and left-half Gunnar Anderson of Ski & FK Lynn had 27 caps. His club team-mates Per Skou and Otto Aulie had 28 and 23 caps respectively. The Norwegians also had a trainer with his own particular motivation: James McPherson was a Scot.

29 August 1920
Olympic Stadium, Beerschoot. England vs Norway
McPherson sent his team out to face his Auld Enemy in front of a crowd of between 5,000 and 10,000 people. The holders' support came from a group

of rowdy English fans behind the northern goal but the rest of the ground was behind the Norwegians. A crowd of film and press photographers stirred on the touchline as Knight led his team out. The sun was sinking into the Belgian skyline behind the backs of the defending champions. The strong wind was also behind them. The holders might have had the elements in their favour, but not luck. Dutch referee Johannes Mutters tossed a coin and everything started to go wrong for Knight's team. Norwegian captain Gunnar Andersen won the toss. He sensibly opted to change ends. Now Norway would have the benefit of the wind and the sun behind them for the first half.

The press photographers and journalists scrabbled to change ends before the kick-off, when Andersen demonstrated his confidence by dribbling around the surprised English attackers and surging into their half. Play stayed there until Einar Wilhelms robbed an inattentive English player and passed to Einar Gundersen, who slammed the ball past Mitchell after 15 minutes.

The shocked holders increased the pace and forced a save from Norwegian keeper, Wathne. After 25 minutes, Nicholas on the right wing caught out the Norwegian backs to equalise but the English gentlemen's casual approach to preparing for the game soon told, as Dick Sloley and Bert Prince went down with injuries. With no substitutes, England had to battle on.

Sensing their chance, Norway attacked relentlessly in the second half. Helgesen and Gundersen drew good saves from Mitchell. A Norwegian interception prevented a certain GB goal in a breakaway but most of the action was in the opposing half, where Wold boldy began to take long-range pot shots at Mitchell's goal. Six minutes into the second half, a move involving Asbjørn Halvorsen, Per Holm and Helgesen found Gundersen, who scored Norway's second.

The Belgian crowd got even noisier. The Englishmen, a washed out replica of Vivian Woodward's teams, were constantly hemmed into their own half by confident, fitter opponents. Twelve minutes after Gundersen's goal, Per Holm shrugged off an ineffective Basil Gates challenge to send Einar Wilhelms through for a third.

Stunned Norwegian fans urged their team to play defensively to secure a victory. Captain Andersen nonchalantly waved back then urged his team into attack again. This high pressure game eventually wore the Norwegians out. Wilhelms went down with an injury but at 3-1, there was no way back for England. Knight's team won a late corner but the Norwegian defenders easily pounced on the in-swinging ball. When Mutters blew the whistle, the holders had managed not more than half a dozen shots on goal all game.

The Sportsman blamed the defeat on the injuries to Prince and Sloley, a "weak performance" from the halves and the side's overall age, but could not argue about the result: the holders deserved to lose. *The Scotsman* was more forthright, saying: "The pups are beginning to bite back." Citing a woeful lack of preparation, *The Scotsman* concluded:

> "The defeat of Britain at her own national game is still the topic of conversation. It is generally acknowledged that the team was not representative of Britain's best amateur talent but the point which provokes the most criticism was the poor condition of some members of the team. It was obvious to the spectators that they were in want of physical training and their physical fitness was an unpleasant contrast to the fitness of the Norwegians."

The Scotsman continued to refer to the team as "our boys" but one Scot who quite obviously saw the dividing line between England and Scotland clearly enough was James McPherson. As weary, dispirited English players shook hands with the Norwegian party and posed for team photos, they were bewildered to hear a familiar caterwauling. In a bizarre moment of anti-English triumphalism, McPherson led a Scottish bagpipe band into the arena playing the Norwegian national anthem watched by the bemused and outraged Wreford-Brown and Colonel Kentish. The dejected Ted Robbins stood to one side, not quite sure what to make of the spectacle.

The defeat and the holders' loss of their title was greeted with no more coverage than the run-up. *Athletic News*, which covered all sports but favoured professional football, opined: "[Defeat] is the result of very haphazard and indifferent preparation." There was no inquest in the media. The weekly *Athletic News* devoted articles in consecutive issues on FA secretary F.J. Wall being presented with a gift from the Swedes thanking him for all his work in the footballing world.

Would England have beaten the Norwegians if their reluctant captain, Max Woosnam, had played? Who knows, but Woosnam went on to win gold in the doubles and silver in the mixed doubles in Antwerp.

A Briton footballer did pick up a medal in Antwerp but George Hebdin was turning out for the hosts not the holders. A 31-year-old British centre forward, who had moved to Belgium in 1917, Hebdin made three appearances for Belgium while playing for Union St Gilloise. In March 1909 the Belgians realised that Hebdin only held a British passport. In deference to Fifa he was rapidly dropped, only for the rules to change in 1912. Fifa decided that any player who had been in a country for a decade could turn out for his new home, a rule that remains today but with a far shorter qualification period. So Hebdin returned to the Belgian side in 1913 and was in the Belgian squad that reached the final in Antwerp.

Vivian Woodward did not get to play in front of the stand he designed, but he would surely have approved of how his great rival, Nils Middelboe, warmed up for the Antwerp Olympics. In 1913 Middelboe moved to England. After initially signing for Newcastle he switched clubs before making an appearance for the Magpies and joined Woodward's old club, Chelsea, becoming their first overseas player. With his last chance of Olympic glory in Antwerp in 1920 only weeks away, Middelboe played in the Chiswick Park Tennis Members Singles Championship.

There was to be no glorious end to Middelboe's career. Denmark went out in the first round, losing to Spain 1-0. The Spaniards were then eliminated by Belgium to set up a final between the hosts and Czechoslovakia. In Antwerp, with nothing to do, Ted Knight and Wreford-Brown volunteered to run the line. In the centre with the whistle was another Englishman, John Lewis, who endured a difficult match. The Czechs disagreed with most of his decisions, some with good reason. *The Times* reported that Lewis ordered off a Czech back for kicking; other reports suggested the Czechs took umbrage at the second Belgian goal. What happened once the Czechs got annoyed is not disputed. Their entire team mobbed Lewis. When the Englishman would not defer to Bohemian umbrage, the Czechs stormed off. The baffled Belgians were left with no one to play against. Lewis, Knight and Wreford-Brown tried to persuade the Czechs to come back out, but to no avail. The organisers had little choice but to disqualify the Czechs and award the Belgians gold.

The watching Wreford-Brown had been welcomed onto the FA Consultative Committee shortly before the Olympics. Ironically, in their former guise as Bohemia the Czechs had sided with the AFA during the Great Split but the final only hardened Wreford-Brown's views on how the game should be played. No one knows how many times he related the stormy events of the final to his fellow gentlemen back home but the 1920 Olympics certainly had a big impact with the Home Nation FAs.

In 1912 Fifa had laid down new rules on amateurism to try and sate the British but these were subsequently broken with reckless abandon in Antwerp. Players were paid openly and well in excess of hotel and travel bills and "broken time". This issue – the payment of players for unpaid time taken off work – would later seal the British game's international exile. After their miserable performance against Norway, the FA stormed back home in a high-minded dudgeon. "British amateurs have been playing against professionals of other countries; we shall never again take part in Olympic football," fulminated one unidentified FA official on his way out of Antwerp.

Ironically, the Norwegians were not one of those teams. Apart from England, Norway, who were thrashed 4-0 by Czechoslovakia in the next round, and Middelboe's Danes were probably the only truly amateur sides in the tournament. The Norwegians, Danes and English would not return to the Olympic football tournament for a sporting generation. Nils Middelboe stayed with Chelsea until 1923, playing 175 matches, then like the true amateur that the Great Dane was, he turned out for Corinthians and Casuals for three years and also refereed. In 1936 he returned to Denmark and coached briefly at his old club.

The English team's coach, George Latham, returned to Cardiff City and became the only manager to take the FA Cup outside of England, winning the trophy in 1927. He coached Cardiff up until 1936 and his home town club's stadium, Newtown AFC, was named Latham Park in his honour.

Many of the players drifted off into the unchronicled ether of amateur football. Basil Gates and his brother Eric returned to London Caledonians and won the Amateur Cup in 1922/23. A year later, Basil turned out for Southend in a Football League fixture but that was his only flirtation with the professional game. The Gates brothers remained staunch amateurs. Between 1920 and 1931 these two sons of a Scottish mother collected 15 caps between them for the England amateur XI but never played in the same international XI together. George Atkinson won the Amateur Cup again in 1921/22 and proved a one club man, later becoming Bishop Auckland's honorary secretary. Bert Prince, who went on to win five amateur caps for England, stayed with the Army and rose to the rank of lieutenant colonel, but Wesley Harding, another England amateur international, was to die five years later, aged just 32. The headmaster of Bishop Auckland School at the time, his death was blamed on his war injuries.

Olympic keeper James Mitchell made a more lasting impression on the football world. After graduating from Manchester University, Mitchell joined Preston North End but stayed a gentleman. PNE had beaten Wanderers 3-0 in the 1889 FA Cup Final with an amateur keeper, Dr Mills Roberts. Mitchell also reached an FA Cup Final, but made a far more lasting impact.

PNE reached the 1922 final, which was played at Stamford Bridge in London. Uneventful until the 67th minute, the game exploded when Huddersfield and England winger Billy Smith was brought down in the box. A penalty was awarded. As Smith prepared to take his kick, Mitchell, also the first and last goalkeeper to wear glasses in a cup final, began dancing around in his goalmouth. One match report likened his routine to "an excited monkey on a stick awaiting the offer of a bag of peanuts". Smith still scored. Huddersfield went on to win 1-0, giving manager Herbert Chapman the first of many trophies. After the game, the rules were changed because of Mitchell's behaviour so that goalkeepers had to at least stay on their line when a penalty was taken. After the cup final Mitchell joined Manchester City for five seasons but left when the club were relegated in 1925 and briefly played for Leicester City.

Mitchell's cup final antics would not have been appreciated by those Corinthians in the Antwerp side like F.W.H. Nicholas. In 1922/23 Corinthians entered the FA Cup, a competition which would provide the club and Nicholas with some great days. In only their second season, Nicholas was in a team of Corinth gentlemen that eliminated northern powerhouse Blackburn Rovers. Nicholas went on to score 28 goals in 54 games for Corinth and he also went on private cricket tours led by the Honourable Lionel Tennyson, who became godfather to his son. Nicholas played for Essex until 1929. His best season was 1926, when he made 726 runs, including his only century with a knock of 140 against Surrey.

His captain in Antwerp, A.E. Knight, played for Portsmouth at the Dell against rivals Southampton a few days after returning home. The result was no better than Antwerp, a 2-0 defeat. To make matters worse, he suffered an injury that meant Knight was unable to captain Portsmouth in their first Football League season in 1920/21. He left Pompey in 1922 and played the remainder of his career at Corinthians, where he was granted life membership and helped, along with Jackie Hegan, produce a brief flicker of renaissance at the grand old club.

Knight and Woosnam were, to a degree, men increasingly out of step with their time, but they helped Corinth turn back the clock. In the 1920s Corinth produced a number of memorable FA Cup performances. The team made the third round on a number of occasions and drew big crowds for their "home" games even though Corinthians had no home ground. In 1926, 30,000 fans turned up to Crystal Palace for a 3-3 draw with Manchester City. Hegan was among the scorers that day and again in 1927 when Corinth made the fourth round. The team went down 3-1 to Newcastle United but an incredible 56,338 fans swelled Crystal Palace.

Hegan eventually won 23 amateur caps and four for the full team, scoring twice on his debut in a 6-1 mauling of Belgium in 1923 and playing in England's first senior game with France. He scored 50 goals in 167 games for Corinthians before finally hanging up his boots in 1933. A professional soldier all his life, he was awarded the OBE during World War Two, when he attained the rank of lieutenant colonel and retired in July 1949. Hegan is card number 15 of 50 in the 1926 cigarette card series Football Caricatures by "Mac", issued by John Player and Sons.

Hegan and Knight were content to play when work allowed. Northern Nomads also only played friendlies but professional clubs had few free slots and often sent reserve teams. This provided little opportunity for gentlemen to test themselves and their disappearance from the top of the game seemed inevitable. Joining the Football League had been mooted at Corinth but the club averred. Most Corinthians agreed that raising a decent squad for 42 matches in Division Three South would prove impossible but the Corinthians were also decidedly sniffy about the prospect of entertaining the leading southern amateur league, the Isthmian.

Not all the Corinthians agreed. Something had to be done to save the gentlemen's game or their doctrine would be lost. Sitting on the deck of the ship going back from Antwerp was one of those modernists, who had an idea how to prevent a repeat of the Antwerp humiliation.

CHAPTER FIVE: IN/OUT, NORTH/SOUTH

"The real point at issue is – can an Amateur XI compete successfully in the League? If it can, few will deny that to all the other members and to the game itself the Club will be a boon."

Dick Sloley

DICK SLOLEY WAS STEAMING – BOTH LITERALLY AND metaphorically – back home from Antwerp. The manner of the Olympic defeat to the Norwegians stung the London schoolteacher. Sloley had signed as an amateur, first with Aston Villa and then his local side Brentford, and he knew that playing friendlies was no longer enough for himself or the purists from the bastion of the AFA. Sloley was close to the AFA and turned out for their representative team against Cambridge University in 1921. But he was a modernist. The World War One veteran – with the Royal Flying Corps – lobbied diligently for Corinthians to join the Football League. Sloley was ignored but remained convinced that if there was a gentlemen's club in the Football League, it would be a natural home for the best amateurs – like Queen's Park, who still held their own in the Scottish first division.

In 1922 Sloley left his teaching post at Harrow to become joint headmaster of Golden Parsonage School in Hemel Hempstead. And, after 37 games for Corinth, he left and signed for Ealing Association FC, a stalwart of the AFA. Sloley went on to win the Southern Amateur League and cup double in 1927, and later he left Golden Parsonage School to become secretary of the medical school at University College Hospital, London, where he looked on as Corinthians drew big crowds in the FA Cup. About to hang up his boots, Sloley began to put into action a plan that had been simmering since that long, doleful journey back from Antwerp – a plan to revive the gentlemen's role in football.

The spur was a chance meeting in the winter of 1927 with Bob Alaway, who was behind the formation of Middlesex Wanderers, an amateur team of some repute that toured overseas. Sloley and Alaway retired to the Sports Club at St James's Square in central London and the 1920 Olympian enthusiastically explained his plan. If nearly 60,000 people were willing to watch Corinth in the FA Cup, then, reasoned Sloley, surely a southern amateur team in the league would garner sufficient support. "[Sloley] foresaw that with so many of the public schools going over to rugby, the Corinthians, unless they amended their qualifications for membership, would gradually fade away as a telling force", recalled Alaway in his memoir, *Football All Round The World*.

The pair agreed to put a plan into action. The Earl of Lonsdale was recruited as a club president with the vice presidents including the headmasters of Harrow and Westminster Schools. A handful of impassioned former amateur players including Alaway and his brother Horace joined as committeemen and vociferous media support came from *Athletic News*, then edited by 1908 Olympic gold medallist Ivan Sharpe.

Sloley met the Football League and their president, John McKenna, who were surprisingly receptive. This was not common cause but financial common sense as the Football League were all too aware of the huge attendances that Corinthians had drawn in their FA Cup matches in recent years.

"Dick sought and was immediately granted a meeting with the management committee of the League to place our suggestions before them," added Alaway. "The encouragement, advice and helpful suggestions he received were of untold value."

After their first meeting the Football League had made only one condition. Corinthians played mostly away matches and had to find a ground like Crystal Palace for popular home games, such as FA Cup ties. This, McKenna made clear, would not do in the Football League. A permanent ground was needed for Sloley's new team, whose name suggested just what sort of players he hoped to recruit. No working-class amateurs, only classics-reading gentlemen for the Argonauts.

In February 1928 Sloley agreed a deal to rent White City – home of England's 1908 Olympic success – much to the fury of nearby Football League clubs Brentford and Queens Park Rangers, who vowed to block his proposal. So Sloley made contact with Arthur Elvin, the impresario who owned Wembley Stadium, and agreed a deal to rent the new home of English football that had opened five years previously.

Although the days of Corinthian supplying the bulk of the full England team were long gone, a handful of amateurs still occasionally featured in internationals, such as Sloley's Antwerp team-mate, Jackie Hegan and fellow Corinthians, such as F.N.S. Creek and Alfred "Baishe" Bower. There were also amateurs playing in the Football League such as Rigger Coates at Southampton, while Edgar Kail would soon go on to play for England while at Dulwich Hamlet.

If players of this standard would join the Argonauts, the club could prove a success but Sloley would not disclose the names of players who had pledged allegiance to his plan, refusing to break any confidences. Despite this and a Football League recommendation to vote for the two clubs up for re-election, at the end of the 1927/28 season the Argonauts gained a surprising 16 votes from sides in the Third Division South. This was fewer than the two sides seeking re-election, Torquay and Merthyr, who gained 42 and 27 votes respectively. The other three challengers for a place in the Third Division South – Fletton, Kettering and Peterborough – gained just five votes between them.

Sloley had agreed a lease with Elvin and his old club Ealing played a handful of games at Wembley, but the attendances were paltry. Sloley had said that the Argonauts would only apply to the Football League once. He seemed unlikely to change his mind until, in January 1929, Corinthians put in their last, great FA Cup performance, routing Norwich 5-0 at Carrow Road in the third round. The following month, *Athletic News* reported that the Argonauts would attempt to set sail again.

The names of Sloley's committeemen and putative players for the first Argonauts bid had remained shrouded in secrecy but club notes acquired for this book identify some of those involved. The committee included former Labour prime minister Ramsay MacDonald, the eminent geologist Sir

Arthur Holmes and the former Mayor of London, Sir Charles Wakefield. The notes also claim that the Prince of Wales, whom Sloley had met while at Golden Parsonage School, was also supportive of the project.

In early April, Sloley invited some of the players who had committed to play to a meal at the Arundel Hotel and they seem unlikely to be names to fill Wembley. The star was Doctor Donald Fairbrother, who in 1926 had captained Northern Nomads to victory in the Amateur Cup. Fairbrother was an England amateur international. So was Frederick Gregory but these players' experience in the Football League was limited. Gregory had been on the books of Wimbledon and Leyton but had made just three appearances in the Football League for Millwall and those were two seasons ago.

Fairbrother had been on the books of Manchester United and Manchester City but his solitary league appearance at Blackburn Rovers was in 1923. The most experienced player was Albert Miles, who is credited with 16 appearances for Cardiff City between 1927 and 1929. Sloley's ex-Ealing team-mate Arthur Isaac was among the diners and his Football League experience was limited to a couple of appearances for Brentford back in 1924. Another Ealing player, FC Probyn, was also at the Arundel Hotel along with AM Eastman of Leytonstone.

Sloley had met with Casuals, a club for ex-public schoolboys playing in the Isthmian League, who pledged support but there was none from Corinthians or the FA. This drew the ire of Ivan Sharpe in *Athletic News* but Sloley's biggest public supporter was also tiring of the refusal by the Argonauts founder to name any of his potential players.

At the 1929 annual general meeting of the Football League, Sloley spoke to the assembled clubs. "So much has been said as to the possible playing strength of the Club, so much as to the many difficulties which will have to be overcome, that there is a danger of losing sight of the fundamental object of the proposal," said Sloley to the massed ranks of the league clubs. He continued:

> "The real point at issue is – can an Amateur XI com-
> pete successfully in the League? If it can, few will deny
> that to all the other members and to the game itself the
> club will be a boon … In making this final appeal for
> your recommendation, we would urge that not for many
> years – even if ever again – will it be possible to revive

this movement. The Argonauts is the only amateur club which has ever made such progress in its organisation to be in a position to make an application for admission to the League. To all other applicants a further opportunity will arise – to the Argonauts this is the last. The Argonauts bring something to the Third Division which no other applicant can offer – an entirely new interest. Isn't the experiment worth a chance?"

Only half a dozen clubs thought so on this occasion and the Argonauts finished a distant third in the election. The Argonauts had been thwarted by self-interest among the league clubs and a lack of leadership from the FA, which Ivan Sharpe condemned. The continued flight of the public schools from football to rugby union would accelerate and after this second failure, Sloley's fellow Olympian, the Reverend Kenneth Hunt, wrote in *Athletic News*:

"I think it is an awful pity from what I call the social point of view, if you like, that what are commonly called the classes and the masses are being educated to understand that there are two different games. It is a dreadful mistake. Let us diminish rather than increase this separating of people who like good sport into two different games. I believe that if those Corinthians who are good enough would sign as amateurs for some professional team in the League and would play for them regularly it would do an enormous amount of good not only for the game itself but to reduce the feeling that gentlemen play another game, which is called 'Rugger'."

After Hunt's plea appeared, Dick Sloley resolved to try one last time but his refusal to name any players had lost the Argonauts their biggest supporter. In the 1930 Football League election for the Third Division South, the Argonauts' final bid was ignored by *Athletic News* and the club failed to win a single vote. That some professional clubs had earlier voted for these amateurs was partly a reflection of self-interest among their owners, who relished the big crowds that Corinthians had drawn in the FA Cup.

After the third bid Sloley abandoned his quest for a gentlemen's team in the Football League, much to Alaway's dismay. "I am convinced that we could have made the Argonauts the Queen's Park of England," wrote Alaway shortly before the 1948 Olympics in London. "It might have cut across the notions of even certain amateur clubs, but, had the scheme succeeded we should not now be worrying about the chances of our Olympic side. The material would have been there – with experience against professionals."

Instead, just as after the formation of the Football League and Old Carthusians' exclusion, the amateurs' role in football would pan out rather differently. Sloley's venture having failed, the gentlemen would have to exercise themselves in the grand halls of the sport's administration rather than on the pitches of the Football League.

SLOLEY'S FAILED DREAM HAD PARTLY BEEN MOTIVATED by the English/British response to the two Olympics that followed Antwerp. At the meeting held during the 1920 Olympics, Fifa had ruled that neutral members could play who they wanted but the British had taken their balls and their boots back to home to play mostly among themselves. In the two years after Antwerp, England played just one game against a continental side – Belgium in 1921 – and the other Home Nations continued their record of playing only each other.

The Antwerp meeting had been simply a Fifa meeting rather than a full official congress including representatives of all the world body's members. A congress followed in 1923, which the Austrians and the Germans did not attend but the Hungarians did. Also in attendance was the Football Association of Ireland (FAI), which joined Fifa in 1921 – two years before formal political independence was achieved from Britain. Ireland had two senior amateur clubs but independence saw Dublin-based Bohemians leave the Belfast-based Irish League to play with clubs from the south. Independence also led to a rule allowing Northern Irish athletes a choice over whether to represent Britain or what would later formally become the Republic of Ireland providing they had an RoI passport.

Before the 1924 Olympics in Paris the Home Nations begrudgingly returned to Fifa, but their restoration was on a couple of strict provisos: no Fifa interference in the Home Nations' relations with each other, and no percentage of gate receipts from their internationals to help fund the world body's growth. With the return of the British, Fifa made a renewed attempt to define the slippery concept of what an amateur really was.

Professionalism began to take hold in central European countries such as Austria, Czechoslovakia and Hungary, replacing the shamateurism that had become rife as associations reconciled gate receipts with players left out of pocket for broken time. Agreeing on what defined an amateur had become even harder but the British knew. You took no money for anything. If you did, you were a professional. Fifa board member Rodolphe Seeldrayers argued this punished less well-off amateurs but the world body's future president could not sway the British, whose position was dominated by privileged traditionalists.

In December 1923 Fifa asked the British to consider a middle ground, taking into account broken time. The result: all four Home Nations walked out again, this time accompanied by the Danes, who agreed with their stance. There would be no British footballers in Paris, but perhaps that was for the best.

After the ignominy of the defeat to Norway in 1920 the England amateur team went into decline. The days when only English gentlemen could go on overseas tours to teach the world how to play had long vanished. Footballing standards improved not only in neutral Scandinavia but also in countries even more decimated by the mass slaughter of World War One than Britain.

Around 885,000 military deaths were recorded by the UK during the Great War compared to 1.4 million in France. The UK's population of 45.4 million was greater than France's 39.6 million, and its sporting infrastructure had not been trampled on by the Central Powers. Yet football in France and across Europe was rapidly catching up.

Months after the 1920 Games a radically changed England amateur XI journeyed to Paris to play the French Olympic XI. Only Harold Prince remained from Antwerp. The army man was installed as captain but his charges lost 2-1. Three years later, the Olympians A.E. Knight and Jackie Hegan returned to the amateur side for matches against Belgium, but England lost 3-0 and 2-1.

The gentlemen that had traditionally populated the England amateur team and been the mainstay of earlier successful Olympic efforts were disappearing, but the AFA's influence also sidelined the working- and middle-class amateurs. In 1921 Corinthians had resumed touring overseas, going to France. In 1923/24 the club won their first 11 matches, including wins over league sides Queens Park Rangers and Southampton, and toured North America with Wreford-Brown among the leaders of the touring party. Finally taking part in the FA Cup provided some real moments of glory for Corinth, but winning that competition was unrealistic for the gentlemen amateurs.

The purists had also given up on winning the FA Amateur Cup. The Old Boys' teams had decamped for the Arthur Dunn Cup by this time and the Amateur Cup was firmly the province of working-class amateur sides. Even the Casuals refused to take part until 1923/24, when their return was marked by a 3-1 defeat in the first round to Southall. Staunch defenders of the amateur credo, such as London Caledonians and Cardiff Corinthians, entered but with no discernible success other than Caley's win in 1922/23. Between the 1920 Olympics and the next British entry in the Olympics in 1936, the only Amateur Cup final victory for an upper-class amateur side was the Casuals' 2-0 win in 1935/36. The footballing amateurs from the privileged backgrounds of the public schools and the business houses had been overwhelmingly usurped.

As football became more professional, more moneyed and more boisterous, the upper classes withdrew. An increase in attention from the betting industry would end many public schools' affection for football in favour of rugby union, where the young gentlemen produced by the public schools were increasingly funnelled after the Great War. Here, those upwardly mobile gentlemen could find qualities they had tried – and failed – to uphold in football. Rugby would also be plagued by shamateurism for decades but would hold back the tide of professionalism for much longer than football.

For those gentlemen amateurs holding the fort in football, their only real power lay in valiantly trying to hold onto their embattled ideals through the influence gained by the AFA's settlement with the FA. This saw the likes of the Casuals return to the Isthmian League in 1919, but after 1920 and the Antwerp disaster another tilt at the Olympics was gone – for now at least.

Some football clubs still donated to the fund-raising for the 1924 Olympics. Woodward's old clubs were among the most generous, with Chelsea donating 100 guineas and Tottenham Hotspur providing 50 guineas, but no footballers would journey to Paris.

At the 1924 Olympics, the ongoing row over definitions of amateurism meant that neither an English or British side, nor Denmark – the finalists in 1908 and 1912 – took part. Austria and Germany did not feature either but a record field of 22 countries entered. The Republic of Ireland made their debut alongside the United States, Estonia and the first South American side, Uruguay. The Irish made the quarter-finals but Uruguay cruised to the gold medal. On their way to the final, Uruguay thrashed France 5-1 – an indicator of what might have happened had the English amateur team entered in 1924. The tournament established football as a serious source of revenue for the IOC. Gate receipts from the 41,000 fans who watched Uruguay beat Switzerland 3-0 represented a twelfth of the Games' overall income.

The following year another milestone passed in Corinthians' long slow fall. Alfred Bower was called up from Corinth to the full England team in 1924 for a 4-0 rout of Belgium. For the next game he was handed the captain's armband. His reign was brief, ending in 1926. Alfred George Bower played the last of his five full internationals against Wales in 1927 but holds one record for eternity. No amateur would ever captain the full England team again.

By the time Bower's full international career was ending, Fifa was confident enough to declare that a world football competition was possible, "without one single FA official, or British journalist, professional manager or British manager". Fifa made a last attempt to bring the British back for the 1928 Olympics in Amsterdam but this only made matters worse, far worse.

At a Fifa congress in 1926 the Home Nations were persuaded to attend only to see the Swiss put forward a motion saying: "It is not allowed to pay compensation for broken time, except in some well-circumscribed cases, to be fixed by each national association." The Home Nations would have none of it. The FA dissented but the motion was carried by 12 votes to 8. Returning home to the land of the much-hunted shamateur, the FA warned: "We are of the opinion that at present it is doubtful whether our amateur regulations would be observed."

In 1927 the divide between the Home Nations and Fifa developed into a gaping chasm. Fifa insisted that the IOC accept the condition over broken time payments. So the four British associations quit the Olympics. A few months later, all four Home Nations also walked away from Fifa yet again. This time, seemingly, for good.

This uncompromising attitude over amateurism permeated deep into the English game, dividing not only the FA from Fifa but the strongholds of the English amateur game, which remained the North East and South East. In 1927 an anonymous letter sent to the Durham FA accused Crook Town of breaching rules over payment of expenses. Clubs then paid a flat rate for "tea money" but the FA duly suspended Crook. The club's officials claimed "tea money" payments were rife and cited another 20 north-eastern clubs who did the same. The FA insisted that this was no excuse and the next year 341 players and many club officials were suspended – all from the North. Bishop Auckland alone had 46 players declared "professional", rivals Ferryhill lost the same number and Cockfield lost 37.

Players could be reinstated as amateurs but only at the discretion of individual county FAs. Entire playing squads of working-class amateur men were lost by the witch hunt. Cockfield's captain R.W. Harrison summed up local perceptions: "The amateur who sports plus-fours and knows the best people, travels in comfort, lunches before the match, dines after it and stays at the best hotel keeps his status," said the brusque but honest Harrison. "The stocky built, bow-legged Durham pit lad goes without lunch, crowds into a United bus, receives five shillings for tea, contents himself with a pie or snack in a side street and consequently is a professional."

To those traditionalists running the FA, there must be no form of compensation whatsoever. In 1899 Wreford-Brown summed up this position when interviewed by *Chums* magazine, saying, "Anyone who wants wine has to pay for it out of his own pocket." Little had changed since then. The players of Cockfield were not drinking wine, they were happy with tea, but even that was unpalatable to the FA unless they had paid from their own pockets.

With the AFA's influence being felt, the selection policy of the England amateur team looked suspiciously similar. England continued playing full international and amateur friendlies outside Britain, mostly against France, Belgium and Luxembourg. The English usually won. A first overseas defeat in a full international did not come until 1929 when a visit to Madrid resulted in a 4-3 loss to Spain. Confident of their pre-eminence, the FA did not need to join anyone else's club and would run their own game, amateur and professional, as they saw fit.

The other Home Nations had a clear sense of their own position inside the UK, but less so overseas. The SFA looked into travelling to France and Germany for matches in the late 1890s and early 1900s but interest diminished. The focus was retrained on Britain and the popular Home Nations championship. In the 1920s the SFA sent touring parties to North America but the first match as a full international with a non-UK side was not until May 1929, when Scotland travelled to Oslo to beat Norway 7-3. Fifa had advised members not to play the Home Nations but there is no record in the SFA archives of any special arrangements needed for the match.

That same year that Scotland visited Oslo the FAW sent a team of 18 Welshmen to Canada for a lengthy tour. The Wales squad travelled 13,000 miles, playing and winning 16 games against provincial teams. Only in 1933 did the Welsh take the plunge and go to Paris to help the French, who had been let down by another country for a scheduled friendly. The game finished 1-1.

Ireland never played an international against any team other than England, Scotland or Wales before independence for the south. A Northern Irish side was invited at short notice to visit Norway in 1922, losing 2-1 in Bergen to a team featuring some of England's conquerors from Antwerp. When the Norwegians discovered that the visitors' hastily assembled team contained a handful of professionals, they asked Fifa to scrub the match from all records. The IFA did not discover this until the 1990s.

Northern Ireland continued to select players from the Republic until 1950. Their first full international against a side outside of the Home Nations was a year later, a 2-2 draw with France in Paris. Fifa spent many years trying to pressure the IFA into dropping the name "Ireland". Only in the 1970s did the team become known more widely as Northern Ireland.

In the late 1920s isolationism gripped football in all four Home Nations. Frustrated by the British and keen to avoid dependence on the IOC, Fifa set up a commission to finally organise their own world championship. This would be for all players, amateur or professional. No discrimination, no dividing lines. If that could be achieved, tedious British-inspired debates over amateurism, broken time and professionalism would be banished. Fifa's dream accelerated as more members joined from outside Europe such as Cuba and Costa Rica, and regional confederations were established.

The IOC tried to provide its own solution and went back on a vote passed at a 1925 Prague congress – by a thumping 66 votes to 12 with 5 abstentions – opposing broken time. After sitting on this decision for two years, the IOC ruled that football would be an exception to sports like athletics. Broken time payments could be made without penalty. The British sporting establishment virtually choked with outrage. To ensure players were really amateur, broken time payments would go direct to athletes' employers. Even this was unacceptable to the British sports' ruling classes. The Home Nations had a conference in Liverpool in late 1927 to debate the IOC's new stance. All four associations would not deviate from their vision of what defined an amateur. The stalemate nearly forced the BOA to quit the entire Olympics until everyone finally accepted that GB's amateur footballers would have to stay at home – again.

"Payment or reimbursement for loss of time at work is quite contrary to British ideas of amateur sportsmanship," railed BOA secretary Evan Hunter, continuing:

> "The present decision affects football only because in virtually all other sports payment for the loss of salary is already forbidden by the international federations governing these sports. There is therefore no reason why Great Britain should not enter for any of those sports. As to football, if players are to receive this payment I am quite certain the Football Association will have nothing to do with the Games – more's the pity."

At the BOA's annual pre-Olympic dinner at the Connaught Rooms in April 1928, the Metropolitan Police's string band entertained future Olympians, who dined on *consumer de tortue* and grilled lamb. No footballers sat among the athletes, boxers, weightlifters and swimmers.

Fifa and the FA had brief, terse discussions in 1928 but there was to be no last-minute agreement. GB's footballers would not be in Amsterdam. An amateur football tournament between a Great Britain team, Sweden and Denmark at the same time as the Olympics was briefly mooted but never materialised.

The rows over amateurism spread like an ague and entrants into the football tournament dwindled to 16 nations. Argentina and Chile joined Uruguay in travelling over from South America. Other non-Europeans included Egypt, Mexico and the US. Uruguay swept to victory again although a replay was needed to finally see off neighbours Argentina 2-1.

In Britain, there was no third way between amateurism and professionalism. The traditionalists at the FA were the spur for this divide, but outside of England mixing money and sport was equally unseemly. Amateurs who had gone over to the other side and played for money could ask for reinstatement as gentlemen but the FAW were as unflinching in their enforcement of this divide as the English. At the start of one season, 28 players asked the FAW to be allowed to return to the amateur game. Just six were allowed.

In Scotland, there was similar disdain for money's involvement. The Scots went on a first overseas tour in 1931, visiting Austria, Switzerland and Italy. The tour, which ended in defeats to the Austrians and Italians and a win over the Swiss, provoked a furore in Scotland. The tourists were paid £2,600 for the three-match tour, which had been watched by an aggregate of 85,000 people. This fee was described as "scandalous" in *The Scotsman*.

An editorial shortly after in the *Observer* summed up the prevailing mood on playing football in continental Europe. "Why send teams there in our close season?" asked the paper's leader writer, adding:

> "It is quite another matter to dispatch teams from England and Scotland to tour distant parts of the Empire. The players there are Anglo-Saxon and adhere to the laws of the game. They share the British ideals of this sport and are not so interested in some so-called world championship. It is surely our task to raise the standards of the game in England; not to trouble ourselves touring on the continent and of arranging matches with these countries."

That sideswipe was aimed at Fifa, which in 1930 achieved its dream of staging a World Cup for all players, whether amateur or professional. Having won two Olympics, Uruguay hosted the tournament – not a universally popular choice – and again beat neighbours Argentina in a final watched by 93,000 people. After this tournament, Olympic football would never be the same. Fifa did not need the IOC. Having been homeless for many years, an almost ephemeral organisation only existing in meeting rooms and on paper, Fifa set up a permanent office in Switzerland. A footballing behemoth was born.

For the IOC, football briefly disappeared in 1932, sunk by the rows over amateurism and a lack of enthusiasm for the sport in the US, the Olympic hosts. The US had sent a football team to Amsterdam but football was hardly established back home. At the 1932 Olympics in Los Angeles the game did not feature. The sport was clearly too much of a money-spinner for the IOC to drop altogether, however, and in 1936 the Olympics were scheduled for Berlin. Before the event, the IOC forecasted that receipts for the football matches alone would pay for the entire Games.

Outside the Olympics, Fifa and the Home Nations rubbed alongside in an uneasy truce on the IFAB, where the world body finally gained admittance in 1913. Fifa had two votes but so did each of the four associations from the Home Nations. Fifa was relatively powerless but football was so much more advanced in the Home Nations that most other nations accepted British authority over setting the game's rules.

England finally played the old Central Powers in August 1930, drawing a full international 3-3 with Germany in Berlin and then playing out a 0-0 draw with Austria four days later. In 1933 Norway asked the FA to raise a British team for an amateur tournament with the northern countries of central Europe. Even that was too much for the traditionalists within the FA, such as Wreford-Brown, whose power in the FA was growing. Under Wreford-Brown's guidance the FA's amateur committee played a defensive game. The Norwegians' offer was rejected.

Gradually the AFA's role had diminished as powerbrokers like Wreford-Brown moved onto the FA's committees. In 1931 the AFA agreed to a revision of the original pact that sealed the truce. At the FA's request, the organisation was renamed the Amateur Football Alliance. A dozen new member clubs could be added to the AFA roster each year but membership must never top 500. The AFA gained two concessions: the FA allowed representatives from the AFA, Oxford and Cambridge Universities and another from the public schools onto its main council.

Wreford-Brown had taken up the role as Oxford University's representative within the FA back in 1920. This latest breakthrough enabled the old Carthusian to bolster his power base, as the AFA was also allowed a voice on the international selection committee, providing a voice to lobby for the dwindling number of amateurs playing at the top level of the professional game. Here too, Wreford-Brown would have plenty to say as participation in the next Olympics began to look more likely.

In 1934 Fifa held another world championship. The Home Nations' isolationism continued even though the tournament was far closer to home. The hosts won again as Italy beat Czechoslovakia 2-1 after extra time in front of 45,000 people in Rome. The 1934 World Cup produced earnings of nearly 56,000 Swiss francs for Fifa, whereas levy on the 105 international matches played in 1935 by the organisation's members provided just 50,000 Swiss francs.

The World Cup became a financial necessity for Fifa and the role of football at the next Olympics seemed likely to shrink by comparison to the new world championship. Except these Games would not be quite the same as any previous Olympics. Adolf Hitler would see to that.

CHAPTER SIX: BERLIN 1936 AND A BRUSH WITH HITLER

"I've been washing my hand ever since."

1936 GB Olympic footballer Sir Daniel Pettit
on meeting Adolf Hitler

FOR PETTIT, THE MOST INFAMOUS SPORTING SPECTACLE
of modern times could so easily have been passed up. "Young people didn't
see the aura that you see in the Olympics that you see today," he says. "Then,
you were likely to be saying what will I be doing in August? Will I be on
holiday or is there a marriage in the family?"

Daniel Pettit – he was knighted many years later for services to industry
– was certainly a gentleman, but no child of privilege. One of six children
born in the poor streets of Liverpool, Pettit's family managed to send him
to Quarrybank School. He proved a star pupil, playing junior football
for Everton and Liverpool Football Clubs and winning a scholarship to
Cambridge University in 1935 to read history and French. Pettit was a
gentleman because he would not play football for money.

Richard Pettit vividly remembers his father banging his fist on a table
and shouting, "You don't play football for money." Even into his early
nineties, his working and footballing career left long behind in the distance,
Daniel Pettit smiles at his son's impersonation. "You were regarded as rather
special just to be an amateur then," he says with a smile. An amateur he

stayed. Pettit would go to the 1936 Olympics even though he did pass up an international amateur cap in favour of a family wedding.

The kudos associated with being an amateur and a gentleman had seeped into the grammar school system that educated Daniel Pettit. After graduating from Cambridge, Pettit inevitably started turning out for Corinthians and – when back on Merseyside – for Northern Nomads. For Corinthians, the sun was setting on the club's independence and the grand aims of Pa Jackson would soon begin to flounder.

Pettit went on Corinthians' four-match winless tour of Denmark and Germany in April 1936. He was called up for England's amateur team twice, playing the first game against Wales but missing the second to go to his brother's wedding. Aged 79, Pettit told BBC Radio Worcester: "In 1936 it was still very much an amateur game that you took part in as a form of relaxation. Not something that preoccupied your life to the point that you became almost a fanatic about what you were doing in the sports arena instead of something relaxing and a team game with your fellows."

There were no weddings in the Pettit family in the summer of 1936. When Tom Leek, a half-back with Moor Green and teacher at Buckhurst Hill School, dropped out of the Olympic squad, Daniel Pettit packed his boots for the experience of a lifetime.

DANIEL PETTIT WAS NOT THE ONLY LAST-MINUTE ENTRY for the 1936 Olympic football tournament as there was very nearly not any GB football team at all. Since Antwerp, football in Britain had become an insular affair. A 16-year harrumph meant that the only competitive international football competition for the British teams was the Home Nations championship. Scotland and Wales emulated England and tentatively embraced Europe, but since 1920 two Olympics featuring football and two Fifa World Cups passed without any British involvement at all.

When the 1936 Olympics in Berlin moved into sight, Britain was not certain to be involved in any sport, let alone football. The problem was not raising £4,000 to send a squad of athletes but the malevolent persecution of Germany's Jewish minority that spread like a cancer into all walks of life. "Hands off sport, politicians," roared Sir Noel Curtis-Bennett, Britain's representative on the IOC in 1936, when a boycott was mooted. It was fine, of course, to say that in complacent Britain but not in Berlin, where the

Nazis' tentacles wove into everyday life with hideous effect.

A British boycott lobby was organised by the National Workers' Sports Associations but few potential Olympic players were in the NWSA. As the threat of another world war edged ever closer, football's administrators in Britain were isolated by their own boycott – not a political one, but over that same hoary old chestnut: amateurism.

As the British associations withdrew during the 1920s they were gripped by an English inspired paranoia over the rest of the world's inability to play by their Corinthian standards. After 1920, payments for broken time became commonplace in Belgium, Italy, France, Norway and Switzerland. The FA were suspicious of most countries outside the British Isles, who were suspected of lax standards. No one understood the principles of the British game. Or so the FA thought. When the BOA's members assembled at London's Dorchester Hotel for their 1934 annual dinner, no footballers or administrators from the sport were present – a pessimistic portent for anyone hoping for a return to the Olympic football tournament in Berlin.

The Home Nations were so entrenched that sending a football team to Berlin barely merited discussion until the very year of the Games. In April 1936, reports circulated that football's return to the Olympic Games after an eight-year absence would involve no more than eight teams. The Germans were furious amateurs with standards akin to the British. This was demonstrated to sinister effect after the Germans annexed Austria in March 1938. Professionalism was soon outlawed as "unworthy of a German man".

The problematic ideals of amateurism, however, threatened to blight the 1936 Olympic football tournament. The organisers could not afford such a paltry turnout, which would have been disastrous. Football was expected to offset much of the cost of staging the overall Games. A quickly spun PR rebuttal was fired off. The hosts bullishly insisted that 19 teams, including the likes of China, Haiti and India, would play in Berlin.

Other countries cited as confirmed entrants ranged from Lithuania to Japan. The Home Nations were absent from this wishlist along with France, where the professional game was burgeoning. Talking up the tournament, the organisers reiterated that their football tournament would adhere to the amateur rules that strictly governed Germany's 600,000 senior players and the 900,000 juniors. No broken-time payments would be made, a claim which was made to win over the uncompromising British.

In April 1936 the Germans wrote to the FA asking for a team of not just English but British footballers to come to Berlin. But a British side would endanger the new independence that Scotland and Wales found by embracing Europe. According to their records, the FA wrote to the Scots and the Northern Irish but not the Welsh about the Germans' missive. By June 1936 they had not received any reply. Having been absent since 1920 and with little sign of entering Fifa's nascent World Cups, the traditionalists wanted a return to the Olympics. The FA's power-brokers gave the other Home Nations two options: nominate players for a British team or let England represent Great Britain – yet again.

In the spring and early summer of the Olympic year, officials from the four Home Nations' FAs met all across the land, from Shanklin in the Isle of Wight to Troon in Scotland. But they only met their fellow countrymen. Divided by four, the English met only other Englishmen, the Scots with the Scots, and so on. The Scottish administrators in particular remained in a dudgeon. In 1909 the SFA had complained by letter to the FA over their participation in the 1908 Olympics as Great Britain. That letter went unanswered.

For the Scottish administrators, the principle of a joint team was so "great" according to SFA records that a simple sub-committee could not decide whether they would participate in a joint team. Only the main Scottish FA board could rule on the notion of Scots playing as Britain on a football field. The next meeting of the main Scots FA board was 5 August – and the Games started on 2 August. As British football's bureaucrats shuffled from one provincial town to another, incapable of talking to anyone but themselves, the Games moved ever closer, marked only by inaction.

On 4 July, the four Home Nations' associations finally sat down. A statement was issued two days later confirming that a team of gentlemen would go to Berlin on the proviso that the tournament was conducted within the British definition of an amateur. No other objection was lodged or definition asked of the Germans about the competition.

The FA typically took charge but each of the four Home Nations would be allowed to send two officials – all at England's expense as the FA would foot the entire bill. Promisingly, for the future, the 4 July meeting had concluded with a decision to form a British Olympic Football Committee for subsequent Games.

A year earlier, the FA relented under pressure from the Yorkshire and Middlesex county associations and formed an amateur international selection committee, which helped nominate players for Berlin. On 13 July, less than a fortnight before the BOA party was due to leave, a squad of 22 players was named. There had been little time for watching players. Lobbying within the FA for individuals played a part in selection, as did the writing of journalists, who were then much closer to the players than today. Reporters and amateurs often socialised together in the bar after the final whistle. The doyen of journalists writing on amateur football then was Norman Ackland. The gentleman's game had a curious ambassador, one whose personal life would have concerned such men of probity as the FA.

Sydney Norman Ackland – he preferred his middle name – was born in southern Ireland in 1890 to a family of rich bankers. His CV showed he went to Trinity College Dublin and fought in the trenches and at sea as a purser in World War One. That was all true, but the words between the lines of the life of Ackland, a frustrated creative writer, were far more lurid. At 16 he was working as a bookie's runner and was sent to England after getting the family's maid – to use the words of his son, Joss, the distinguished English actor – "in trouble". After the war, Ackland drifted into the arena of so many frustrated scribes – journalism. Indulging in the heavy drinking that typified many men of Grub Street, he married and had three children but preferred to live with a mistress in Maida Vale.

Ackland first began writing on amateur football under the pseudonym, Philistone, in the *Westminster Gazette* in 1923. Over the years, his knowledge for the subject took him to *The Times*, *Morning Post* and the *Daily Telegraph*. In the 1930s he was writing as Pangloss in the *News Chronicle*. Ackland took his by-line from the French satire *Candide* written by the philosopher Voltaire. "He believed in everything for the best in the best of all possible worlds," says his son Joss. "I've worked as an actor in Africa and America and met players who said he started them off in football. He did a lot for amateur football."

Many Olympians over the years found themselves championed by Ackland, including the man who would captain the 1936 squad. Even without such positive press, Bernard Joy would surely have been the team's obvious leader. Gentlemen capable of playing at the top of the professional game could still be found in the amateur game but they needed time to train frequently to meet the amateur players' standards. Dulwich Hamlet's Edgar Kail – a wine and spirit salesman with three full England caps in 1929 – and Wilfred Minter of St Albans City were often feted as being of the quality but lacked the desire or the time to join the players. With the advantaged upper-classes in retreat, few amateurs did. In the early 1930s, Rigger Coates played for Southampton and Aubrey Howard Fabian for Derby County. By 1936 Joy was the most prominent amateur of his era, a man who took on the mantle of Vivian Woodward in his own forthright fashion; the last gentleman to play at the very highest level.

Just nine years old when A.E. Knight's holders were humiliated by Norway, Joy was born in Fulham and went on to the University of London, where he played centre-half for the university XI. After graduating he signed for Casuals and played in the Football League as an amateur for Southend United and Fulham. In May 1935 Joy signed for first division champions Arsenal as an amateur but played mainly in the reserves. His first-team debut took nearly a year and he played no part in the 1936 FA Cup win, but that season lifted the Amateur Cup for Casuals. A.H. Fabian was also in that Casuals team but his best days were behind him, unlike Joy.

Joy played in England amateur internationals, and after lifting the Amateur Cup found himself drafted into the full side for a game with Belgium, a depressing 3-2 defeat. There was no other player with Joy's experience and his role as captain in Berlin was assured.

The Casuals had not been in the FA Amateur Cup semi-finals since 1893/94, when they were defeated by Wreford-Brown's Old Carthusians. Players would frequently switch between Casuals and Corinthians but, by the late 1920s, Corinth were routinely weakening the sister club by calling on players for less-than-important friendlies. This culminated in a huge row between the two clubs after Corinthians claimed a number of players for a friendly with Reading. W.E. "Wag" Greenland, Casuals' secretary and also assistant secretary at the AFA, brokered a deal that players selected for his side must honour that selection. The lure of league games was a strong pull for many gentlemen. In the season before the Olympics, Casuals were among the strongest amateur sides in England and supplied a total of five regular players for the Olympic squad, including their giant, enigmatic goalkeeper, Terry Huddle, whom Greenland had introduced to the club.

Born in Sandhurst, Huddle spent time in South Africa, where his father conducted the Durban Philharmonic Orchestra, then returned to the UK and signed for Casuals. Huddle measured 6ft 3in and could throw a ball further than some players could kick one – a skill that also saw him keep goal for the Middlesex water polo team. For Terry Huddle, sport was a game. He played for Casuals and Corinthians. When Sunderland offered him a contract after a superb performance for Corinthians in a 2-0 defeat at Roker Park in 1934, his response was automatic. For amateurs like Huddle, these offers had little or no attraction. The maximum wage was firmly in place alongside the restrictive retain and transfer system, which kept players at clubs until they agreed to accept the offered wage or were sold to another side at the management's discretion. By 1936 Huddle had signed as an amateur for Arsenal but played in the reserves. He had no intention of ever turning professional. The professional game probably had little allure for the other two Casuals players in the 1936 squad, Bertram "Bill" Clements and Frederick Riley, a speedy outside-right in the tradition of Jackie Hegan.

Clements was scoring a goal on average every other game for Corinth but the club's 1933/34 season had been a disaster. A mere three first-team wins were recorded and Corinth withdrew from the FA Cup in protest at not being given a bye to the third round. Their form briefly improved in the 1935/36 season with a 6-3 win over Tottenham but many opponents no longer fielded full first teams. As the Olympics got closer the club were on a downward trajectory. Those FA Cup performances of the late 1920s, when giants like Manchester City and Newcastle were run close and Norwich thrashed 5-0, were like the final flowering of a dying tree, the leaves deceptively lush despite the canker within.

Corinthians' days were numbered but, with Pettit's late inclusion, the club supplied three regular players to the 22-man squad for Berlin – an indication of the AFA's influence on the selectors as much as Corinth's quality. Another Corinthian going to Berlin was Edgar Donald Reid Shearer, who eventually played 50 games and scored 35 goals for the club and toured Germany, Holland and Denmark with the team in 1933, alongside Jackie Hegan. That Shearer made so many appearances is incredible as he lived and worked mainly in Ireland.

Born in Hendon and educated at Aldenham Public School, Shearer went to work in Ireland at 17 for the textile firm that employed his father as a London agent. A fine all-round sportsman, he briefly turned out at fly-half for Derry's rugby team then switched to the city's football side on one condition: Corinth always had first call on his services. As Derry were professional, Shearer – like the true gentleman he was – insisted that his match fee went to the "player" whose place he had taken. Known by his middle name, Donald, Shearer was a pivotal figure in the Irish League's back-to-back victories over the Football League in 1935 and 1936. He was another automatic choice for Berlin and listed as a Corinthian despite playing more often for Derry.

Even with the AFA's influence, the make-up of the 1936 GB squad better reflected the growing strength of the provincial southern amateur game than in Antwerp. But with lobbying needed within the secretive halls where the FA's selectors met, this recognition was only gradual. Ilford – Amateur Cup runners-up in the Olympic season and winners in 1929/30 – supplied England amateur international Guy Holmes. Wimbledon lost their first Amateur Cup final in 1934/35 to Bishop Auckland but the south London club were on the rise and 18-year-old Maurice Edelston was the first of their many Olympic players. Edelston's father played in the Football League for Hull, where Maurice was born. The family later moved to London and Maurice would eventually emulate his father and join the professional ranks, but in 1936 he was still a promising young gentleman.

The Athenian and Isthmian Leagues were the stronghold of the southern amateur game. Barnet were Athenian champions in 1930/31 and supplied Lester Finch. Born in Barnet and educated at Monken Hadley School, Finch joined his hometown club in 1928. He was a regular scorer in the amateur leagues but refused to go professional, combining work as a printer with football. Finch only got one week's holiday but would be away for two weeks in Berlin. "I decided to take my week's holiday at that time and apply for extra time with loss of pay," he said. "However, my employer was so pleased that he paid me for the whole time I was away. What a holiday – you might say it was the holiday of a lifetime."

For players like Finch, football was just not a game to be played for a wage. The title of his autobiography – *Playing for Fun* – makes that clear enough. Shamateurism existed and was sometimes referred to as "the vat that didn't need its lid lifting", but to many players amateur football was a fraternity, a brotherhood that transcended class. Playing for clubs like Corinthians, Casuals or Northern Nomads that only played friendlies outside of cup competitions meant that players could play for different clubs in the same season. There was no money or league involved, so no transfer was necessary.

Haydn Hill played for Corinthians, Yorkshire Amateurs and made a handful of Football League appearances for Sheffield Wednesday, while his rival for the goalkeeper's shirt, Terry Huddle, was a Casuals player but turned out for Corinth and Arsenal reserves.

The Scottish FA had not initially divided gentlemen and players as the English had done but a Scottish amateur international side finally got off the mark in 1926/27 with a game against England. The new classification proved an immediate success, with the English humbled 4-1 at Leicester. The matches were then played annually and in the decade before Berlin a side made up mainly, although not exclusively, of Queen's Park players won six of the ten fixtures. During the SFA's early years, English-based players had been banned but now even Scottish amateurs from clubs like Romford were selected. Professional Scottish league sides including Ayr United and Stenhousemuir supplied amateur players to the Scottish amateur side but Queen's remained the dominant force in the gentlemen's game north of the border. The club still offered players a chance to test themselves against the best in the country – albeit for no pay. In the 1935/36 season, Queen's played in the first division of the Scottish League and finished 13th out of 20, the other 19 clubs all professional.

Amateurs at full international level in Scotland were disappearing. When Scotland played England at Hampden in April 1933 in front of a record 136,259 crowd, two Queen's players featured. Jimmy Crawford was a talented footballer and champion sprinter who equalled the Scottish record of ten seconds flat in the 100 yards in 1929. He won the last of his five caps that day, when his Queen's team-mate Bob Gillespie took the captain's role after Rangers' Davie Meiklejohn was injured. Gillespie retired at the end of that season and is the last amateur to play for Scotland, but Crawford would go to Berlin. So too would two more Queen's strikers, Joe Kyle and John "Mac" Dodds, who were expected to start. The club's masseur, Robert "Bert" Manderson, would also travel with the GB squad. Scotland's most prominent amateur club had the most to lose by releasing four first-team players in the early part of their season; for the greater British sporting good, Queen's acquiesced. The other Scotsman in the squad was Coventry

Brown, an amateur international forward then serving with the RAF as an air craftman first class.

The year of the Olympics was fraught for sporting relations in Ireland as the Football Association of Ireland – representing footballers from the Irish Free State – unilaterally decided to compete internationally as Ireland. This did not go down well with the football authorities in Ulster, who remained titled – then, as now – the Irish Football Association. Fifa kept out of this row but the FAI enthusiastically embraced the world outside of the British Isles, unlike their counterparts in Belfast. Northern Ireland had still to play a team outside the British Isles although amateur internationals began at the end of the 1920s, mostly against Scotland.

Two Northern Irishmen went to Berlin. Cliftonville supplied amateur international T.J. "Jimmy" Gibb. Gibb's countryman Bertie Fulton was an established full international. Born in Larne in 1906, left-back Fulton initially played for his home town and then moved to England in 1925 to train as a teacher at Strawberry Hill College and played for London Caledonians. He won his first amateur cap in 1926. Two years later Fulton made his debut for the full side in a 4-0 defeat against France that has never been recognised as a full international. In 1929 he made the first of 15 appearances for the Irish League representative side. He taught at St Comgalls in Larne and was seen as years before his time, often overlapping on the touchline to cross balls onto the near and far posts and would play systems that were then unheard of in Irish football. After leaving his home town side for Belfast Celtic, he became, unless teaching or injured, Northern Ireland's regular left-back.

The Northern Irish and Scots FAs made player nominations, unlike the Welsh, whose amateur game was not as strong as in the rest of the United Kingdom. Welsh amateur internationals began in 1908 with a 1-0 defeat against England in Stockport, but they only embraced the Scots in 1929/30 and Northern Ireland were shunned. Cardiff Corinthians became focused mainly on young players during the 1930s who often went on to play amateur internationals. The club became an unofficial nursery club for Cardiff City later in the decade.

Len Evans, a policeman and PT instructor, had picked up four full caps playing in goal for Wales as an amateur. The last – against Northern Ireland – was when he was with Birmingham City in 1933, but he had retired by the time Berlin came around. Longstanding FAW secretary Ted Robbins, who had been in the post since 1910, would travel to Berlin and had some input on the selection of the two Welshmen for Berlin, who were both in the Royal Navy and played in England. Stoker Bill Peart played for Gloucester and Ifor Fielding, a maths-loving half-back with a degree from Aberystwyth University, would join him when on shore leave from HMS *Ganges*.

The Welshmen's inclusion made the squad a truly British effort, but for the players, this did not matter. "Back then, it wasn't important who you played for. England one week then Great Britain the next," says Pettit. This much was evident in how the Liverpudlian has noted the nationalities of his squad mates in his own programme. He has written an E for England by Donald Shearer's name which was later crossed out and replaced by an NI for Northern Ireland, while Peart is down as English not Welsh.

With their entry confirmed late, there was no real time for squad sessions. The BOA team was led by Lord Burghley, who sent a type-written letter to all the British Olympians about their travel arrangements. As the footballers lacked time together and were out of season, Burghley added a hand-written postscript to the letters, saying: "As there is a month to go before we leave for Berlin kindly take some exercise."

The team would be coached by Fulham trainer Bill Voisey and had two joint managers. One of those joint managers was also the FA's choice as "member in charge" and a familiar face. More than a decade and a half after seeing his gentlemen humiliated in Antwerp, Wreford-Brown was back. In 1899 Wreford-Brown had been selected as the captain of a team of amateurs and professionals to go to Germany to take on the emerging German national side. At the last minute an injury struck and Wreford-Brown's younger brother Oswald went instead.

Oswald was killed in WWI and Charles Wreford-Brown's boots had finally been hung up, but he remained heavily involved with the FA. He accepted that standards among the amateurs had fallen but could content himself with the rising number of players embracing the credo.

"The amateur of today shows no great advance in skill but for every good player we had then, we have fifty today," wrote Wreford-Brown in the *Evening Standard* in 1934. "Professionals as a whole have improved out of all knowledge. There are few weak spots in their game and the facilities and supplies to strengthen the league teams are immense. The extra training that the professionals now get makes them more than a match for any amateur side."

Now established as a solicitor, Wreford – as he was known to his friends – admired the professionals' skills and accepted the penalty kick as "a concession to the modern onlooker, who is annoyed by foul play", but some aspects of the game were abhorrent to this paternalist, such as the trade in men. "I am not an admirer of the transfer system," he wrote in 1934. "As a matter of fact I loathe it, although as a man of business I can appreciate the position of clubs when they say 'we must get the players'."

Still heavily involved in the upper echelons of the FA and often leading touring parties, the grand old Carthusian would lead the 1936 Olympic party jointly with Stanley Rous, his love for the game undimmed. As recently as 1929, Wreford had turned up for a Corinthians game at Eton to find his old club a man short. "His son offered him a pair of stockings, which the father had worn at Charterhouse 40 years before and he proceeded to play an excellent game at centre half-back," wrote *Athletic News*. Wreford-Brown was in his 63rd year.

Rous, his companion in Berlin in 1936, had retired far earlier to concentrate on refereeing, first in the Football League then taking charge of internationals at home and in Europe. In 1934 Rous refereed the FA Cup Final between Manchester City and Portsmouth, went to Belgium the next day for the last of his 36 internationals as a referee, then laid down his whistle to become FA secretary, taking over from F.J. Wall.

Rous, already the consummate sporting politician, always suspected that – amid all the bluster – a side would go to Berlin. With this in mind, he asked Voisey and fellow Fulham coach Joe Edelston to hold twice-weekly training sessions at Craven Cottage for the six London-based players, including Edelston's son, Maurice. Lester Finch wrote in his memoirs that similar arrangements were made for the other nationalities but with only two Northern Irish and Welsh players, these must have been pretty desultory sessions. The Scottish contingent had at least started pre-season training with Queen's Park but the squad's preparation was lacking as they drifted into Liverpool Street Station on 29 July 1936.

The station was pandemonium, a mass of athletes of all sports and nationalities milling around in a chaotic atmosphere using London for a staging point. Eventually the BOA squad boarded the 8.15pm train to

Harwich for a night ferry to the Hook of Holland, when alcohol was available for a nightcap or two. At 7.21 the next morning, the weary Britons boarded the North German Express train to Berlin. During their trip, the athletes were handed leaflets telling them of the sights on offer. In addition to the Teutonic, intimidating glory of the Olympic village, the GB party should see happy workers cheering their leaders and "unmolested Jews" eating and drinking in Berlin's cafes. That was the German organisers' story. The British athletes were encouraged by the BOA to seek out the rotten heart of Germany, the Jewish doctors unable to practise, the torture chambers.

Arriving in Berlin, the British footballers found a melee of spectators, press and a band waiting for them. The players had to fight through crowds to get into the village; the footballers marched up to the entrance in military formation supervised by Lord Burghley and the British standard was run up the flagpole. Segregated into male and female sections, the village was surrounded by pine, silver birch, weeping willow and rolling meadows. It was almost idyllic but for the barbed wire perimeter fences and tight security. "It was impossible for anyone to get in or out without their pass," wrote Finch in *Playing for Fun*.

The 22 footballers were all in one hut together with attendants, a masseur and two stewards to make the beds and tidy up. The Germans spared no expense. The village featured 38 dining rooms, each with their own chef, a giant gymnasium, theatre, indoor swimming pool, post office and a training field that replicated the main stadium. The Games would sate the complacency that then gripped many British politicians. Hitler wanted to use the Olympics as a public relations exercise. His preening party members would take any chance they could to impress the British and use them for unspoken credibility in their PR stunts.

"The Germans were very anxious to have the English-speaking people and by that I mean the British Isles rather than America on their side," says Pettit. This manifested itself early on, when the Germans attempted to force the British party to give the Nazi salute at the opening ceremony on 1 August. Pettit adds:

> "The Nazis were very strongly of the mood that we should give the Nazi salute on the inaugural parade and we re-fused quite strongly to do that. We preferred to march

past … with us giving an eyes right. We had no intention of giving the Nazi salute. The people round about, some would give the Nazi salute and some would not but as the Games went on, more and more people would give the salute as if the Games were for their benefit."

The Games opened on a Saturday but GB's first match was not until the Thursday. Wreford-Brown and Rous watched over twice-daily training sessions. Some players would also take a ball onto the practice ground used by the other athletes for an impromptu kick-about. "This could be a bit hazardous with the odd javelin or discus flying about," said Finch.

The main arena was nine miles from the village and Berlin itself ten miles distant. Regular buses took players to both. The footballers also mingled with the other athletes. Daniel Pettit became friendly with legendary US track and field athlete Jesse Owens, whom Hitler refused to meet due to the colour of his skin. One footballer's wife travelled to Berlin and stayed in town, where the player made conjugal visits. Other players got the bus to Berlin to visit the amusement parks and many of the team took in the athletics events directly before playing matches. "It was the wrong sort of preparation," admitted their captain, Bernard Joy, later in *Association Football*. "Our approach may have been typically amateur but it was not realistic in view of the efficiency of our rivals."

The 16 teams, which included China, Japan and Peru but not, as the Germans earlier claimed, Haiti or India, were seeded into two groups according to perceived ability. Despite a lack of recent track record at the Olympics, GB were seeded joint favourites with the hosts. "The staggering fact is that the players, still complacent about the standard of Continental football, accepted the judgement as proper," said Joy.

The players may have deluded themselves but the media did not. As the squad left for Germany, some newspapers expressed concern that defeat was likely sooner rather than later. In Scotland this was met with derision. Surely, SFA stalwart Bailie Coltart told the Edinburgh Corporation's annual lunch on 5 August, "they were able to take a defeat. It did not matter one iota who won; the game was the thing."

Wreford-Brown might have approved of Coltart's approach but, even with only a handful of practice matches for the hastily-drawn together team, the prospect of losing to China in the first round seemed outrageous; just as defeat to Norway had 16 years previously. The Chinese were making their Olympic debut and were an unknown quantity – just as the Norwegians had been in Antwerp. In common with the Norwegians, the Chinese had also played together regularly. To pay for their passage to Berlin the Chinese had embarked on a mammoth world tour. En route to Germany, China played 28 games and, ominously for GB, they won them all.

6 August 1936
Mommsen Stadium, Berlin. GB vs China

All four Queen's Park players were in the starting line-up, which caused consternation in the non-Scots players. "We English understood that because they were to miss their club's first league games, the selectors had insisted that they be guaranteed places in the side [for the first Olympic game]," wrote Joy later.

Football not involving the hosts was often played at smaller outlying stadiums and GB were despatched to the Mommsen Stadium to face the Chinese, whose ambassador to Germany was in the crowd. A dry wind gusted across the field and the temperature hovered around 15 degrees.

As the players donned their kit, they found that this new "British" team would play in the regular England kit with an Olympic patch.

China won the toss and chose to play with the evening sun and the breeze behind them. When the game kicked off, GB's lack of practice was evident. Crawford and Finch on the right and left wings respectively delivered chance after chance into the Chinese penalty area. All were passed up or easily mopped up by China's centre-half. Honed by regular match play, China's ball control, sharp tackling and positioning were more than a match for the British and Joy had to be at his best to repel Chinese attacks led by their forward, Lee Wai Tong.

Fulton was, according to Rous, more used to playing centre-half, yet was deployed bizarrely at left-back. Confused by his role, the Irishman did not pick up the Chinese winger, which gave GB's opponents free reign down that wing. At one point, the brusque Joy seethed to Fulton: "Don't you feel safe outside the penalty area?"

GB were amazed to be beaten to headers or in the tackle by smaller opponents. More than 20 minutes passed before the first chance on goal for either side, Chinese keeper Pau Ka-ping fisting out a Kyle shot. GB were then shocked after Suen forced the ball into their net after a goal-mouth melee but German referee Helmut Fink ruled the goal out for a foul by Ip.

As the game wore on, the excited Chinese put in some rash tackles but Fink controlled the match tightly. GB kept up the pressure but China held on with the confidence of a team at ease with each other and Hill had to tip a 30-yard shot from Fung King-Cheng over the bar. At half-time, Joy's team were dazed, the match goalless.

All four Scotsmen were, according to the *Manchester Guardian*, guilty of missing chances, and the entire side of poor ball control. This continued into the second half. As the game restarted, China nearly took the lead in a moment of confusion in Joy and Pettit's defence.

From the resulting goal kick, play transferred immediately to the other end and Kyle and Dodds both nearly scored with successive chances. After 55 minutes, GB finally broke through when Dodds latched onto Crawford's pass to open the scoring. Eight minutes later, Kyle sent Finch through for a second. Crawford and Finch continued to create more chances but no one could score. GB crawled to an edgy win.

THE *GUARDIAN* DESCRIBED GB'S PERFORMANCE AS "NOT an impressive display," adding: "On the form displayed in this match the British players can entertain little hope of beating Poland tomorrow." Rous admitted that the game was not a good one. He and Wreford-Brown hoped that after a full game together, GB would show some improvement against the Poles in the second round.

The selectors laid the blame for the size of the win over China with the Scots. Dodds, despite his goal, and Kyle were dropped. An injury kept out Pettit, who was replaced by John Sutcliffe. Donald Shearer also came in. Poland were viewed as one of the stronger teams. A Polish selection visited London prior to the Games, losing only 2-0 to Chelsea. Leading Polish club side Wisla then beat the west London club 1-0. Joy's defence would be far busier this time and his team would have far fewer chances to score.

Between the two games, the British footballers spent more time enjoying the Games, but at some point during their time in Germany the team were taken to meet Hitler. According to Terry Huddle, the squad were taken to Berchtesgaden, his castle nearly 400 miles away from Berlin. Huddle even saved a photo showing the squad escorted by black-suited SS guards towards Hitler. All the footballers had to shake the dictator's hand. Into their nineties, Terry Huddle and Daniel Pettit had still not forgotten. "I've been washing my hand ever since," says Pettit six decades after diplomatic niceties forced him into shaking hands with Adolf Hitler.

8 August 1936
Post Stadium, Berlin. GB vs Poland

The game, which would be refereed by a Swede, Rudolf Eklow, was to kick off at 5.30pm. This gave the players time to watch other events in that afternoon's Olympic programme. Their opponents were mostly in the Polish Army and had spent the past six weeks practising together. The GB team's amateur approach faced a massive test but even the realist Bernard Joy later admitted he underestimated the Poles after watching them dismiss Hungary 3-0 in a testy first round match.

Joy's misplaced confidence was quickly eradicated. The Poles immediately had the better of the play. When one of the new players in the side, Bill Clements, put GB ahead this was against the run of play. Far quicker to the ball, the Poles surged into attack. Wodarz sent a fierce shot crashing towards the GB goal, which Haydn Hill kept out, but Gad scored from the follow-up for the third consecutive game for Poland. Three minutes before half-time, Wodarz put Poland 2-1 up.

In a six-minute spell after the restart, the British were annihilated. Wodarz and the Polish left wing Gad tore GB apart with the former claiming a hat-trick. At 5-1 down, GB were facing an even more humiliating exit than in Antwerp. Gardiner responded by body charging a number of the Poles. When Gardiner knocked over Gad, the crowd booed the Scottish half-back. Bernard Joy was not impressed. His GB team would not descend into a vicious kicking game. They would fight back by playing football and, incredibly, produce a stunning comeback.

As the Poles eased up with the game seemingly won, Joy sent all his players forward bar Hill. With just 17 minutes left, Joy sent a shot crashing against the crossbar and Shearer pounced onto the rebound to reduce the arrears. Six minutes later, Joy scored with a shot from the edge of the penalty area. The crowd were on their feet, whistling with excitement as Joy sent his team upfield again. Three minutes later, Shearer scored his second.

GB had eight minutes to claim a highly unlikely draw but the British gentlemen lacked the experience and training of their shocked opponents, who recovered to close out the game. GB were out. Wreford-Brown was stunned, but the Poland captain Wodarz was not so surprised. He said:

> "We looked a bit lost after British goals [but] we played much better than them. Even if we would go into extra time, we had won for sure. You know, there are moments when one team play excellent, and then another one. But as a team Poland was minimum a half class better than British. We had a really strong side."

For a second Olympics in a row, the British had been undone by arrogant over-confidence. The score-line was respectable but did not reflect how badly Joy's team were outplayed early on. Every time Finch beat the Polish right-back for pace, the Barnet printer's shirt was pulled. Finch claimed this was his first experience of shirt-pulling but admitted: "We did not play well." GB got through a round – an improvement on Antwerp – but the performance over the two matches had not impressed anyone. Poland were clearly the better team. To Wreford-Brown's chagrin, the amateur ethos of simply playing the game was no longer enough to win against such committed, highly trained opponents as the Poles, whose jobs allowed them to prepare as well as any professional side – a depressing augur for the future.

Rous held the amateur game in high regard but for him the professional code was the peak. He found the endless bickering over definitions of amateurism absurd. Quite what relationship the FA secretary enjoyed with Wreford-Brown is hard to judge. The Old Carthusian is not mentioned in Rous's autobiography. Many of the GB side had featured for the Middlesex Wanderers at some point and Bob Alaway was in Berlin. Alaway and Rous took dinner with their Dutch, Swedish and German counterparts but Wreford-Brown was not at the table.

Rous's only experience as an international manager (albeit joint) at the Berlin Olympics merited just two pages, but his experiences in Berlin seemed to have coloured his views. Four decades later, Rous said: "It has always proved a more satisfactory arrangement to select as Great Britain's representative the winning side in the home championship, rather than have a mixed team."

Many of the players from 1936 agreed. Lester Finch said: "I think the cause … was the mixing of different styles of play for we had no opportunity to practise together as a team." Their captain Joy, in typically forthright fashion, agreed. "My experience – and this is entirely my own view – is that it would have been better to have selected an entirely English side," said Joy. "The attempt to blend the different styles and temperaments in so short a time was a failure."

Poor preparation, helped little by dithering over whether to enter at all, and time spent enjoying the Games rather than training, was just as much the cause of the team's undoing.

After the Poland game the footballers went to the British embassy in Berlin, where ambassador Neville Henderson and his wife put on a function for all of the Commonwealth athletes. To the surprise of Daniel Pettit, he and his team-mates were met by many of Germany's leading politicians. The footballers mingled with senior Nazi party officials at the meet-and-greet. Pettit found himself unwittingly engaged in conversation with the likes of Nazi head of propaganda, Doctor Joseph Goebbels, and Joachim von Ribbentrop, who two years later became Germany's foreign minister.

Pettit adds:

> "Every one of the senior Nazis were there in person and being extremely genial and friendly and talking to you and having what you might call quiet conversations. You left reluctantly convinced at the time that there was nothing especially wrong with them. It was only gradually that [you realised] they weren't all like the people that you played football and cricket from Germany with before the war, which I had done quite a lot.
>
> "They were a very mixed bag whose real purpose was not social or economic development of Germany and a good relationship with us based on those principles. They were more interested in dominating Europe and making sure they had a country such as Great Britain on their side.

"There were strong attachments between us and Germany and I had many friends who were young people in Germany but disillusionment was beginning and this came from realising that they were not interested in positive social benefits. This was drawn out more and more [for the players] as [we] got in touch with the Games."

After two matches GB's footballers were out, but they were in good company. Hitler was not a football fan and had not planned to watch the hosts' quarter-final. Maybe the Germans' 9-0 first-round pasting of Luxembourg changed his mind. Norway were also back after a 16-year absence and a far tougher proposition than the Grand Duchy, having thrashed Turkey 4-0 in the first round. Again, the Norwegians produced the shock of the competition, as they put two goals without reply past Germany. Disgusted by this unexpected humiliation of the best gentlemen footballers from the master race, Hitler stormed off before the game even finished.

With Hungary and Turkey also eliminated, all the Central Powers from the Great War departed by the quarter-final stage when Peru overcame a two-goal half-time deficit to beat Austria 4-2. The Peruvians' equaliser had prompted a pitch invasion and after the end of extra time the Austrians and their British coach, Jimmy Hogan, formerly of Bolton Wanderers, complained of being manhandled by Peruvian players and spectators. One report even suggests a Peruvian brandished a revolver. The organisers ordered the game to be replayed. The Peruvians promptly walked out.

The Peruvians' decision was supported by football authorities in Argentina, Chile, Mexico and Uruguay and prompted stone-throwing at the German embassy in Peru's capital, Lima. Peruvian dockhands even refused to load two ships in the port of Callao – one German, one, oddly, Norwegian. The decision stood. The Austrians walked unopposed into the semi-final and beat Poland 3-1. Norway lost their semi-final to Italy but a 2-1 win over Poland secured a bronze medal. In the final, Italy beat Austria 2-1 as the World Cup holders added the Olympic title to their trophy cabinet.

With the British and the Germans both at a premature loose end, a match was scheduled for 12 August. Terry Huddle took over in goal, George Roylance and Bill Peart were at right- and left-back respectively, while Lance Corporal Stan Eastham and Ifor Fielding joined the recalled Daniel Pettit in defence. Coventry Brown was in at outside-right, the Irishman Gibb at inside-right. Dodds and Edelston returned as centre forward and inside-left respectively. Only one man – Lester Finch – played in all three of GB's games in 1936. What was the full German national team romped home 4-1. GB's scorer is not even recorded but Finch recalled a vastly improved performance. "It was an excellent match and we played much better as a team than in either of the two games," he said. After the match, the British and German footballers ate together and everyone received a medal to mark the game.

Terry Huddle did not play a competitive game in the Olympic football tournament but he did, according to his family, participate in another sport. Huddle's talent for water polo saw him called up after an injury to the GB team's keeper. GB's water polo side qualified for the semi-final groups after wins over Yugoslavia and Malta but their progress ended there.

The football squad also watched other sports, listened to a concert by the Berlin Philharmonic Orchestra at the village and even took in a play before eventually returning home. When they got back, the British footballers found that their first-round opponents had followed them. China's enormous tour rolled on and a match was arranged at Arsenal's Highbury Stadium against Islington Corinthians, a club set up only four years previously.

The Olympians Eastham, Huddle and Finch lined up for the home side, who won 3-2. On 1 September the Chinese were later entertained by the Casuals at Restaurant Frascati on London's Oxford Street with a seven-course dinner hosted, of course, by Wreford-Brown. Inspired, Islington Corinthians then went on their own mammoth world tour in the 1937/38 season with 95 games played in the Netherlands, Switzerland, Egypt, India, Burma, Malaya, Singapore, Vietnam, the Philippines, China, Japan, Hawaii, the United States and Canada.

Islington Corinthians did not visit Germany but English and British football did not shun the Hitler regime after 1936, despite the worsening political situation. The Games is seen today as probably the greatest usurping of a sporting event in modern history. Some historical perspective is available now and the advent of World War Two was needed to emphasise that to Britain's amateur and professional footballers.

Before World War Two was to break out, Britain's gentlemen and players both returned to Germany. Corinthians sallied forth on a brief tour of Germany, playing two matches in March 1937. In April of the following year, Corinth returned again for games in Kaiserslautern, Karlsruhe and Schweinfurt. In May 1938, the full English team returned to Berlin for a match with Germany as complacency morphed into appeasement.

The FA party was once again led jointly by Rous and Wreford-Brown. Unlike the Olympians, the professionals reluctantly agreed to give the Nazi salute during the playing of the German national anthem. Who actually told the team to give the Hitler salute is the subject of some debate but England's captain Eddie Hapgood recalled that Rous, citing the upset caused by the Olympians in 1936, insisted that the players must not emulate the gentlemen. The decision was only reached after a lengthy debate between Wreford-Brown and Rous and the Old Carthusian insisted on telling the inevitably outraged players rather than leave the task to Hapgood.

England trounced the Germans 6-3 but as the years passed, the significance of that salute typified the attitude of British prime minister Neville Chamberlain's government towards the Nazis. Daniel Pettit has certainly never forgotten. "Eyes right only," he recalls darkly more than six decades after his own greeting to Hitler.

A few months after the English professional footballers' ill-advised salute to Hitler, Fifa held another World Cup, this time in France. Again the Italians retained the trophy. Again the Home Nations sat the competition out on their side of the Channel.

After 1939, football ground to a halt in the sense that the game's players and administrators were used to. With players often away, Corinthians' fixture list had been shrinking in the run-up to the outbreak of war. The grand old club of the traditionalists qualified for the 1938/39 FA Cup only to be thumped 3-0 by Southend in the first round. The end was close. Corinth's last first-team fixture was on 12 April 1939, when Daniel Pettit and Maurice Edelston played in a 1-0 defeat to a combined Royal Navy & Royal Marines XI. The end of the club's independence had been signalled the previous Christmas, when secretary G.A. Strasser called an extraordinary general meeting at the Sports Club in St James's Square. The reason was to vote on a merger with the Casuals. The two clubs had been run by one committee since June 1937 and jointly toured Jamaica that summer. The vote was duly passed: "In the best interests of football," insisted Wreford-Brown.

Corinthian-Casuals, who would still play a part in GB's future Olympic efforts, were formed and quickly forgotten as the Nazi machine stormed across

Western Europe and pushed the British Expeditionary Force, quite literally, into the Channel. As the world set at each other again, the Olympics had an enforced break. An Olympics scheduled for Tokyo in 1940 was no longer possible. The gap before Britain united on the Olympic football field again would prove too long for any of the 1936 squad. The war severed their footballing careers.

Donald Shearer was a blunt man and a realist. He knew when his football career was over. An officer in the Territorial Army, he joined the Royal Artillery for the war and reached the rank of lieutenant colonel and was awarded the OBE. Whilst stationed at Tobruk in North Africa in 1944, Shearer played in an army match. His side won 2-1 but Shearer had had enough. Concerned that the ability that once attracted an offer of a trial from Arsenal (rejected, of course) had gone forever, Shearer threw his boots into the sea.

He did not give up on sport though. A talented cricketer and right-hand bat, he played regularly for Ireland before the war, notching up his first half-century against the prestigious Marylebone Cricket Club (MCC) in 1934. Four years later he batted for three hours to score 56 against the touring Australians. After the war, he forsook football but returned to the cricket crease, scoring 43 for Ireland against the touring South Africans in 1947 and playing a match-winning stand against the MCC at Lords in 1951. He retired the following year and joined public life in the province, taking a number of roles, including the chairman of the Sports Council of Northern Ireland in the late 1960s. Donald Shearer returned to the land of his birth later in life, dying at Sudbury in Suffolk in July 1999.

Like Shearer, Jimmy Gibb went into administration and was the secretary of the Irish Football League for several years after WWII. The other Irishman in Berlin, Bertie Fulton, played on, winning 21 full caps for Northern Ireland, the last two years after the Berlin Olympics. He rejected numerous offers to go professional and remained a teacher. He played most of his career with Belfast Celtic and won five league titles and two cups with the club, which he left at the end of the 1942/43 season in sad fashion. Celtic's final game was a title decider with Linfield. The scores were level into the dying minutes, when Celtic were awarded a penalty and the ball was handed to Fulton, who faced his friend and former team-mate Tommy Breen in the Linfield goal. Breen saved the penalty, Linfield took the league trophy; Fulton's career with Celtic was over.

The Scotsmen, whose en masse appearance in the first game against

China had so upset Bernard Joy, went back home and straight back into the Queen's Park side for the next match against Partick Thistle at Hampden, which ended in a 2-2 draw.

Lester Finch went back to Barnet and his job as a printer but was off again to New Zealand and Australia in 1937 on tour with the England amateur team along with Terry Huddle. In 1940 Finch joined the Royal Air Force but found time to play plenty of football, including matches for Bournemouth, West Bromwich Albion and Wolverhampton Wanderers. He played wartime matches for the full England team, which are not classified as full internationals, but never turned pro. The last line of his autobiography explains why: "Sport has given me a lot of fun and enabled me to make many friends and for that I'm very grateful."

He returned to his beloved Barnet FC and won the Amateur Cup in 1945/46 and reached the final again two years later. Unlike Shearer, he was loath to call it a day. His last game for Barnet was for the reserves in 1953, when a player failed to turn up. He scored in a 6-1 win over Sutton. After 476 appearances and 226 goals, the moment that Shearer saw so clearly in Tobruk arrived and Finch retired. He was 44. A keen cricketer, Finch also played cricket for Barnet and continued this sport into his early sixties, which enabled him to play with his two sons.

Maurice Edelston played in wartime internationals for Fulham, then Brentford and Reading, where his father took over as manager in 1939. Edelston stayed an amateur with Reading until 1952; he left having played 223 matches and scoring 80 goals. After a season at Northampton Town in 1953 he retired and went into broadcasting. He was a summariser for the BBC during the 1966 World Cup finals, covered European and England football matches and tennis. The author of two books, *Masters of Soccer* and *Wickets, Tries & Goals*, Edelston died in 1976 from a heart attack. The library at Blue Coat School and an award given by Reading FC to their outstanding academy player are both named after Edelston.

His Olympic captain Bernard Joy would also go into the media but only after enjoying a more prominent career. Joy began to play more regularly for Arsenal after Berlin, usually deputising for regular centre-half Herbie Roberts. When Roberts broke his leg in October 1937, Joy took his place and won a league championship medal and a Charity Shield winners' medal as an amateur. In World War Two, Joy joined the Royal Air Force but continued to turn out for Arsenal and found time to play more than 200 wartime games for the Gunners.

After the war, Joy briefly resumed his top-flight career with Arsenal only to retire in December 1946 after 95 first-class games (excluding the war). Joy continued with the Casuals for two more years as he moved first into teaching and then journalism, writing for the *Evening Standard* and the *Sunday Express*. In 1952 he wrote one of the first histories of Arsenal FC called *Forward, Arsenal!* and a number of other books. Joy proved a keen chronicler of sporting history, including the GB Olympic team.

After the war, another of the class of 1936 also moved into teaching. Ifor Fielding served on HMS *Excellent* and HMS *Hood*, and turned out for the Combined Services and the Navy at football. He then settled in Portsmouth and, after leaving the Navy, he returned to teaching maths in his new home on the south coast and was still working part-time in his 1970s.

Many of the Olympians played their part in World War Two but only Frederick Riley is reported to have died in the conflict. A flight lieutenant in the Royal Air Force, his 542 squadron plane was shot down over France in 1942 and he is buried in Boulogne. Terry Huddle spent his war mostly in the Far East and returned home to tragedy. Having not seen his wife for the entire six years of the conflict, Terry Huddle woke up one morning a few months after returning home to find she had passed away in her sleep. He later happily remarried, working mostly as an estate agent in Wokingham. "He was an estate agent, a book-maker, a bit of a rascal really but a great father," says his step-daughter Roisin, who took Terry Huddle at the age of 79 back to Berlin and Berchtesgaden. Hitler's castle was demolished at the end of the war but for Terry Huddle the site was still redolent of his visit decades before, riddled with the ghosts of the dictator and his leather-gloved Nazis. Terry Huddle lived most of his life in his native Sandhurst and died in 2004, aged 93.

One man outlasted all the 1936 Olympians. Daniel Pettit returned from Berlin with 100 signed postcards from Jesse Owens with which he would reward well-behaved pupils. He taught briefly at Bury Grammar School and then went to Foix in the Pyrenees to work as an English tutor.

When war broke out, teaching was a reserved occupation and Pettit did not have to fight but signed up all the same, joining the Royal Artillery. He was despatched on a troopship to El Alamein in North Africa, just as his wife had fallen pregnant. Pettit learnt Swahili and was sent into the Kenyan countryside to raise an army to fight in Burma for the King's African Rifles. Away for four years, including a long stint in the Burmese jungle, Pettit returned to the UK and met his five-year-old son Richard for the first time.

When peace was declared, Pettit returned to football, turning out for the enlarged Corinthian-Casuals even though he worked in his native Merseyside for chemical group, Lever Brothers. He worked in personnel at their Port Sunlight division and as part of this role in the late 1950s had to discipline two workers, who consistently struggled in late. The pair's excuse was that they played in a skiffle band but Pettit had to let both workers go – one of whom was Paul McCartney, who used his new-found freedom to form the Beatles. Decades later, the pair met again. McCartney thanked Pettit for doing him a big favour.

In the 1970s Pettit was appointed chairman of the government's National Freight Corporation and later knighted for this role. After the death of his wife, Pettit went to live with his son Richard and his daughter-in-law in Worcestershire. Football is still not, Pettit thinks, a game to be played for money but he enjoys the modern game. He says: "I think football today is rather special, they are really very good."

Sir Daniel Pettit died in July 2010, aged 95.

CHAPTER SEVEN:
1948 AND THE BUSBY BOYS

"I handled them as I would professionals, worked them
like slaves and not once did I hear a word of complaint
… it was a pleasure to work with such men."

Matt Busby, 1948 Olympic football manager

THE END OF WORLD WAR TWO LEFT MILLIONS DEAD
and, more prosaically, took out the best part of the footballing careers of
many players. Coming back from the war, upwardly mobile men were racked
by insecurities. Going into professional football in your mid twenties did
not always seem so attractive. Rob Hardisty, whose father Bob was probably
the most eminent post-war amateur of them all and a great Olympian, says:

> "It was a tougher game then. Players didn't last so long
> and it was unusual for people to play much past their
> early thirties as there was less protection and it was a
> tougher game. The rough and tumble of the game took
> its toll more. If it hadn't been for the war, I honestly
> don't know what Dad would have done, but they were
> the last generation that didn't have to turn pro to get a
> good standard of football."

At just 17, Bob Hardisty played for Bishop Auckland in the 1939 Amateur Cup semi-final. Then came the war and later that year he signed up with the Hong Kong & Singapore Signals. Hardisty was billeted in Dalmahoy, south west of Edinburgh, where he struck up a friendship with the unit's physical training instructor, a Scotsman whose professional career at first division giants Manchester City and Liverpool had been ended by the war. Matt Busby still played in wartime internationals and games for the United Services team alongside Olympians Maurice Edelston and Bernard Joy, but was 36 when the war ended. Busby knew his options on the field were diminishing and wanted to manage. He had coached the Army Physical Training Corps on a tour to Bari in Italy in 1945. Maurice Edelston's father Joe offered Busby an assistant's post at Reading but he went instead to Manchester United. The rest is well-repeated history. Busby took Manchester United to runners-up in the first division in 1947 and 1948 and won the FA Cup in the Olympic season. One of the best young managers in English football, and a Scotsman, he was the perfect choice for a new Olympic side that would move away from the influence of the southern traditionalists and the Corinthian attitude that had, arguably, undermined the 1936 effort.

Busby would later describe football at the Olympics as a "cleft stick", saying:

> "Those nations who continue to act according to the book are faced with two alternatives. They must either refuse to compete against such unfair odds, or enter for the Olympics knowing they have no earthly chance of victory. In Britain, since the Berlin Games of 1936, the policy has been to enter, presumably on the assumption that it is better to have the Union Jack trampled into the turf than not to show the flag at all. I think it is the only possible decision, even though, every four years, it exposes Britain's footballer-clerks, footballer-grocers and footballer-pitmen to something akin to ridicule."

Busby detailed these thoughts on the Olympics in his autobiography, *My Story*, which was published 1957. These were unlikely to be his feelings as he approached his first international challenge as a manager in 1948. He was referring to efforts after his 1948 campaign as, despite playing against such "unfair odds", no one would ever ridicule the team that Busby put together for the 1948 Olympic Games or their performances.

BEFORE THE GAMES RETURNED TO LONDON, TOKYO and Finland had been mooted as hosts for a 1940 Olympics. After Japan sided with Germany in the war, the Olympic flame never arrived and the Finns would have to wait a little longer before staging the greatest sporting event on Earth. The IOC was quicker to recover than Fifa and the Olympics resumed in 1948 with a tournament that would be very different from the previous Games, which had been typified by the grand ambitions of the Nazis in Berlin. Rationing ruled and the London Olympics would be the Austerity Games, staged at a cost of £750,000 with a make-do-and mend approach. London won the right to stage the Games in 1946. Though lacking in infrastructure, staging the competition was seen in some quarters as part of the victory celebrations.

The Games would also give the embattled gentlemen administrators with the FA, such as Wreford-Brown, who had been made a vice president in 1941 by Rous, an opportunity to strike a blow for their credo even if their representation on the pitch was declining. Wreford-Brown's successor as the Oxford University member at the FA was a young chemistry professor called Harold Warris Thompson, who would later become the scourge of the shamateur. Secret payments persisted but the amateur credo was boosted by talented players, who relished the social standing that being a gentleman provided in the post-war footballing world and, having survived the war but lost much of their career, now wanted something more out of life.

Corinth's merger with the Casuals before World War Two had seemingly ended the era when public schoolboys played friendly matches purely for the sport against leading professionals. With no floodlights, gaps in the fixture schedule between league matches were rare. Clubs that persisted in only playing cup and friendly matches, like Northern Nomads, whose only Amateur Cup win was back in 1926, suffered. Nomads' goalkeeper Brian Wakefield recalls: "It was getting ridiculous and we were really struggling and losing our good players like George Bromilow because people wanted regular matches."

After the Corinthians and Casuals merger, the enlarged club took over the latter's Isthmian League commitments. This competition remained the strongest of many southern amateur leagues, whose names – Athenian, Corinthian, Delphian, Parthenon – indicate the influences or aspirations of their middle- or upper-class founders. The backgrounds of these founders not only contrasted starkly with most of the players, but also their counterparts in the North, where there was not such a proliferation of well-off gentlemen who could afford to cling to the amateur ideal. In the North of England, the main amateur competition was simply known as the Northern league.

According to Norman Ackland, the AFA had become less of an organisation or even an acronym, more an ideology: "A continuance of the real old-fashioned amateur football, emphasis on amateur spirit, good sportsmanship and good fellowship."

At the start of World War Two, Ackland had been promoted to major and fought at Dunkirk with the British Expeditionary Force. His journalistic career on hold, he was then posted to Poona in India for most of the rest of the war. On being demobbed, he threw himself back into journalism with gusto.

Under his pseudonym, Pangloss, Ackland became a standard bearer for the amateur game. His coverage of the code paid for the drinks at his regular watering hole, the Press Club, where the waitresses were regularly the target for his overtures.

Ackland had divorced his first wife and intended to marry an 18-year-old girl only to find out that his old mistress, Maureen, was ill with tuberculosis. Instead of abandoning Maureen, Ackland remained with her until her death, only then taking up with a Press Club waitress, Jane. Against a background of this colourful personal life, Ackland embraced the AFA ideal and when not at the Press Club could often be found drinking with the amateur players.

Amateurs playing at any first-team level in the Football League were increasingly scarce but the surge in the game's popularity sent attendances soaring. The 27,000 spectators that saw Bernard Joy lift the Amateur Cup in 1936 would soon seem paltry. With the amateur game exempt from entertainment tax, more and more clubs were able to pay generous "expenses", indulging in the shamateurism that the FA's traditionalists had fought so hard against. Yet this practice also buoyed the game, raising standards by tempting good quality players like Hardisty, who were attracted by the pre-war notion that being a "gentleman" carried social kudos.

As life got back to normal within the confines of rationing and austerity measures, countries shattered by World War Two began the task of rebuilding, and the post-war period saw a new sense of Britishness pervade the Home Nations. Immediately after WWI, the Home Nations' sporting character had been too immature to allow a GB football team to be created in Antwerp. After WWII, this changed. When Russian champions Dynamo Moscow toured Britain in November 1945, matches were played in London, Cardiff and Glasgow. Fuelled by a mixture of paternalism and arrogance based on Britain's self-appointed role as the home of football, GB would unite again on the football field and not just for the Olympics.

As early as May 1945, newly liberated Danish teams played teams of British soldiers in front of big crowds. In July that year Bernard Joy took a British team to Copenhagen for a match with the reconstituted Danish national team. All the British players were still in the military. Joy, as an officer, was captain and joined by Arsenal team-mate Eddie Hapgood. That game was about revitalising Danish football, but a match that was to be held at Hampden between the Home Nations and a Rest of the World XI had bigger ambitions.

Fifa's operations had been crippled by the war. Mail took months to arrive, there had been no dealings with any eastern European associations since 1940 and contact lost completely with countries such as China, Japan and the Philippines. By 1944, Fifa's resources were spent, the organisation paralysed. Contacts were slowly made at the end of the war but the prospect of another World Cup was distant. Fifa needed help. Such help arrived due to a brief sense of Britishness on the football field.

Despite the austere times, the maximum wage made football cheaper to put on and even cheaper to watch. The game boomed at all levels. Led by the FA, the four Home Nations returned en bloc to the Fifa fold in 1946 on the proviso that their individual independence was never again questioned. This was underwritten by a guaranteed Fifa vice presidency rotating between the four British associations – a role that remains today. In return, Stanley Rous suggested that Great Britain would stage a match between a united Home Nations team of professionals and a Rest of the World XI to raise money for Fifa's empty purse. The Rest of the World were duly thumped 6-1 at Hampden Park in Scotland in front of 135,000 people, with up to

£35,000 raised for Fifa's cash-starved coffers. Rous may not have favoured a mixed team but a GB side had guaranteed the Home Nations' autonomy. A British side would also play in an international tournament before any of the professional UK national sides in a glorious flowering of the Olympic side led by Busby.

Preparations for the Olympic team started when the Home Nations Olympic committee, including Rous but not the now ageing Wreford-Brown, convened in the Great Western Royal Hotel in Paddington, central London on 10 September 1947. The committee met up again in Liverpool on 5 November 1947 before taking in an England vs Ireland international in the same city. Each Home Nation would supply two representatives and a secretary to the effort – enough administrators to field a team with a man to spare! In the interim, Manchester United was sounded out and Busby agreed to take the role and council members and county associations were asked to suggest potential players.

The war's influence pervaded all levels of football as many players remained in the military or started national service. This provided a major boost for the Army, Navy and RAF representative sides and helped develop a strong England side. Wartime internationals did not count officially, but in one encounter Scotland were trounced 8-0 by the English. The Scots, Irish and Welsh, however, did not have the same level national base within the armed forces and a disparity developed with England winning the first two Home Nations tournaments staged after the war in 1946/47 and 1947/48.

This English dominance was reflected in the amateur code with England crushing Ireland 5-0 and Wales 7-2 in the 1947/48 season. Against overseas opposition England were more frail. The team suffered their first ever home defeat to European opposition, France winning 2-0 at Bromley, and Luxembourg were only just edged out 2-1. Scotland's amateur team was slow in recovering and recruitment of Scots for the Olympic GB squad again focused on Queen's Park, then playing in the Scottish first division. Amazingly, though, Busby would have no part in selecting the squad for the Olympic tournament as council members and county associations were asked to suggest potential players.

When the committee men trudged off to the Imperial Hotel in Llandudno in the New Year for an update, a friendly against the Netherlands in June was confirmed, yet no players seemed to have been watched. That started the following month when Queen's Park took on a putative Olympic XI drawn from the rest of the UK. The selectors also took in England amateur internationals against Northern Ireland, Wales and France over the next two months before drawing up a list of probables and possibles. Many players from those first few games would go on to feature in Busby's starting XI.

The role of amateurs in the professional game – on the field at least – was shrinking, but the gentlemen had not completely vanished from the top of the game. Bernard Joy was the last amateur picked for the full England team but not the last one selected for an England squad.

Peter Kippax was the son of a wealthy Lancashire factory owner. When not playing for Yorkshire Amateurs, he turned out for Burnley. He did not feel any need to go pro. Kippax was on the wing for the Clarets in the 1947 FA Cup Final and picked for a full England international against France that May. Though Kippax never started due to a bout of flu and no gentleman was ever selected for the full England team again, he made the Olympic squad.

Kippax played in that first game against Queen's Park – won 4-0 by the possible Olympians – alongside another Yorkshire Amateur playing in the Football League. Harry McIlvenny's father Jimmy played for Bradford City but Harry signed as an amateur for rivals Bradford Park Avenue. Bill Amor, a policeman who combined playing for a works team at biscuit maker Huntley & Palmer and as an amateur with Reading, was also selected.

Like Bob Hardisty, Jack Neale's career had been cut short by the war and the maximum wage remained a deterrent, but perhaps more than any of Busby's squad, the Walton & Hersham player identified with the AFA's tenet. His son Graham Neale says: "Dad was very much the amateur sportsman. Lower division players weren't paid much better than Walton & Hersham then but Dad wasn't driven that way. He was into the sport for the sake of the sport and the camaraderie afterwards."

When war broke out, Neale served in the RAF, spending time in South Africa and playing in Durban, then returned home in 1945 and worked as a civil servant. He played in all five England amateur matches in 1946/47 but at 29 was unlikely to get an offer from the professional game. Some younger players also lacked the confidence to join the professionals.

"I felt I was too old to go pro," says Jack Rawlings about his ambitions on being demobbed from the East Riding Yeomanry in 1946 aged 23. He had been approached by Arsenal but instead joined oil giant Castrol and played as an amateur for Enfield.

Some of the squad were fortunate to be even playing football, like left-half Eric Fright, who overcame infantile paralysis to play with leading amateur side Bromley, and Denis Kelleher, who was one of two Northern Irishmen who played in the first probables versus possibles game at Blackpool. Hardisty and Neale lost the best days of their career to WWII but Kelleher was lucky to be alive at all. Born in Dungarven in November 1918, Kelleher was first capped by the Northern Irish amateur side in 1937 before he moved to London and signed for Barnet. In the war he joined the Royal Navy and made lieutenant, only for his ship to be sunk off Tobruk. Taken prisoner, he spent 18 months in various camps before being transferred to a German prisoner of war camp near Bremen, where he took part in one of the most daring escapes ever undertaken.

Kelleher had learnt German while in captivity and, in 1944, along with Stewart Campbell, a lieutenant in the Fleet Air Arm, he simply strolled out of the camp. Posing as Dutch merchant navy officers, the daring duo evaded the Germans and escaped to neutral Sweden. Anyone who has seen *The Great Escape*, which is partly influenced by Kelleher's nonchalant getaway, will know what faced the two POWs had they been caught.

Kelleher enjoyed the fortnight he spent in neutral Sweden waiting for a boat home. He admitted as much in a letter to Barnet's secretary Lionel Purrott, saying he had smoked too much but could not wait to get the club's black and amber strip back on. Five days after boarding a cargo ship from Stockholm, Kelleher returned to the Barnet side and two days later scored both goals in a 2-0 win. The stuff of a *Boy's Own* adventure, Kelleher was later awarded the MBE for his daring escape. In 1948 the dashing forward was offered a place in the Republic of Ireland's football squad but was training to be a doctor at St Mary's Hospital and joined Busby's squad. The other Northern Irishman from that Blackpool game was Kevin McAlinden, a goalkeeper with Belfast Celtic, whose father was a shareholder at Glasgow's Celtic and businesses on Belfast's Shankhill and Falls Road.

Three Welshmen featured, this time all from Welsh clubs. Electrician Frank Donovan played for his local side Pembroke Borough, whom he captained to promotion in 1947/48. Donovan came recommended by the FAW and featured in the early matches. More trial matches were played, at Blackpool on 8 May and Hampden Park on 29 May, and another three Welshmen entered the frame. Only Gwyn Manning of Troedyrhiw, near Merthyr Tydfil, and Barry Town's Julian Smith made the final squad.

The Scottish influx again all came from Queen's Park, who were then struggling at the foot of the Scottish first division. Three Queen's Park players played in victory internationals in the 1945/46 season but these are not classed as full internationals. The days of a Queen's player featuring in the full Scottish side were gone but the club did their cause a great deal of good with a league victory over high-flying Rangers during the selection process.

After this shock win, seven Queen's players were chosen for Busby including the youngest player in the entire squad. Ronnie Simpson might have been 18 but did not lack experience. As a schoolboy, Simpson suspected the worst when called into the headmaster's office at King's Park Secondary School in Glasgow. Instead, two Queen's Park officials were looking for a keeper. Simpson had been spotted playing for his school team and the committeemen wanted a stand-in for their regular keeper, who could not get shore leave from the Navy. At 14 years and eight months, he made his first-team debut at Queen's Park in a game at Hampden against Clyde in 1945. Queen's won 5-2. To start, Simpson trained after school but at 15 and a half, he left for a job as a clerk while waiting for a vacancy to train as a newspaper sub-editor. By the time Busby was looking for a keeper, Simpson was a Queen's regular and in the reformed Scottish amateur side.

Simpson was joined by a man who could have been teaching him. Half-back Davie Letham was a schoolteacher at St John's Street School in Glasgow and had something in him of Kenneth Hunt, the Footballing Parson from 1908 and 1920. Before school football matches, Letham – a colour sergeant in the Boys' Brigade at his local Methodist church – would twist the sideburns of errant pupils. Like the Footballing Parson, Letham was popular with his male pupils and his good looks made him equally admired by the girls. Joining Letham in the squad was Dougie McBain, another half-back, who played a handful of games as an amateur for Hamilton and Dumbarton before going to war as an air gunner. On demob, he signed with Queen's and worked as a civil servant. When McBain was selected, he wrote to his employers asking for unpaid annual leave for the Olympics. His request was turned down – so he had to take his holiday – and to add insult to injury, McBain was also congratulated by his employers on being selected – for England!

Team-mate Angus Carmichael – by some distance Busby's tallest player – was approached by Aberdeen in 1946 with a contract offer of £1,500 a year, but had his sights on becoming a vet after being turned down by the RAF due to a mild heart problem.

As with many previous Olympics, the choice of squad captain seemed obvious, but Bob Hardisty, for all his undoubted ability, did not like leading teams. This, the Bishop Aucklander worried, would upset his game. For his friend Busby, Hardisty overcame his natural inhibition and agreed to take the captain's armband with Letham vice captain.

Recruited by committee, the squad reported for their first training session with Busby on 17 May. Before that there was a triangular amateur series between the Netherlands, Luxembourg and English players in the running for the GB squad – a telling sign of the FA's influence. The results augured badly. A narrow 2-1 win over Luxembourg was followed by the would-be Olympic Englishmen being thrashed 5-2 by the Netherlands at Dulwich Hamlet.

As Busby was introduced to the squad, he realised just what he had taken on. "Most of the players were strangers to each other," he recalled. "My first task was to shake hands all round and try to remember some of the names. I wondered what I had taken on. This was a job presenting a real challenge and I realised right from the start that many hectic weeks of hard graft lay ahead."

All these players were in the squad but not certain of an Olympic place. The squad would only be confirmed after the friendly match against the Dutch in Amsterdam on 20 June. The fixture was one of three friendlies organised for the team by Rous, who played a wider role in organising the overall Olympics. Rous was a special aide to Lord Burghley and on the 12-man organising committee, but took a keen interest in the football. To help train the squad, Busby brought in Manchester United trainer Tom Curry and a handful of first-team players, including Jack Rowley, Stan Pearson and Johnny Carey. United's physio, Ted Dalton, also joined the GB squad and some of the initial training sessions were held at Old Trafford.

The main training base was a country mansion in Twyford near Sunningdale golf course. "We found there was a net and some racquets and started playing tennis and then we kicked the ball over the net. We had to more or less make the most of what was there," Jim McColl told *The Scotsman* in 2008.

Rous was a regular visitor to Twyford, where players wore blazers and ties for meals together. At mealtimes, the FA secretary would pick out players and invite them to join him. Between training sessions some players made quiet trips to the bookmakers to back tips passed on by a team-mate. With rationing in force, special rations, including tinned fruit from New Zealand, were brought in to build the players up. This provided some compensation for players left out of pocket by missing work. All the squad had to take their annual holiday entitlement to coincide with the Olympics. As the British obsession with amateurism meant no broken time payments were tolerated, those with unsympathetic employers were left out of pocket. But not one player missed those sessions, which impressed the professional Busby.

"By this time I was getting to know the lads and what is more important, they were getting used to me – and appreciating my requirements," Busby recalled. "I handled them as I would professionals, worked them likes slaves and not once did I hear a word of complaint … it was a pleasure to work with such men."

As the Dutch game loomed, players knew they were playing for their Olympic place. Fortunately the days of stormy ferry trips were long gone. The team's coffers had recently been boosted by a £250 FA grant and the side flew to Amsterdam on KLM. The Dutch had yet to embrace the divide between amateurs and professionals and sent out a team of players from their top flight, the Eredivisie.

The start was not encouraging. After just 13 minutes, a McAlinden error gifted van der Tuyn a goal. Leytonstone's Leon Joseph equalised just before half-time but six minutes from the end van der Tuyn played in Rooseberg for the winner. A loss, but the setting had hardly helped. "The game was in Amsterdam on the day of the Dutch Olympic trials in front of 65,000 people," recalls Rawlings. "Although we did get to see Fanny Blankers Koen [winner of four gold medals in various sprint disciplines] run."

Despite scoring, the talented Joseph, who had won an Amateur Cup winners' medal that season with Leytonstone and also played for Spurs, was controversially left out in favour of Kippax, who overcame an injury. Two Welshmen from Cardiff Corinthians and Lovells Athletic also missed the cut, along with three Queen's Park men and England's amateur keeper, R.B.

Carr. Closing of nominations was left to the committee.

This goes some way to explaining the exclusion of a player who would have most likely made both the squad and Busby's starting line-up. Cyril Martin was a nippy little winger who played for Bromley until his job took him to Marseilles. Shortly after arriving, he was signed by Olympique de Marseilles and was a regular in the French first division in 1947/48. Busby took his newly confirmed squad to train at Bill Amor's home ground, Elm Park in Reading, and Martin turned up at an early session under the impression he had been nominated. The Home Nations Olympic Committee, however, had forgotten a player who had just won that season's French league title.

The next warm-up was in Basle against a local side. On the day that Angus Carmichael graduated as a veterinary surgeon, he caught a night sleeper to London and a flight to Switzerland. "When we got to Switzerland, I couldn't believe what they had in the shops," recalls Carmichael. "There was nothing in our shops like the watches they had there. When I got engaged to my wife Anne I couldn't even get her an engagement ring back home."

After the game, Carmichael and the rest of the players were ushered into a room in their hotel and offered the pick of a show of expensive Swiss watches. The prices were slashed and most players bought one, some half a dozen. The Swiss, worried about the thin-looking Britishers, also gave Busby's players food parcels. When the squad ambled into the entrance hall at the airport in Switzerland, Busby took the customs guard to one side and explained that as his charges were poor footballers they had nothing to declare. No questions were asked.

Gripping food parcels and laden down with watches, the GB team boarded their plane home ticking in unison. "As we flew back to RAF Northholt, you couldn't hear the engines, all you could hear was all these watches ticking," laughs Angus Carmichael.

On 25 July, GB ventured to Nantes for a game with the French amateur side. Busby recalled the game finished a draw. FA records show a 2-1 win for the visitors. Newspaper reports suggest GB won 3-2 with Alf Hopper scoring after 17 minutes and Kelleher adding a second seven minutes later. Simpson produced a point-blank save just before half-time and GB added a third from a McIlvenny penalty, only for France to rally with late strikes from Strapp and Coerbin, but GB hung on. Afterwards the players received a Dunhill cigarette lighter each, but that was little consolation to Davie Letham, who was injured in the game.

After the friendlies, Busby realised what quality there was among his amateurs. He knew of Hardisty's abilities but was particularly impressed with Kelleher, Fright and Bromley's Alf Hopper. Squad comedians McIlvenny and Eric Lee, a schoolteacher playing in the Football League with Chester, kept their team-mates amused. Spirits were high as the tournament approached. Team selection was left to Busby but some choices were forced. Letham's injury persisted and a dead leg kept Jack Rawlings out.

Expectations were generally reasonably high, based not on self-delusions later to be exposed but on recognition of what Busby had achieved with his squad. The *Guardian* wrote: "A determined fight by Great Britain – dare one say into the semi-finals – will satisfy the national pride. A victory in the final, as in 1908 and 1912, would be a glorious surprise indeed." Not everyone was so confident. "The standard of play and quality of British amateurs now is a long way behind the 1936 vintage," sniped the influential *World Sports*.

With the British game in the close season, there were no amateur or professional club sides for the other Olympic teams to play warm-up matches against. The only opposition was the Metropolitan Police side. Otherwise, the teams had to practise against each other after arriving in England. By comparison, GB's preparations were – for once – thorough.

At the opening ceremony at Wembley on 29 July, Busby's gentlemen led the entire British squad out. The war was over three years ago but danger from the skies remained, albeit of a milder kind. "There was this American, not an athlete, walking around at the ceremony with a trilby asking all the athletes for a dollar. He said 'whoever gets hit by the most pigeon shit gets what's in this hat'," recalls Angus Carmichael.

31 July 1948
Highbury Stadium, London. GB vs the Netherlands

Two days after the opening ceremony, GB's campaign kicked off. The Dutch side in Amsterdam had been a trial side. In London, the Netherlands fielded their first choice XI and thumped the Republic of Ireland 3-0 in a preliminary before the game at Highbury, which would be watched by the Dutch Prince Bernhard. As in Berlin a dozen years previously, the GB team's competitive strip was again the England kit with an Olympic badge.

There is no evidence of objections from the Irish, Scots or Welsh over the kit. Perhaps what the team wore did not matter as the side was, once again, truly British.

The Dutch were robust tacklers and Bromley's Tommy Hopper was concussed after one early challenge. His response typified the belief engendered by Busby. Rather than leave his team with ten men, Hopper ignored medical advice to leave the field and carried on playing even though he was obviously in no condition to do so. Relishing the physical approach of his opponents, Hopper, his face covered in blood, put in his own telling tackles and dribbled round the shocked Dutch players.

The Dutch were technically superior, but they were matched by GB's overwhelming spirit. Gwyn Manning – preferred at left-back to Carmichael – was also injured by a Dutch tackle but again refused to come off. In baking heat, Hardisty opened the scoring and goals from McBain and Kelleher, whose dribbling was magnificent, established a 3-1 half-time lead.

In the second half, Eric Fright continued to play superbly and a member of the Olympic committee with connections to a Scottish professional club yelled across to the watching Stanley Rous: "May I approach him? May I approach him?" The astounded Rous had no reply. During the last 45 minutes, the Dutch rallied and equalised with a superb left-foot volley from their inside-left, Wilkes, to take a thrilling match into agonising, exhausting extra time. The fitness schedules imposed by Busby on his amateurs would be tested at the first hurdle.

As extra time began, the exhausted British soldiered on, refusing to lose a game seemingly won. When Harry McIlvenny popped up to score a last-minute winner, Tommy Hopper was so overcome by McIlvenny's goal that he passed out. After the game he was taken to the Royal Northern Hospital, where Hopper was found to have played almost the entire match with a fractured cheek bone.

"Every man played his heart out," said Busby. The game had been won but at a cost. Busby lost not just Hopper but Ronnie Simpson and Manning for the quarter-final against the French. The latter two were replaced by Kevin McAlinden and Jim McColl with Frank Donovan coming in for Hopper.

The French would surely not be as difficult opponents as the Dutch if their first-round win over India was a guide. The Indians only had two pairs of boots. The other nine players made do with bandages and plasters on their toes and a 2-1 loss to France was respectable in the circumstances. The French were not much better organised, forgetting to bring a ball, which made training interesting.

5 August 1948
Craven Cottage, London. GB vs France
In the first ten minutes, a frenzied opening saw a dozen free kicks shared between the two sides for fouls. McAlinden was soon pressed into a save from Hebinger but McColl and Jack Neale dealt easily with the rest of the French attacks. At the other end, French keeper Rouxel indulged in flamboyant dives to keep out GB. McIlvenny came closest to scoring, skimming the French crossbar with a back-header before Hardisty – from a Donovan corner – headed home the opener.

The French had little response but GB were equally lifeless, drained by their heroics against the Dutch. Busby's team were the better side throughout; Lee, Fright, McBain and Donovan were all far too good in defence to give the French forwards any space. GB closed the game out easily, saving their energy for the semi-final. Busby and his team had surpassed all expectations by reaching the last four and were starting to believe some of their more optimistic supporters. Could they really emulate Vivian Woodward's two victories in 1908 and 1912? "The further we went, the more confidence that we could actually win it came into it," recalls Jack Rawlings.

The Olympic matches had been spread across a wide variety of venues from Highbury and Craven Cottage to Portsmouth's Fratton Park, Crystal Palace's Selhurst Park and Tottenham Hotspur's White Hart Lane. With a nod to the amateur community, games also went to the homes of Dulwich Hamlet, Ilford and Walthamstow Avenue's Green Pond Lane. Other places suggested as venues included Bournemouth, Brighton, Southampton, Watford and Worthing. Only the semi-final and final would be at Wembley. Admission prices for group games were kept low in these ascetic times, starting at 1/6d – 7.5p in modern money – rising to £1-1s, which is the equivalent of £1.05. The likes of Bournemouth lost out on a chance to stage a game, when five teams dropped out. China, led by Lee Wai Tong from 1936, returned only to be thrashed 4-0 by Turkey.

In the semi-finals, Busby's team were joined by the Swedes and the

Danes, who were both coached by Britons, George Raynor and Roy Mountford respectively, plus Yugoslavia. In the first semi-final, Raynor's Sweden edged out Mountford's Denmark 4-2 before Busby's side took on the relatively unknown but fancied Yugoslavs at Wembley. Communism meant that all players in Yugoslavia were classed amateurs even if they were in the forces or civil service and spent most of their time playing football for the best teams in the country. This would be the first time – but certainly not the last – that GB would face such an unequal battle.

11 August 1948
Wembley Stadium, London. GB vs Yugoslavia

With austerity ruling, Busby's squad once again got the tube to the match at Wembley, where 40,000 fans wondered if the improbable was possible. That belief hardened when twice, with the game 0-0, McIlvenny was clear on the Yugoslav goal, but the Yorkshireman could not convert his chances.

As the game progressed, Busby could see that the Yugoslavs were quicker to the ball and made every pass count, unlike his side. McAlinden had kept his place after his clean sheet against the French but fumbled a Bobek shot to give the Yugoslavs an early lead. The British lacked the Yugoslavs' skills but again compensated with resolve. A minute after Bobek's goal, Donovan sent a thumping shot through a crowd of legs to equalise. In the first two games Britain's defence held steady, but they faced a bigger challenge now and were found wanting. Volfy was left unmarked to restore Yugoslavia's lead.

After half-time, Mikajlovic hooked back a high centre into Mitic's path for a third. GB responded with vigour and matched Yugoslavia without being able to make a breakthrough. Busby's side had been undone by their opponents' quick manoeuvring and rapid, short passing. Man-to-man marking might have been a counter but it was too late. Busby's dream was over. His team, *The Times* said, had played "their best match of the tournament", with Hardisty to the fore, but simply lost to a better side.

For the play-off for third place, GB would return to Wembley to face Mountford's Denmark, whose players remained amateur although not perhaps to the rigid English definition. Danish football was an increasingly working-class game and players could be compensated for lost pay. When England were scheduled to play Denmark in 1922, the FA asked for separate

Danish amateur and professional fixtures.

The Danes refused, saying that every player was amateur – a definition that would remain until 1978 – and missed the 1930 World Cup on the grounds that other teams were professional. After World War Two the Danish game slowly evolved into a form of semi-professionalism, but the Danes only travelled to London in 1948 because their federation, the DBU, felt a debt was owed to the British, the English in particular, for their help in developing the game over the years.

13 August 1948
Wembley Stadium, London. GB vs Denmark
Britain's chance of a gold medal had gone and the crowd inside the cavernous Wembley Stadium dwindled to 5,000. Busby made seven changes to give as many players a game as possible, such as Angus Carmichael and the fit-again Jack Rawlings. Simpson was also restored in goal for a game played in wet, slippery conditions.

Busby's side were no match for the Danes' speed or stamina, perhaps not even tactically, but that spirit remained to bridge the gap and produce a thrilling game. Bill Amor proved more effective than Peter Kippax, who he replaced. Eric Fright, once again, was outstanding. The rain hammered down as the game went on, making the match one to forget for Simpson and his opposite number Nielsen. Both had woeful games and between them were at fault for four goals.

McIlvenny opened the scoring for GB and added another to equalise after the Danes had gone 2-1 up. The downpour continued and the slippery pitch made ball control increasingly difficult. The Danes again took the lead before an Amor penalty restored parity. At 3-3 Denmark's outstanding centre forward Karl Praest showed his prowess by scoring two goals to win the match. Even the consolation of a bronze medal was to elude Busby.

George Raynor's Sweden went off with gold, beating Yugoslavia 3-1, but the sun was setting on the Western Europeans. The rise of the Eastern bloc would become all encompassing. For the Danes and Nils Middelboe, there was revenge for 1908 and 1912 but GB were not disgraced. Jack Rawlings says: "We did fantastically well to get as far as we did. I felt we could have beaten Denmark but that was their full team."

Busby rued McIlvenny's early missed chances against the Yugoslavs and suggested that an even better performance could have been produced if he had chosen the squad. "It was not really an encouraging start to have 26 unknowns thrown at me in the hope that Matt Busby will sort them out," he said without taking away anything from his players.

"As manager of the British team on that occasion I did a job of work which I shall always regard as one of my best," added Busby. "Steering Manchester United to the championship of the Football League first division was child's play beside the problems of sorting out a winning team from twenty-six spare-time footballers drawn from four different countries."

Busby made this astounding claim in his autobiography in 1957 before both his only other international experience, briefly taking charge of Scotland in 1958, and also successfully rebuilding Manchester United after the Munich air crash that same year. Under Busby, United won the first division title in 1965 and 1967 and the European Cup the following year but the GB job would be his only role in charge of an international team in a tournament. He managed Manchester United for 24 years and was later knighted. Busby died in January 1994, aged 84.

After the Danish game the squad had a final night together in Uxbridge and Busby came up to Simpson. "Well, thanks a lot Ronnie. Good luck to you and if you ever consider turning professional, give me a ring," Busby said to his fellow Scotsman, as recalled by Simpson in his autobiography, *Sure it's a Grand Old Team*.

The teenage Simpson had never been paid such a compliment but then could not countenance turning pro. First, he had to get his national service out of the way with the Royal Armoured Corps in Catterick. In July 1950 Simpson was demobbed and decided to join the "players". He recalled:

> "A number of English clubs including Blackpool, Middlesbrough, Arsenal and Portsmouth were immediately in touch with me, along with a number of Scottish clubs. I thought about that Olympic farewell I had with Matt Busby. Should I phone him? Well, I've always been a bit of a home bird. If I were to turn professional, I didn't want to travel too far – so I signed for Third Lanark, just a few minutes' walk from where I stayed with my parents."

Simpson still went on to win trophies in England and Europe despite not calling Busby at Manchester United. After Third Lanark he signed for Newcastle United and won the FA Cup in 1952 and 1955. Five years later, the "home bird" went back to Scotland and Hibernian, whose then manager Jock Stein sold Simpson to Celtic in 1964. A year later Stein joined Simpson at Parkhead and in 1967 the pair would lift the European Cup for Celtic. In 1967, aged an astounding 36, Simpson made his Scottish international debut in a famous 3-2 win over then world champions England. He retired in 1970 and moved into management with Hamilton Academical, later working in the hospitality suites at Parkhead for Celtic.

Busby may have been impressed by Simpson but Spiders team-mate Andy Aitken was not. "We scored three … but let in five," Aitken told *The Scotsman* many years later of the Denmark game. "Our keeper was better to watch than to play with." Aitken quit the Spiders in 1948 after asking for his contract to be cancelled after a disagreement and was offered £5,000 by Aberdeen and Clyde to go pro, but remained a "gentleman", later becoming general manager of Colville.

Ronnie Simpson was not the only player that Busby thought might have a future in the professional game. "Matt Busby asked dad to Old Trafford but I'd just been born and my mother didn't want him to go," says Gwyn Manning's daughter Avril Besley. But Manning never left Wales, playing instead as a semi-professional for Brecon Corinthians and Merthyr Tydfil. His son Doug says: "Dad just wasn't very ambitious. He worked at Hoover as a painter on the maintenance team and had a chance to progress but stayed on the brushes instead."

Frankie Donovan went back to Wales and along with Manning and Julian Smith received a commemorative medal from the FAW. The trio played for the Welsh amateur side against India, who stayed on after the Olympics. Kitted out with the same inferior footwear, the Indians prevailed in Wrexham and drew in Swansea against the Welsh gentlemen. Donovan briefly joined the "players" at Swansea City but after a handful of Football League games returned to Pembroke in July 1951. He helped the club to the Welsh League "double" in 1953/54, managed there and at Milford United, and then opened a sports shop.

When Busby's players had left Uxbridge, their manager told them to all keep their official tracksuits. Shortly afterwards, the FA wrote to all the

Olympians, who had each given up a month without pay, asking them to stump up £5 or return their tracksuits. That sounds harsh but the Games had proved costly for everyone involved. Tournament accounts show a £5,019 deficit. At a subsequent meeting of the Home Nations Olympic Committee, a vote was passed by three to one – Scotland opposed – that each association would make payments based on the number of participating players. This left England stumping up £2,281, Scotland, £1,597, Wales £684 and Northern Ireland £456. For the FAW, this expense was offset against income of £1,837 from the two post-Olympic friendlies against India.

Despite the penny-pinching from the Home Nations Olympic Committee, Busby's approach endeared him to his Olympians. After the tournament, Jack Rawlings wrote to the GB manager to thank him for such a great experience. Back at Old Trafford and deep in the 1948/49 season, Busby found time to send a two-page hand-written reply on club paper to Rawlings. While overseeing United, Busby was even keeping an eye on the scores of his early charges and noted Enfield's winning start to the season. Busby wrote to Rawlings: "[The Olympics] was an experience I will never forget and again besides the honour of the position, to me it was grand to be associated with such a wonderful band of chaps. I only wish I could see that chap Hopper now. Keep up the hard training and most of all the sharpening up. You have the rest."

After the Olympics, Rawlings signed for Hayes and went on to win 14 England amateur caps, citing Busby as revitalising his career. "He was great. Very understanding," Rawlings says. "I was never a fast player and he put two years of pace on me." Rawlings played for Hayes 178 times and scored 43 goals before leaving for Hendon in 1955, but had to retire two years later with a back injury. He later managed Southall and remained in west London, working for Castrol all his life before taking early retirement at 59.

Busby's affection for his Olympic players extended beyond letters. Manchester United trained in Weybridge ahead of fixtures or cup finals in London. Jack Neale's son Graham recalls regular visits. "When Manchester United won the European Cup when I was a bit older, I realised who had been calling round all these times."

A civil servant at the Ministry of Agriculture, Fisheries and Food, Neale was most of all a football man. After retiring at 35, he continued to help Walton & Hersham as a committee member until the early 1970s and helped the club gain admittance to the Isthmian League in 1971. He was also instrumental in recruiting Allen Batsford, who managed the club to victory in the 1973 Amateur Cup.

The two Northern Irishmen remained gentlemen too. Kevin McAlinden returned to Belfast Celtic, who on Boxing Day following the Olympics took on rivals Linfield in one of the most infamous football matches ever played in sectarian Northern Ireland. With the two clubs occupying the top two places in the Northern Irish League, the game was highly charged. McAlinden was particularly prominent as his father was involved in Ulster's nationalist political scene. The match finished 1-1 but as the teams left the field, Celtic's players were overwhelmed by a horde of Linfield supporters. Centre forward Jimmy Jones was kicked unconscious, with McAlinden and defender Robin Lawlor also seriously hurt. McAlinden never played for the club again. In 1949, amid concerns their players could not be properly protected, Belfast Celtic folded. The war hero Denis Kelleher devoted his life to the sick. In 1952 he joined London's St Mary's Hospital as a general practitioner. A staunch Catholic, he regularly accompanied trips by the Handicapped Children's Trust to Lourdes as their medical officer and worked as a GP until retiring in 1989.

Scotsman Davie Letham stayed amateur too, partly due to injuries, and later became president of Queen's Park and the Scottish League. Wage offers to more established amateurs could be derisory in Scotland. Dougie McBain was offered a contract by Rangers in 1948 but was unimpressed and signed for Queen of the South, then a strong provincial side with a smattering of internationals. He opened a sub-post office while still playing, but after retiring, retrained as a lecturer in economics and worked in Edinburgh.

Jim McColl joined McBain at Queen of the South then played for Falkirk, Cowdenbeath, Berwick Rangers and Montrose before being forced to retire at 32 through injury. He promptly took up badminton and worked as an insurance broker, and then set up a solar heating business. The father of six children, he always supported Hibernian and never lost touch with his good friend Angus Carmichael, who after the Olympics moved to a veterinary practice in the Lake District.

Bob Hardisty tried to persuade Carmichael to join Bishop Auckland but the giant Scotsman was having none of it; he was going to stay a vet. The ambitious young manager of Football League side Carlisle also got in touch but even Bill Shankly could not tempt him to go back to football. "Shankly offered to send a taxi for me but I had to explain I worked on Saturdays," says Carmichael, who never lost his love of the game, only the time for it. Years later he would play games with farmers from Cartmel, who were dumbfounded at their vet's hidden ability. Carmichael turned out for Cartmel FC a few times but there was no comeback. After a handful of games, he hung his boots up for good.

In 1998 he was invited to a get-together of the 1948 team at Wembley by the British Olympic Association. Four of his Scottish team-mates were with him and they all met Princess Anne. No Englishmen were present. Carmichael, who moved to Lincolnshire to practise and retired there, has never seen a single English player from Busby's squad since 1948.

In the Olympic year, one of Busby's English players travelled up to Carmichael's Queen's Park. Impressed by the prospect of playing regularly in the Scottish first division at Hampden Park, the player wanted to sign for the Spiders – until he discovered that the Scots gentlemen were only paid bare minimum travel expenses. Not impressed with this Corinthian approach, the "gentleman" went back to England and an "amateur" club with less stringent accounting methods.

As post-war life settled down, the maximum wage inched up but remained unattractive for some amateurs, even those playing at the top level. Peter Kippax represented the Football League twice but left Burnley at the end of the 1948 season. He was later on the books at Liverpool and Preston but remained an amateur. The Chester schoolteacher Eric Lee made more than 360 appearances for his home-town team up to 1956/57 but also stayed amateur, preferring to earn his money teaching. The uncle of comedian Bob Mills, Lee immigrated to Canada after retiring.

For some amateurs like Harry McIlvenny, playing at the foot of the Football League was unattractive compared to the top of the booming amateur league. Exempt from entertainment tax and with no official wages to pay – only expenses that could be written off against tax – the amateur game evolved at a rapid pace. A major fillip came in the Olympic year when, after nearly 60,000 fans watched that year's Amateur Cup final, the FA shifted the final to Wembley. A mere 3,500 people watched Wreford-Brown and his Old Carthusians in the competition's first final at Richmond in 1894. Since then, the game of the purists had become the people's game.

In the first final at Wembley in 1949, an amazing 95,000 spectators turned up to watch Eric Fright's Bromley side beat Romford.

Impressed, Harry McIlvenny quit Bradford Park Avenue and the Football League for Bishop Auckland. In 1950 he went back to Wembley with Bishops and played in front of 88,000 people in the Amateur Cup final. McIlvenny lost that game but went back again a year later. This time 100,000 fans turned up but the Bishops lost again, this time to a new team called Pegasus.

Pegasus had been formed in May of the 1948 Olympic year. A meeting was called at the East India Sports Club in St James's Square in central London – not to divide the amateur game again but to embrace that credo. Representatives of Oxford and Cambridge Universities and Corinthian-Casuals filed in along with Wreford-Brown, now in his eighties. According to Joss Ackland, his father, the *Candide*-reading, hard-drinking journalist Norman Ackland was also in attendance. A new team was formed, named Pegasus after the winged horse of the classics and to be exclusively the preserve of Oxbridge graduates.

The driving force behind this new club was a fellow at St John's College, Oxford, the chemistry professor Dr Harold Warris Thompson. "While admiring the skill of the professional game, [a few soccer enthusiasts at Oxford] saw with some dismay the effects of prejudice by others against it, for this prejudice was providing a channel for the flow to rugby football in many schools all over the country," said Thompson. "Within a generation, this might prove disastrous and damage our national prestige even in the world of international soccer which this country has done so much to create, for without a veritable host of amateurs behind them, the professional ranks must surely dwindle."

With this grand ambition in mind, true to the spirit of their forefathers, the club would not play in a league but would challenge for the Amateur Cup. As a figurehead, a familiar figure was brought in. Also present in the room for the birth of Pegasus was the Footballing Parson, and Kenneth Hunt was elected president of football's flying horse.

After the 1920 Olympics, Hunt had gone back to his job as housemaster of Highgate School's Grindal House. He took boys on extra-curricular trips, such as camping in the Isle of Mull, to broaden their outlook and approached teaching with the same passion as he had previously displayed for football.

If boys failed to pay attention, Hunt – showing dexterity that suggested he could have been some basketball player – would bounce a football off the rear of the classroom onto the back of the offending pupil's head. The Footballing Parson also kept a cane on his desk, which ex-Highgate pupil and motor racing commentator Murray Walker felt the force of.

In his autobiography *Unless I'm very much mistaken*, Walker remembers being called to the front of the class for a misdemeanour. Hunt told the effervescent Walker: "I'm going to give you three strokes, Walker, but before I administer justice, have you got anything to say in mitigation?"

"I thought you would be interested to know that I will be the second generation of Walkers you have beaten because you beat my father," suggested Walker. "Oh, did I?" responded an indignant Hunt. "Well now I'm going to give you six for that." Walker cites that caning as the major reason in persuading him to have less to say for himself in future.

The Footballing Parson was a popular housemaster – the house colours remain black and gold in a tribute to his footballing career at Wolverhampton Wanderers – and by the post-war period the name Grindal was synonymous with Hunt to most Highgate pupils. He wrote an instruction book called *Association Football* and in 1929 became Highgate's deputy head. During WWII he helped evacuate the school's 400 boys to Devon during the Blitz. His affection for football and Wolves never dimmed. He often returned to the club and even played in a practice match during WWII.

While in Westward Ho!, Hunt became ill. His health took a further downward turn after returning to Highgate in 1943 and having a fall while on air raid precaution duty. He retired in 1945 to Heathfield in Sussex and was a fitting figurehead for Pegasus, with Thompson doing all the hard work as secretary.

Initially, only players at Oxford or Cambridge during that or the preceding season were allowed to play. To keep Pegasus strong, players outside of this remit would be needed, suggested the likes of Kenneth Hunt. "The rule of qualification for only one year after going down should be altered at once otherwise the club will die a natural death in a very few years," urged Hunt from his deathbed on 26 April 1949. Two days later, the Footballing Parson passed on, aged 65.

The new Pegasus constitution was not welcomed by Corinthian-Casuals, who had lost in the first round of the first two post-war Amateur Cups. For the next four years, Corinthian-Casuals endured the ignominy of having to qualify for the first round of the country's premier amateur competition. With qualifiers staged so early that many players were still in whites on the cricket field, the club did not make the first round again until 1951/52, when the FA finally relented and gave the club a guaranteed first round slot. By that time, the new rule over eligibility had gone through and Pegasus were flying.

In 1951, a Pegasus team featuring seven England amateur internationals defeated Bob Hardisty and Harry McIlvenny's Bishop Auckland 2-1 at a full Wembley in the Amateur Cup final. Over the coming years, Pegasus would boost the GB team's playing roster and reinforce the social standing of the "gentlemen", of players who could somehow afford not to go professional. The club's Amateur Cup matches routinely drew crowds of 10,000 or more to Iffley Road in Oxford and Pegasus would emulate that 1951 Amateur Cup win. Wreford-Brown, the one amateur administrator within the FA, who had championed the Olympic team more than any other, would not be there this time. A few months after that first cup win, the great bastion of the amateur game passed away, aged 85. He was still Oxford University's representative on the FA Council. Wreford-Brown would not get to see Great Britain's next Olympic performance either. Maybe that was just as well.

CHAPTER EIGHT:
1952 AND WINTERBOTTOM'S WOES

"It really was terrible."

Derek Grierson, 1952 GB Olympic squad player

MATT BUSBY'S FREE HAND IN SELECTING A TEAM IN London represented a step away from the FA's autocratic formula of teams picked by committees of grandees. A committee chose Busby's squad but the starting XI had been the manager's choice. The catalyst for this change came in 1946, when the FA appointed a director of coaching in Walter Winterbottom. A favourite of Rous, Winterbottom had played for Manchester United in the 1930s, when he also took a physical education course at Leeds's Carnegie College. After serving as an RAF wing commander in WWII he had been offered a job back at Carnegie after the war, but the thoughtful Winterbottom had other aspirations. He wanted to develop a national coaching scheme and took the less well-paid job on offer with the FA.

Soon after Winterbottom was appointed, England trounced Ireland 7-2 and the following year Winterbottom became England's first manager in the modern sense. A selection committee held sway but he ran the team. Over the years Winterbottom would be castigated for his handling of England, for seemingly ignoring the growing overseas challenge. Three results in particular are held up as evidence.

In 1950 the British Championship was used by Fifa as a qualifying group for the first post-war World Cup in Brazil, much to Rous's satisfaction. As part of the deal with Fifa, all four Home Nations agreed to enter the first post-war World Cup. The top two countries in that year's British Championship would be awarded places in the 1950 World Cup finals. The SFA, however, insisted that the Scots would only travel to Brazil if they were the Home Nations champions. After losing out to England the Scots stayed at home and Winterbottom's side went on to reach the quarter-finals in Brazil, but not without suffering a woeful 1-0 defeat to the USA. Three years later, England were savaged 6-3 by a majestic Hungarian team at Wembley – an infamous first home loss to a side outside of the British Isles. A year later Winterbottom took his charges to Budapest, but England were pulverised 7-1. Those defeats are cited as the former schoolteacher's worst moments as an international manager. Yet lost in history's crumpled pages lurks another defeat that ranks with that hat-trick of humiliations – Great Britain's performance at the 1952 Olympic Games in Helsinki.

The Finnish capital had been expecting the Olympics since 1938, when Helsinki had been lined up as a possible venue for the 1940 Games. That never materialised but even then the Finns were fretting about whether the home of football would send a side. Helsinki's then vice mayor Erik Von Frencknell said: "It would be sad indeed if Great Britain to whom the world owes so much for the science and spirit of football is not represented."

The concept of a united British team had not died with Rous's post-war World Cup deal with Fifa. In 1952 a match was staged in Wales between a Welsh professional XI and players from the rest of the Home Nations to celebrate the FAW's 75th anniversary. The home side won 3-2 but this was a one-off celebration match, unlikely to be repeated. All four Home Nations were embracing the new world order independently. The idea of a GB football team was withering but a GB side would compete at Helsinki after the Home Nations Olympic Committee reached an agreement to send a team after a meeting on 17 September 1951 at Lancaster Gate. The only snag was the cost. In 1936 the entire BOA team cost £4,000 to send to Berlin. To go to Helsinki, the cost of sending just a squad of footballers and officials was put at £7,000. Unlike Fifa's World Cup, where teams played in groups guaranteeing more than one match, the Olympics was knock-out. So Helsinki would involve spending £7,000 possibly for just one match.

On 19 November 1951, FA officials attended the BOA's annual dinner at the Savoy to help the BOA start raising an estimated £30,000 to send a squad to Helsinki. The FA's budget was a quarter of the bill for sending the entire Olympic team of 340 athletes and officials. Not long after, the Northern Irish and Welsh associations admitted they could not afford to contribute financially. Busby offered to return as manager but as the Scotsman was busy with Manchester United, squad selection was left to Winterbottom. With the other Home Nations providing seemingly no impetus, the FA agreed to underwrite the cost of the entire venture. Busby was overlooked as an English manager became a political necessity for a team funded by the FA. Winterbottom's appointment as manager was a formality.

Few gentlemen like Bernard Joy played at the top level of the professional game in the early 1950s, but Winterbottom had a booming amateur game from which to pick his players. That first Amateur Cup final at Wembley in 1949 produced gate receipts of £20,500. Winners Bromley banked £7,000 from the final and semi-final. Amateur clubs' finances were strengthened further in 1951, when the FA decided to pool Amateur Cup receipts and share them between the clubs. This would provide a steady income and help change amateur football, allowing the shamateurs to dominate more than ever. The traditionalists faced a dilemma: if the grand experiment of the winged horse was not to crash and burn, change was needed. The Pegasus committeemen realised that the bulk of the current talented XI, which was drawn from students in residence, would all graduate and leave. Scrapping the one-year qualification rule would draw off some better ex-Oxbridge students from Corinthian-Casuals, who not surprisingly objected. Pegasus went ahead anyway, finally agreeing to Kenneth Hunt's suggestion to drop the one-year rule in 1951 and setting the traditionalists' leading clubs against each other.

For the gentlemen within the FA, the pursuit of the shamateur remained a preoccupation. Identifying culprits was as difficult as ever and some northern gentlemen still felt they were the subject of prejudice by the southern FA. When Bob Hardisty, figurehead at the strongest northern side, Bishop Auckland, married in 1948, the Durham FA had to ask Lancaster Gate if a gift could be given. The FA agreed on the proviso that the sum involved did not top £100. To some that felt like interference from the southern purists, but the gift was phenomenally generous as the average professional footballer was on £5 a week and a manual worker only took home around £15 a week.

The numbers of players like Hardisty, who had lost their best years to the war, was diminishing in the Olympic Squad, but most young men still gave up an early part of their prime footballing life in the armed forces. Conscription began in 1939, and became known as national service after the war, remaining until 1960. This ate away at the youthful confidence of men leaving the services with thoughts of turning pro. A prime example occurred in 1952, when Bromley's Stan Charlton was due to come out of the army and was offered a deal by top-flight giants, Aston Villa. "I was 23 and thought I was too old and would end up starting out in their third team and didn't want that," says Charlton, who reluctantly turned Villa down.

That same spring the Olympic committee sent scouts to Scotland's amateur internationals against Wales and Ireland to draw up probables and possibles to take each other on before the season's end. Having agreed to bankroll the venture, the English soon took over the entire enterprise. A squad of 22 British Olympic players and four reserves were due to travel to Germany and Luxembourg during mid-May for a brief training camp. Only Englishmen travelled to the Grand Duchy. A more British-looking team of Olympic probables took on the professional England B team at Highbury on April 30, losing 3-0. A few more names were trimmed and when Winterbottom unveiled his squad, the notion of a Great Britain football team in Helsinki became a marginal conceit.

Few amateurs played in the top level of the Football League. The season after Busby's Olympic near miss, the only amateurs playing in professional teams were Eric Lee, Harry McIlvenny, Bill Amor and Harry Parr at Lincoln. Their numbers had not grown since then but Winterbottom was able to call on a gentleman with an FA Cup finalist's medal. Having given up a large slice of their young life to the war or national service, a generation existed that were more upwardly mobile and wanted a degree to better themselves. Bill Slater was one of those men.

Slater was called up in 1945 and spent most of the next three years in Germany before being demobbed in 1948. Originally from Blackpool, he played for his local team a handful of times during national service but football as a career was not attractive. When he re-signed for Blackpool it was only on amateur forms. Slater explains: "I'd set my mind on teaching as [football] didn't strike me as being a career. You thought twice about signing [as a professional] and the reward wasn't so great. If it had been more rewarding some more of the [amateur] players might have gone professional but I was keen to have a career."

Slater enrolled on a teacher training course at Leeds University, and Blackpool sent a car across the Pennines to pick up the young inside-forward for the Tangerines' matches. In 1951 Blackpool reached the FA Cup Final. Slater played but his side lost and no amateur would ever feature in an FA Cup Final again. At the end of that season Slater left Blackpool for London to be closer to his future wife. The FA Cup finalist had to resort to ringing round looking for a game, eventually settling on Brentford, the home of his fiancée.

One of the best England amateur internationals was George Robb, who broke into Finchley's first team before joining the Navy for national service. After demob, Robb went to Loughborough College then returned to his native Finchley to become a master at Christ's College and re-signed for his old side, but often played midweek for Spurs. The regular England outside-left, Robb, was also a definite starter in Helsinki.

The only other amateur also at a big professional club was Bill Holmes, a blond-haired teacher from Hunslet, who was a prolific scorer with Blackburn Rovers. In 1946, aged 20, he played briefly for Morecambe and then signed for Lancaster City, while he took a degree in physical education at Leeds University. Holmes won the first of five England amateur caps while still a student in 1950 then had trials with Burnley. "I travelled all the way from Leeds to Derby for a Burnley game but when I arrived the manager Frank Hill told me he'd decided to play someone else," recalls Holmes. "After a brief argument, I left the ground and the club."

Holmes signed instead for arch-rivals Blackburn Rovers and was an immediate hit, scoring on his debut for the mid-week, A, reserve and first teams. Not always available, he only made a dozen appearances in the 1951/52 season but played a big part in Blackburn reaching that year's FA Cup semi-finals. In the fifth round Blackburn drew Burnley and Holmes had great satisfaction in banging in two goals in a 3-1 win. With so few amateurs at the top, Holmes was a shoo-in for the Helsinki squad.

So was Bob Hardisty, who by then had finished his teacher training at Carnegie in the Olympic year and started work as a local authority physical training instructor. Hardisty was named assistant manager. The captaincy went to Charlie Fuller, an outstanding English amateur whose career was even more severed by WWII than Hardisty. Born in Grimsby but with an

East End accent reflecting where he grew up, Fuller played in the 1937 Amateur Cup final for Erith & Belvedere and then joined Walthamstow Avenue, but then war broke out. Serving in the Royal Artillery, Fuller was based near Bromley and switched to his local club. Staying on after hostilities were over, Fuller captained Bromley to the 1949 Amateur Cup. His performance was so impressive that an unidentified Italian club wrote to Fuller, care of Winterbottom, making a double-figure offer (in pounds not lira) to go professional. The Englishman stayed put and was a clear choice for captain and was joined by Bromley team-mate Stan Charlton.

Stan's father had been a professional at Crystal Palace and Exeter but three years in the Middle East with the Army stopped Stan emulating his dad. Posted back to England, he was made a postings clerk at Woolwich Arsenal and was snapped up by Bromley. During an Amateur Cup tie with Barnet in 1951, half a dozen selectors turned up and Charlton had a good match, despite losing 3-1. When the England amateur captain was injured, Charlton came in and stayed in the side for a number of games including the first England vs Scotland amateur international to be played at Wembley in 1951. At that game Charlton was introduced to Field Marshal Montgomery. "[Montgomery] asked me if I was with him in the last war. I said no and he replied 'Well, you'll be with me in the next,'" recalls Charlton with a mixture of a smile and a shiver. England lost 2-1. Again, despite a defeat, Charlton shone and would go to Helsinki.

Alf Noble had been unlucky to miss out on Busby's squad. After being demobbed from the Navy, he signed for Leytonstone in 1946 and made the England amateur side in Easter of 1948. A dismal 4-3 defeat to Wales saw Noble and a number of other English players excluded from the Olympic squad. The Leytonstone player was also dropped from the England team and Noble did not return until 1950 and a match with Switzerland, when he scored to salvage a draw. He was imperious in Leytonstone's 5-0 hammering of league side Orient in an FA Cup match before the Olympics and would not miss out again.

With Wreford-Brown's passing, the purists lost their flag bearer within the FA and the Home Nations Olympic Committee had produced a more egalitarian selection. Since 1948, Pegasus had flown into view with their Amateur Cup win in 1951 under the guidance of former Tottenham Hotspur coach Vic Buckingham and given the FA reason to favour the

Oxbridge fraternity. The traditionalists, with their diehard interpretation of amateurism, were on the verge of another brief renaissance, but Winterbottom was not an Oxbridge man, having trained at Chester Diocesan Training College. This was perhaps why the only Pegasus players selected were Tony Pawson, a Winchester School alumnus from Oxford, and the England amateur keeper Ben Brown, a Dark Blue from Mexborough Grammar School. Corinthian-Casuals supplied Ralph Cowan for trial matches but, dogged by injuries, he missed out.

The bulk of the side were working men like Winterbottom's other keeper, Ted Bennett, who was also an England amateur international. Born in Kilburn, Bennett played a couple of matches as an amateur for Queens Park Rangers in 1948 before joining Southall, where he was playing in 1952. Mixing football with his job as a welder, Bennett was renowned for joining the outfield players to demonstrate his dribbling skills.

The Isthmian League remained the strongest southern amateur competition and most southern players came from that competition. Hendon's England amateur international Laurie Topp was one of only two players from the Isthmian's weaker rival, the Athenian League – the other was George Robb. Like Stan Charlton, Topp never turned professional, fearing he was not quite good enough and deterred by the maximum wage. After leaving school, his mother found him a job at a company that made drills for the RAF, then a reserved occupation, and Topp missed the war, signing for Hendon in 1942.

Pegasus went out of the Amateur Cup to northern side Crook Town in 1952 and Walthamstow Avenue took the trophy. Three of Walthamstow's side went to Helsinki: Derek Saunders, Leslie Stratton and Jim Lewis. A 24-year-old shipping clerk from Ware, Derek Saunders was attracting professional scouts. So too certainly was Walthamstow's main goalscorer, but Jim Lewis would never turn professional and went on to become one of the GB team's greatest ever players.

His father, Jim Lewis Senior, toured Australia and New Zealand in 1937 with the likes of Terry Huddle, played in the Football League for Queens Park Rangers and had a solitary wartime cap for the full England side, but was a devout amateur. He did not make the Berlin Olympic squad but continued playing until his son, "Young Jim", could take his place in the Walthamstow and England sides.

Young Jim would go on to take his father's place in both teams but his football career was interrupted by a stint in the services at Sandhurst and then India. In 1950 he played four games as an amateur for Orient but turned down their contract offer and returned to Walthamstow. "I was on West Ham's books as a youngster too but I'd got a job as a salesman with Thermos so I never turned pro," says Jim Lewis, who was a favourite of Norman Ackland.

In 1951 former player Charlie Buchan had launched a new monthly football title bearing his own name and signed Ackland to write on the gentlemen's game. Over the coming years, a glowing Ackland write-up in Charles Buchan's *Football Monthly* provided a boost for the ambitions of many amateurs, who enjoyed a status unimaginable today. With attendances booming, that year saw a rare live TV match. The broadcast was not a Football League fixture but a friendly between Walthamstow and the Scottish gentlemen of Queen's Park. More than 200,000 people tuned in to see the Scots win 2-0.

One of those two goals was scored by a soon-to-be teacher who would go to Helsinki. The diminutive son of a Largs publican, Derek Grierson had signed with the Spiders in 1948, scoring a hat-trick on his debut for the second XI. On his first-team debut at Forfar, Grierson recalls a sign reading: "Don't throw stones at opposing players". He shunned the pro game for a maths degree at Glasgow University with a view to teaching and played for the Spiders – then enduring their third consecutive season in the Scottish second division – and Scotland's amateur XI, scoring in that 2-1 Wembley win over England in 1952.

Grierson was joined by just two other team-mates: Willie Hastie and Tommy Stewart, who worked in advertising with a soap manufacturer in Newcastle upon Tyne. Another Scot, Bob Paterson, played against England B and Queen's keeper Ritchie trained with the team but neither made the final squad.

In Northern Ireland, Cliftonville remained the most amateur club in the English sense, and two players, Kevin McGarry and Ernie McLeary, picked up full caps in the 1950s. McGarry and McLeary flew over to London for a trial along with another Cliftonville player, Maurice Masters, and another Jim Lewis, this one an Ulster amateur and left-half with Glenavon. Another Cliftonville player, Bruce Shiells, played against England B, but only McGarry, a Belfast doctor and striker, made the cut. He had three full caps and played in that groundbreaking first non-Home Nations international against France in 1951, when he also won the first Ulster player of the year award.

The sole Welsh representative was Idwal Robling, who had broken into the Welsh amateur side in the 1951/52 season. Robling played for Lovells Athletic, the works side of the Newport-based sweet manufacturer of the same name. In 1923 the FAW told Lovells to leave the South Wales Amateur League because the club had professional players on its books. Lovells joined the Welsh League but were looking for a higher standard of football and the FA agreed to let the club move into the English Southern League. Lovells were probably the strongest Welsh side outside of the Football League and Robling one of their star players. The squad was British – with representation from all four Home Nations – but only just. "It would have been a bit upsetting if there hadn't been at least one player from each country in the squad," says Jim Lewis.

The squad was due to fly out of Bovingdon in Hertfordshire on 3 July. The day before, the footballers joined the rest of the Olympic squad at Buckingham Palace for a reception. The royals enjoyed relative luxury in these Spartan times and the footballers were encouraged to take a bottle of beer or wine. One of Winterbottom's squad took a fair few more than one bottle and woke up the next morning in a deck chair in nearby Green Park with a dry mouth and a sore head.

The squad had hardly enjoyed the best preparation but expected to ease through the preliminary round, where GB faced Luxembourg. In five Olympics, the Luxembourgers had won just a single fixture – a 6-0 preliminary round win over Afghanistan at Brighton in 1948. The GB squad of 20 players was accompanied by a giant posse of ten officials, including Winterbottom, trainer Jack Jennings, Rous, who had been knighted in 1949, and selector Leonard Kingston, who was the AFA representative on the FA Council. Four decades on from the split, the AFA was still monitoring amateurism. The party flew out to Finland in a converted Lancaster bomber. "The noise was horrendous," recalls Stan Charlton. The trip was grim but the sponsorship raised by the BOA and supporting federations like the FA was more generous than ever. This ranged from seven Austin cars loaned for the BOA's stay in Helsinki to Braemar sweaters and Horlicks for a bedtime drink.

After arriving, Winterbottom unveiled the team that he, not the selectors, had chosen. All but one of the starting XI – Tommy Stewart – were English, with Billy Holmes left out for the young Jim Lewis. According to Derek Grierson, Stewart also replaced Charlie Fuller as captain. "I was disappointed not to make the starting XI," admits Grierson. "Tommy Stewart and McGarry were the best two players in Helsinki and there were a couple that thought they were better than they were but we all got on okay."

7 July 1952
Lahti, Finland. GB vs Luxembourg

GB's first game was before the Games' opening ceremony and just 3,656 people turned up. The Luxembourgers were more mobile but the British seemingly more confident. Winterbottom's side flew into attack but were predictable and their attacks were easily broken up by the hard-tackling Luxembourg right-back Wagner. Behind him, keeper Lahure seemed assured, only to fumble an early Robb shot from Hardisty's cross to gift GB the lead. GB then conjured up numerous chances but failed to convert a single one.

The scoreline remained until 15 minutes after half-time, when Roller surprisingly equalised. The game opened up with Lahure and Bennett making good saves but no one could find the net. Winterbottom and his players had expected an easy win; no one ever considered the possibility of needing extra time. The surprise of the GB side was evident when, straight from the kick-off, Luxembourg left-winger Letsch was able to advance completely unopposed on Bennett's goal and send a powerful shot past the Southall keeper. GB had been unprepared for extra time and were shell-shocked to be losing.

Driven forward by Wagner, the Luxembourgers found that the Briton's nerve had failed. Roller added his second five minutes later. "It really was terrible," recalls Derek Grierson, watching from the bench. "They lost those two early goals and after that it was all the way down. I'd never had to sit and watch a game like that before and it was really frustrating."

Roller completed his hat-trick before Bill Slater pulled one back but the Luxembourgers restored their three-goal advantage through Gales. At half-time in extra time, Luxembourg were 5-2 up. In the second half, GB poured forward but the crowd were behind Luxembourg. The acrobatic Lahure got an arm or a leg in front of every shot. Jim Lewis grabbed a consolation but GB were routed 5-3, undone by overconfidence and a ten-minute panic attack.

Stories circulated that a couple of Luxembourgers played in the French league but that did not make them professionals, as Bill Slater could attest. "They were just better than we thought," he recalls. For the thoughtful, academic Slater the reason for losing was simple. "It was quite enjoyable and we all got on quite well together but there was no preparation," he says, adding:

> "There were no real practice games before Helsinki, apart from the odd game. We could play among ourselves but that was hardly the same. We weren't a dud team but we were scattered around the country, and not just England, and we didn't have much time to get together. The team and that performance didn't reflect the strength of the amateur game then."

With the game lost, there was only one solution for Britain's footballers if they wanted to stay in Finland for the rest of the Olympics; one that would have sent traditionalists like Wreford-Brown into an apoplectic fugue. If Winterbottom's team wanted to stay they needed to earn some money – and do so playing football. Stan Charlton explains:

> "Before the tournament, Walter said, 'If we go out and enough of you stay, we'll [go on tour] and make enough money to cover our expenses to see the athletics and the rest of the football'. I was in the Army and on special leave and was really keen to stay on as it was fantastic. We all really appreciated what Walter did."

Not all the players were quite so sure. In the changing rooms in Lahti, Bill Holmes, who had been left on the bench, partly due to the impressive form of Jim Lewis and also due to a nagging injury from the FA Cup semi-final, got to his feet to win over the doubters. He says: "I made a big passionate effort to try and persuade some of the players that we should stay on. Some of the guys had families and jobs to go back to, so it was a hard call for them."

Holmes won over enough players to make a tour viable. How many players went back home varies. Bob Hardisty certainly did. Some records suggest a total of five returned but writing in 1958, Derek Grierson recalled that eight of the starting XI against Luxembourg returned to Britain, leaving a dozen for the tour. Bob Hardisty certainly went back but Bill Slater stayed. "That tour was quite enjoyable. By the end we were much more of a team," recalls Slater wistfully.

After the Luxembourg game, Winterbottom's footballers attended the opening ceremony despite having no further part to play in the Olympics, and then the remnants of his team boarded a converted German World War Two bomber for a brief Scandinavian tour. Finnish club side Kuopio were edged 4-3 in the first match before a game with Greece, eliminated in a preliminary by Denmark. The game is classified by the Greeks as a full international with England's amateur XI but with all three Queen's Park players and Robling starting, the team was more British than the one upset by Luxembourg. More than 4,000 fans turned up to Hämeenlinna's Kauriala Stadium to see the home side beat GB 4-2. Club side Vaasa were routed 6-0 in a third game and then Winterbottom met up with another British manager who had endured a sobering Olympics.

Frank Soo was a promising Anglo-Chinese wing-half with Stoke City in the first division before World War Two. He won wartime caps for England but moved into management. In the summer of 1952, Soo was asked to manage Norway's Olympic XI. Like Winterbottom, Soo's experience was brief. His charges were thrashed 4-1 by Sweden in the first round in Soo's only official match as manager. When Winterbottom's touring side arrived in Oslo, Soo was still in charge. Soo looked to have secured a win when, with six minutes to go, Norway were up 2-0, but Winterbottom's team had developed some spirit and late goals from Grierson and Noble secured a 2-2 draw. Grierson played and scored in every game, impressing his manager. "Winterbottom couldn't believe the amount of goals I was scoring because I was very small but I was very strong legged," says Grierson.

The team returned to Helsinki to enjoy the Olympics and the sporting festival around the Games, including the football. Jim Lewis adds: "Walter Winterbottom took us to see a side he said we should watch and lo and behold it was the Hungarians. After seeing them, none of us were surprised when they turned England over later [in a full international at Wembley]."

The prospective teacher Bill Slater was asked to write a report on Hungary, whose innovative approach of playing with a deep-lying centre forward, Nador Hidegkuti, undid less flexible teams – like England. Hungary thrashed holders Sweden 6-0 in the semi-final and beat Yugoslavia 2-0 in the final. They scored 20 goals and conceded just one in five Olympic matches. Ferenc Puskas, Hidegkuti and the Hungarians visited Wembley the next year. Slater's report lay unread. Winterbottom's England team were humiliated, losing by the same score-line as in Helsinki, 6-3.

This experience was presaged for Winterbottom by his return from Helsinki, the footballers flying home to some severe criticism. The day before the GB squad's only gold medal was won in the show jumping. "In the first half, we had enough opportunities to win the tie. The finishing was unbelievably bad," sighed Bernard Joy, while Norman Ackland tartly noted: "As some of the best players had to fly back to England, our touring side's records in those games was quite good."

Winterbottom's predecessor, Matt Busby, had been in Lahti for the Luxembourg debacle and was even more damning. "Luxembourg, who should really be a joke in international football, licked the British team ... Something is radically wrong," said Busby. "There are enough class amateurs in the four home countries, even with the obvious attractions of widespread professionalism, to provide Great Britain with a side that should do better than lose 5-3 to Luxembourg."

Having spent £7,000 on a single shocking game, the FA did not forgive easily. In November 1952 the FA reviewed a report of the Olympic debacle. No verdict was given. The minutes show, "further consideration [was needed] until the next meeting." Quite what that was will never be known as the report on the 1952 Olympics has simply disappeared from the FA library. Luxembourg were narrowly edged out 2-1 by Brazil in the next round so were not bad, but the FA did not forget. In early 1953 an England amateur tour of the Grand Duchy was cancelled and the team sent to Norway instead. No reason is given in FA minutes for the switch.

The scale of the upset is best illustrated by what happened next to some of Winterbottom's players, many who would go on to achieve at the highest levels of the professional game, notably Bill Slater. On his return from Finland, Slater was snapped up by Wolverhampton Wanderers but never went wholly professional, combining football with teaching at Birmingham University. He explains:

> "When I started for Wolves, I was still an amateur and under some pressure from the club to be a part-time professional. They wrote me a contract with a clause in it saying that teaching would get a priority over football if there was ever a clash. I wasn't eligible for the

171

England amateur team due to this new contract and my
university boss was hoping that I wouldn't be pestered
for internationals now."

Amateur internationals were generally shunned by the selectors of the
professional side but, at 27, Slater was finally eligible for Winterbottom's
team. He went on to make 12 full England appearances and played in the
1958 World Cup finals. One of Wolves' greatest ever players, he mixed football
and teaching – missing the odd European away game because of lectures
– for 11 years, during which time he won three league championships. In
1960 he won the FA Cup and was voted footballer of the year. In 1962 Bill
Slater finally left Wolves and returned to London, settling near Brentford
with his wife. He turned out for Brentford again on a handful of occasions
before finally retiring. He was made an OBE for services to sport in 1982
and a CBE in 1998.

For many of the English players in Helsinki, the pro game remained
unattractive, although Ted Bennett joined the players at Watford in 1953.
Despite interest from Italian side Padua, George Robb stayed amateur
until 1953 and after much pestering finally turned professional with Spurs,
going on to score 53 goals in 182 games. Winterbottom put him in the full
England team but, unfortunately for Robb, his debut was Hungary's 1953
visit to Wembley, when the visitors romped home 6-3. Robb never played
for England again and retired due to injury in 1958, returning to teaching
and working at Ardingly College near Haywards Heath.

"I don't think that Walter had quite grasped how good Hungary were," says
Bill Holmes. "Otherwise he wouldn't have invited them to play against the full
England side." Holmes had another season at Blackburn but left in September
1953 after the club signed Tommy Briggs and he lost his place. His appearances
were only sporadic due to college commitments but he notched up 19 goals
in 25 appearances. Holmes moved to Bradford City and then Southport in
July 1954, where he stayed two seasons and scored a hat-trick on his wedding
day. He later worked as a brewery manager in the East Midlands and made
the headlines in 1973, when he and playwright Don Shaw led protests for the
reinstatement of Brian Clough as Derby County's manager – a post Clough
left after a dispute with the club's chairman, Sam Longson.

Holmes returned to the Derby ground for the first time since his fall-out at the stadium with Frank Hill during his earlier brief spell at Burnley. This time he got onto the pitch, racing on to give supporters of his "Bring Back Clough" campaign a wave. Holmes was duly arrested. "My 12-year-old daughter saw me on the TV," recalls Holmes. "The previous day, she'd packed her bags and told me she was leaving home until I'd finished with all this Clough nonsense. She was staying with friends when she saw me being chased and arrested."

Tony Pawson turned out in the first division briefly for Charlton Athletic but remained an amateur and went on to be a successful journalist, writing for the *Observer* for 45 years. Two days after returning from Finland, Derek Grierson and his father went to Ibrox and he signed as a professional for Rangers. He was top scorer with 31 goals in his first season, when he won the league and cup double. In 1956 Grierson left for Falkirk and won the Scottish Cup again. After a final season in Northern Ireland with Glentoran in 1960, he quit and concentrated on teaching. While at Rangers, Grierson had to choose between a final exam for the vocation he would pursue after football and a place in the Scotland professional team for a game against Ireland. "The Rangers manager was very keen on people getting jobs and if you didn't train in the day, you could train at night," recalls Grierson. "I didn't play because of my teaching exam and next time the team was selected, I didn't get in and was never chosen again." After retiring from teaching, Grierson moved to Newton Mearns near Glasgow.

Stan Charlton would not add to his four caps for England's amateur team but his lack of early self-belief proved misplaced. On returning from Helsinki he signed instead for Leyton Orient on £12 a week and after three seasons moved up to the first division, when he and Vic Groves were transferred to Arsenal for a joint fee of £30,000. After 110 appearances for Arsenal, Charlton went back to Orient in December 1958 and captained the team into the top flight for the first time in 1962. Orient only lasted one season in the first division but Charlton did not miss a match. He made 366 appearances for the club in two spells before retiring due to injury in 1965, and then joined Weymouth as manager for seven years. His 1952 Olympic blazer still fits and when the 2012 Olympic sailing competition comes to Charlton's home town of Weymouth, he intends to be on the shore in that blazer.

The lone non-Englishman to play in Helsinki, Tommy Stewart, returned to his job as an advertising executive and had nine years with Queen's Park before work took him to southern England. After a couple of seasons with

Romford he signed for Bishop Auckland and played in two Amateur Cup finals, captaining the team to victory in 1955 over Laurie Topp's Hendon.

The Welshman in Helsinki, Idwal Robling, made 13 appearances for Wales's amateur side while working as a packaging manager but only really hit the headlines after retiring. In 1969, BBC's *Sportsnight* presenter David Coleman reacted to criticism that commentary was easy by running a competition to "find a commentator" for the BBC team to cover the 1970 World Cup finals in Mexico. Robling beat former Liverpool player Ian St John on the casting vote of Alf Ramsey and joined Barry Davies, David Coleman, Ken Wolstenholme and Alan Weeks in Mexico. Despite early criticism, Robling later worked for BBC TV in Wales and continues to work on BBC Radio Wales in Cardiff. The Ulsterman Kevin McGarry never returned to Northern Ireland's full side but won 17 amateur caps up to 1955. After retiring, he coached and became president at Cliftonville.

Helsinki was the end of the road for Walter Winterbottom's stint as GB manager but he took England to four World Cup finals and won 78 of his 139 matches in charge. He was knighted in 1978 and died in February 2002, aged 89.

Winterbottom took a paternal interest in the English players that went to Helsinki and was instrumental in persuading Derek Saunders and Jim Lewis to test themselves at the top. In 1953 Walthamstow Avenue reached the fourth round of the FA Cup and drew against Manchester United at Old Trafford. Busby's team took the lead but Jim Lewis secured a famous 1-1 draw for the amateurs against the reigning first division champions. The replay attracted so much interest that the game was switched to Highbury. Despite being played on a Thursday afternoon, 53,000 people turned up. Walthamstow lost 5-2 but Lewis scored twice. Days later, Chelsea manager Ted Drake offered him and Saunders contracts, which Winterbottom advised them to sign. Both joined Chelsea. Only Saunders went pro, playing five seasons at Stamford Bridge. Along with Lewis, Saunders won the league title in 1954/55 and did not miss a league game that season. In 1959 Saunders left to become a physical education teacher at Westminster School before retiring to Frinton-on-Sea.

For Jim Lewis, his career at Thermos was going too well to join the poorly-paid professional game. He explains:

"When I was at Chelsea, the maximum anyone was on at the end of my time there was £25 a week and an awful lot of the players were on far less. At Thermos, I was doing well and had a company car, which was a big deal back then, so I stayed an amateur. I never really had any problems, only once was it brought up at Newcastle, when one of their players had a go at me for taking money from the professionals, who could have been playing and earning money, because I was playing as an amateur."

Jim Lewis would feature at the next Olympics in 1956 along with Laurie Topp and 35-year-old Bob Hardisty, who had one last challenge left in him. The team would face a new challenge after their ignominious exit in Helsinki and be forced to qualify.

CHAPTER NINE: MELBOURNE 1956
AND TOO MANY BULGARIANS

"You called him 'Sir' or 'Mister Creek'. No one ever dared
call him Norman and we were all called by our surname."

Roy Littlejohn, GB Olympic player

A YEAR AFTER THE LUXEMBOURG DEBACLE, AN UNBOWED
FA took a table at the BOA's annual dinner at Grosvenor House in London.
Rous – now Sir Stanley after being knighted in 1949 – attended and
his party of 12 for once included a couple of players. Not the dedicated
northern schoolteacher and double Olympian Bob Hardisty but the two
Pegasus players left on the bench in Lahti by Winterbottom.

This was an indication of the heights that Pegasus had scaled. The
winged horse won the Amateur Cup again in 1953 with a 6-0 trouncing
of Harwich & Parkeston, widely regarded as one of the finest ever displays
in the final. The club caught the public's imagination and, after two dismal
decades, the exponents of the true amateurism had lifted their credo to a
new zenith. Tony Pawson – a friend of Rous – and Ben Brown both won
the Amateur Cup twice, Brown retiring in 1953 to become a fellow at Oriel
College, Oxford. What the amateur cause needed was a new cheerleader, a
man to beat the drum for the gentlemen's game. Frederick Norman Smith
Creek was that man. He would indeed support the cause, but in his own
quiet, schoolmasterly fashion.

Wreford-Brown would certainly have approved of his successor as Olympic manager. Norman Creek – or F.N.S. Creek as he was more commonly known – was a bastion of the amateur game and one of the great Corinthians: "You called him 'Sir' or 'Mister Creek'," recalls Olympic player Roy Littlejohn. "No one ever dared call him Norman and we were all called by our surname."

During the 1920s when Jackie Hegan and A.E. Knight were helping Corinthians justify their place in the pantheon of the FA Cup, Norman Creek, a lively, diminutive forward, was leading the Corinth line. He played in Corinth's first ever FA Cup tie against Brighton in 1923, the shock win over Blackburn the following year and doughty, narrow defeats to Manchester City, Newcastle and West Ham. In 146 pre-war games for Corinth, Creek scored 152 goals.

Born in Darlington, where he made a couple of league appearances between 1922 and 1924, Norman Creek served in the Flying Corps in World War One and won the Military Cross. On demob, Creek went to Cambridge and won his first Blue in 1920, before joining Corinth the next year. He scored four goals in five appearances for the England amateur team and gained a full cap against France in 1923, scoring in a 4-1 win.

Instead of furthering his footballing career, Creek went – like so many tied up with the Olympic team – into teaching and took a post at Dauntsey's School in Wiltshire, teaching games and geography. In his spare time, Creek played minor county cricket for Wiltshire, wrote for the *Daily Telegraph*, gave many radio broadcasts covering football, organised the Local Defence Volunteers force during World War Two and received an MBE. A decorated war hero, a great Corinthian and a teacher – no one could rival Norman Creek's eligibility for the job as manager of England's amateur team. In 1954 Creek left Dauntsey for that post as the indignity of being forced to qualify for the Games materialised. In July 1954, Fifa had sent the Home Nations' FAs a note explaining that more than 16 teams were interested in playing in the 1956 Olympic football tourney in Melbourne. So qualifiers would be needed. Hounslow Town – quarter-finalists in that year's Amateur Cup and semi-finalists in 1955 – helpfully suggested to the FA that leading amateurs offered pro contracts before the Olympics should be asked to reject the offer until after Melbourne. "Not our policy," said the FA. With a maximum wage and restrictive contracts firmly in place, England's footballers already endured enough restrictions.

In January 1955, the Olympic committee met up at Harrogate's Majestic Hotel as the problems facing a GB team began to stack up. Enthusiasm for the Olympic team was rapidly diminishing. In Harrogate, the Northern Irish and Scots said that as the Games entailed a long trip to the southern hemisphere during their league season, no players would be asked to go. The Welsh, too, would not participate. The reasons were partly cost, partly club pressure.

GB's professionals had united in Belfast in August 1955 to take on the Rest of Europe in a match to mark the IFA's 75th anniversary, but the other Home Nations were asserting their independence more than ever. All four took part in the 1954 World Cup with the British Championship acting as qualifiers and England and Scotland travelling to Switzerland, albeit with little success.

The Home Nations' independence was extending into the amateur game and plans were drawn up for an annual British Championship featuring all four UK amateur teams to be staged in 1956. The euphoric post-war sense of Britishness had gone. Lines were again being drawn.

The FA were left isolated and alone with the thorny issue of fielding a British Olympic team. With no other choice – apart from the politically impossible option of abandoning the team completely – the FA yet again had to underwrite the entire cost. With no funding from outside England, there would be no players from outside England either.

NORMAN ACKLAND HAD NOT TRAVELLED TO HELSINKI in 1952 but remained close to the amateur game, watching and writing up matches, and attending dinners among the sporting gentlemen. "I met him a lot when playing up and down this country as the general press were close to us," says 1956 Olympian Derek Lewin. "He was like all of them – very pleasant – mainly because it was a very different world in sport in those days."

Before the qualifier with Bulgaria, Ackland lobbied for the selection of the Ulsterman Kevin McGarry and the outstanding Welsh amateur Phil Woosnam, who later played for Aston Villa, West Ham and the full Welsh team, to no avail. Had McGarry or Woosnam joined the FA's cause, both would have faced immediate censure from their national FA. Just as in 1908, 1912 and 1920, only Englishmen would be British Olympic footballers. Winterbottom reputedly had some say in selection but Norman Creek was content to let the committee rule, seemingly setting progress back apace.

The FA initially held off entering as they considered how to meet the substantial bill for a trip to Melbourne. The BOA had started an appeal to raise the £75,000 needed for the overall squad but money was sparse in the 1950s. J.P.W. Mallalieu, a Member of Parliament in the Labour government, made clear in a piece in *World Sports* magazine that asking the state for cash was not the British Olympic spirit.

In June 1955, the FA provisionally entered a team. There was one seemingly curious stipulation. The team entered representing GB must take part in the qualifiers and should not be given a place in the main draw. Whether this was evidence of Corinthian ideals or a cynical ploy is unclear but with money short, this provided an easy way out. If GB entered and were knocked out, the FA had at least taken part and at nominal cost compared to sending a squad to the other side of the world. When the draw for the qualifiers pitted GB against Bulgaria, the FA's plan seemed to be working out perfectly.

Bulgaria entered the Paris Olympics in 1924 but lost in the first round to the Republic of Ireland. After WWII, the Cold War solidified Europe into opposing sides. Nations like Bulgaria quickly became even more remote and mysterious but, by the 1950s, the Bulgarians were tentatively emerging into football's limelight. Bulgaria travelled to Helsinki, losing to the impressive USSR 2-1 in the first round and tried unsuccessfully to qualify for the 1954 World Cup in Switzerland. Bulgarian club side CDNA Sofia would enter the second European Cup in 1956/57 but the FA had yet to embrace the competition. The Olympic qualifier would be the Bulgarians' first competitive sporting contact with the home of football. "We only ever met up with the Communist countries in tournaments like the Olympics and I can't recall ever playing against a Communist country apart from that game," says Jim Lewis, who went on to make nearly half a century of appearances for England's amateur team and would return to lead the attack against Bulgaria.

The Bulgaria qualifier provided rare contact with an Iron Curtain country and though politicians had frosty relations with the Soviet bloc the FA attempted some *entente cordiale*; in Corinthian spirit, an opportunity for a cultural exchange was spied. The FA proposed sending an English professional side to visit Sofia with a top Bulgarian side returning the favour. In May 1956, Bulgaria's Olympic team would be FA guests of honour at Wembley for the England professional team's first game against another unknown side, Brazil.

The England amateur team assumed the guise of GB and, as preparation for the first leg of the Olympic qualifiers in Sofia, played a series of fixtures against professional clubs. The first match against Arsenal was a narrow 2-1 loss but this early promise rapidly evaporated. "No progress seems to have been made towards a balanced side since the Arsenal trial," wrote *The Times*. "Indeed, the amateur eleven which lost at Highbury produced the best football of all these tests." One of the few players to emerge with credit during these matches was Roy Littlejohn, an outside-right who scored in a defeat to Queens Park Rangers. Littlejohn had left Bournemouth Grammar School at 17 with dreams of becoming an architect, but loved football. At 18, he was playing for Bournemouth's reserves. When the first-choice outside-right was injured, Littlejohn made his first XI debut and stayed there. Bournemouth's first team were then on £14 a week with a £2 win for a bonus and £1 for a draw, but Littlejohn played for nothing. "To get in the first team of any Football League side as an amateur was pretty unique back then," says Littlejohn. "I wasn't going pro because my dad knew there was no future then in being a professional footballer when I could train to be an architect."

Amateurs bulking out the reserve teams at Football League sides were not uncommon, but by 1956 fewer and fewer made the transition into the first XI. Aware of Littlejohn's appearance in Division Three South, Creek came to watch the Bournemouth teenager and capped him for the England amateur team against West Germany in 1955.

For upwardly mobile young men still deciding what to do with their lives, playing as an amateur was a chance to test their skills and experience the professional game. Payments were rife by now across most amateur clubs. Bishop Auckland paid £5 a game according to one player, Bob Thursby. With two games in a week, Bishop's players earned nearly as much as a pro. Football League clubs were more parsimonious. Roy Littlejohn received only expenses.

Littlejohn was not the only teenage forward in Creek's squad with Football League experience. He was joined by Pat Neil, who played for Corinthian-Casuals and Portsmouth in the first division, and the brief sensation that was Alick Jeffrey. Nicknamed the "Boy Wonder", Jeffrey made his first-team debut at Doncaster Rovers at 15, had an England U-23 cap at just 17 and, in 1955, was seen as one of the most talented players in the country. He was also still amateur.

Playing with the professionals at the very top had not initially benefited

Jim Lewis. He followed Walter Winterbottom's advice and signed for Chelsea – and was promptly dropped by the England amateur team. When Lewis and Chelsea won the title in 1955, the amateur team's new manager Norman Creek relented. Lewis returned for a match against France and by 1955 he was again a regular. He would be joined in Sofia by two ex-Walthamstow team-mates, Tommy Farrar and Stan Prince, and another amateur from Chelsea.

Seamus O'Connell was the son of an Irish horse dealer from Carlisle and started his career with Queen's Park before signing for Bishop Auckland. In 1953 he played three matches for Middlesbrough and scored two goals, but stayed as an amateur with Bishops, playing in their 1954 Amateur Cup defeat. O'Connell was a particular favourite of that Trinity College Dublin alumnus, Norman Ackland. As Ackland savoured a drink at the 1954 annual dinner of the Delphian League, Tom Leek, who lost his place in the 1936 Olympics to Daniel Pettit, told the red-faced Irishman: "I thought you were indulging in eager favouritism when you boosted Seamus O'Connell. But when I saw him ... I realised what a top class player he was."

At the start of the 1954/55 season, O'Connell signed for Chelsea and scored 11 goals in 16 appearances, including a hat-trick on his debut against Manchester United, and helped the west London club win the title. Yet O'Connell never forgot his roots in the amateur game. When he signed for Chelsea, O'Connell promised Bishops that he would return if they reached that season's Amateur Cup. He kept his word, becoming the only player to win the first division title and the Amateur Cup in the same season.

Bishop Auckland had reached and lost four Amateur Cup finals after the end of the war. Then in 1955, Bob Hardisty, playing with his broken ribs in plaster, finally picked up the trophy. The goals in the 2-0 win over Laurie Topp's Hendon were scored by Lancastrian Derek Lewin, who made ten league appearances for Oldham as an amateur in 1953/54 but found the highly restrictive retain-and-transfer system imposed on professionals as big a deterrent as the maximum wage. Lewin says:

> "There was no incentive to go pro. Everyone was earn-
> ing more outside the game than you could in it. Not
> only could you earn more outside, but the contracts were
> so stringent then that you just couldn't get out of them.

Who wants to be controlled like that for £8 a week? My Dad ran a food company and he was happy to see me [working there] and going off to play football."

Lewin's team-mate and Bishop's keeper, Harry Sharratt, would join him in the squad that travelled to Sofia but the first choice goalie was Mike Pinner, who was number one at Pegasus after Ben Brown's retirement and had broken into the England amateur side. The son of a Boston grocer and a product of the grammar school system, Pinner was an unlikely representative for the traditionalists, but Pegasus suited him more than the rough and tumble of the amateur leagues. He could play for Pegasus in the Amateur Cup and still have time to make ad-hoc appearances for leading Football League sides like Aston Villa and Sheffield Wednesday as a stand-in for their injured first XI keepers. Pinner recalls:

"I did think about going pro in the mid-fifties. I was offered terms with Spurs on £14 a week but it didn't seem a financial proposition to me as I was always going to be a lawyer. If you were an amateur then, you didn't need permission from the FA to play for a professional team. You were just put on a register and wrote a very polite letter to Sir Stanley Rous saying, 'Can you please amend your records that from X date I will be playing for X team'. He wrote back telling you the change had been made and that was it. Today, a successful team would not put up with you, whereas I trained a lot in the evening and a lot of my training was squash, which was ideal for a goalkeeper. If you were good enough you were accepted as just another player and that was reciprocal. Everyone was simply a player and there was no discrimination."

Creek's 15-man squad left for Sofia accompanied by Northampton Town trainer Jack Jennings. The overall party was led by former Derby County and England forward, Jack Bowers. To the players' surprise, a huge crowd had gathered at the airport to greet the British team. "The local people made us very welcome," recalls Tommy Farrer.

The game was to be played at the 45,000-capacity Levsky Stadium but this relatively new ground was totally inadequate for the interest stirred up by the visitors. The Bulgarian FA received half a million application for tickets. "The Bulgarians themselves seem surprised that the same interest for this match has not been aroused in Britain," wrote *The Times* correspondent. He continued:

> "All this commotion over a match played by the amateur footballers of England takes some understanding, especially by the players themselves, who have never been caught up in anything on such a scale before. There is an impression in some quarters that the full strength of English football has come to Sofia and it is something we are trying to dispel."

Anxious ticket touts wearing black caps like characters from a piece of Kafka fiction lurked everywhere. Visitors to the Georgi Dimitrov Mausoleum, which had been built in 1949 to hold the embalmed body of the Bulgarian leader, found touts everywhere, often emerging silently from behind a pillar or out of a darkened doorway. *The Times* football correspondent was approached but held onto his ticket.

In these spartan, Cold War times, the black market was rife. Most things had a price – as Jim Lewis found out. His job at Thermos was progressing well and he had bought some expensive nylon shirts, taking four to Sofia. After a trip out into the Bulgarian capital, Lewis discovered that the black marketeers were not just outside. One was in his room and had been sold three of his precious nylon shirts by Lewis' room-mate Seamus O'Connell. "I managed to stop Seamus selling the last one and he was sad because of the price he'd got [for the others]," laughs Lewis.

On the day of the game, a quarter of a million people flooded into the area around the stadium. "It was an experience perhaps unparalleled before in the history of any British football side overseas," wrote *The Times*, about what threatened to be an epic mismatch. In communist Bulgaria, there were no professional footballers. Everyone was a gentleman – of sorts. And the best 11 gentlemen in Bulgaria, who had been training full-time in a top-secret location for the past fortnight, would take on Creek's team of schoolteachers, salesmen and gas fitters.

22 October 1955
Vasil Levsky Stadium, Sofia. Bulgaria vs GB

From the kick-off, GB's game-plan was obvious and not all that Corinthian. For all his faith in the amateur credo, Norman Creek was a realist. His side had come to defend and leave with something to play for in the return leg. The game was played almost entirely in the English half as the corner kick ratio – two for Creek's side, 15 for Bulgaria – shows. Even the experienced O'Connell was overwhelmed in midfield by Bulgarian wing-half, Bozhkoff. GB's heroes were in defence and the tireless Hardisty, whose ball control was the equal of any Bulgarian.

Bulgaria went ahead after 30 minutes when Stefanoff's close-range shot gave Pinner no chance. A second came 15 minutes into the second half through Yaneff after a rare Hardisty error. In between, the Bishop Aucklander and captain marshalled his defence superbly. Pinner made many good saves and Farrer and Hendon's Eric Beardsley both had to head the ball off the line. With ten minutes to go, England finally dared to attack. Littlejohn and Hardisty forced good saves out of Yossifoff but the score stayed 2-0.

A place in Melbourne was possible but not probable. Creek's side had a long wait to try and make up the deficit. The return at Wembley was on 12 May. By then, members of the Sofia squad like O'Connell, Neil and Littlejohn dropped out through injury or loss of form, while Alick Jeffrey was barred after signing pro forms with Doncaster.

Highbury had initially been suggested as the venue but building work was due at Arsenal's home that summer and the home leg was switched to Wembley. That was a brave move by the FA given the sparse crowd for the last Olympic game there in 1948, but interest in the top of the amateur game was stronger than ever, even though the post-war boom in professional football appeared over. Football League attendances peaked in 1952 and by 1956 had dropped seven million to 33.3 million. In contrast, the Amateur Cup remained a massive draw. When Bishop Auckland took on neighbours Crook Town in the 1954 final, the game finished in a 2-2 draw in front of a 100,000 full house at Wembley. The replay at St James' Park produced the same score and a third game at Middlesbrough's Ayresome Park was needed before Crook triumphed 1-0. The aggregate crowd for those three amateur games was 196,727, providing total receipts of £46,787. With amateur clubs exempt from entertainment tax, both finalists walked away with £11,000 each – twice as much as that pocketed by the two finalists in that year's FA Cup Final, West Bromwich Albion and Preston North End. In 1956 the diehard amateurs' renaissance continued with Corinthian-Casuals reaching the Amateur Cup final, and Wembley was almost full again.

The GB team's home leg with Bulgaria was an evening game and proved less fascinating to Londoners than the first tie had been to Bulgarians. Just 28,000 people pitched up at Wembley but the FA still banked gate receipts of £5,000. By this time, the cost of the 11,580-mile trip to Melbourne had been put at £15,000.

In preparation for the return leg, Creek's team trained on Paddington Rec and had a week together. Changes to the team saw former Northern Nomad George Bromilow brought in at inside-left. Bromilow turned down Liverpool to become a schoolteacher and in 1955 signed as an amateur with Football League side Southport. Also in was Charlie Twissell, a 24-year-old amateur then playing with the players at Plymouth Argyle. For his national service, Twissell had joined the Royal Navy and was a regular in the services' representative team. Spotted by Argyle, he signed up as an amateur in April 1955 and played for the England amateur side against Ireland and Iceland in the run-up to the return Olympic tie.

Creek also called up two players from Corinthian-Casuals, who had picked up a handful of players from Pegasus. Gerry Alexander was a Jamaican who moved to the UK to train to be a vet and would later be the last white captain of the West Indies cricket side, captaining the team from 1958 to 1960. After moving to England, he won a Cambridge Blue at cricket and his first England amateur cap while still at university in 1952. He won the Amateur Cup the following year but then switched to Corinthian-Casuals along with fellow winner, Jack Laybourne.

Laybourne, who would play up front with Lewis and Twissell against Bulgaria, was another seemingly unlikely representative of the establishment, who benefited from the grammar school system. The son of a Durham miner, after leaving Hookergate Grammar School Laybourne emulated his father by spending four years underground. After coming up for air, Laybourne went to Cambridge, gained three Blues for football, and scored for Pegasus in the final of the 1953 Amateur Cup. On their journey to the final, Pegasus beat Corinthian-Casuals in a highly charged third-round game in front of a 12,000 capacity crowd at the Oval. Since then, Laybourne had begun work as a sales executive and was living in Bayswater, west London, so he swapped allegiances to Corinthian-Casuals.

From the 1952 Olympic crop, Laurie Topp was back and joined by the likes of the postman Farrer, Prince and "Dickie" Dodkins, a hard-tackling left-half for Ilford, who worked as a clerk at an engineering firm.

12 May 1956
Wembley Stadium, London. GB vs Bulgaria
At Wembley, GB briefly threatened an upset. After 12 minutes Laybourne nodded on a Dodkins free kick and that man Bob Hardisty scored. Creek's plan of all-out-attack – helpfully detailed in the programme for any English-reading Bulgarians – was then forgotten. For 15 minutes not a single save was forced out of Bulgarian keeper Naidenov. Bromilow and the slight Twissell gave the ball away when shooting seemed easier. The game turned. A defensive mistake forced Pinner to come off his line and he was lobbed by Milanov. Six minutes later, Stan Prince went for a centre that Pinner had covered. To his horror, the gasfitter put the ball into his own net.

Five goals were needed to win the tie but Creek's team had not given up. For the second half, GB came out showing great fighting spirit. Endeavour again briefly matched superior overseas skills under the floodlights. Hardisty nodded in an equaliser but GB could not slow the game down. Five minutes later Bulgaria hit back, Dimitrov beating Pinner with a low hard shot. Driven on by the omnipresent Hardisty, GB came back again. Twissell hit a post. When Lewis was hauled down, he converted the penalty himself, but the game was up. The speedy, talented Bulgarians held on for the draw.

Qualification was over. To the secret relief of some in the FA, there would be no gigantic bill for a trip to Australia. The British had done as Olympians should and taken part, unlike many other associations concerned about the cost, including Olympic stalwarts the Netherlands and Sweden. Even Hungary decided that the £17,500 they estimated that defending their title would cost was just too steep and withdrew. Vietnam planned to make their Olympic bow but quit along with the Turks. In the Middle East, tensions were running high ahead of what would become the Suez Crisis and Egypt withdrew. When China also pulled out, the field was decimated. The qualifiers had been pointless.

With so many countries pulling out, Fifa began asking teams that had already been eliminated in the qualifiers to return. Korea had only been knocked out by Japan after drawing lots but still refused. When Poland quit and the IOC came knocking, the FA had no such qualms. Surprising perhaps but Rous was again on the IOC's organising committee. Three weeks after being eliminated, the IOC asked the FA to re-enter and send a side to Melbourne. The FA agreed on the stipulation that a "fully representative team could be selected". Whether that refers to getting the best amateurs during the English league season or a team representative of Great Britain is unclear.

Having lavished £7,000 on sending a team to Lahti to be pasted by Luxembourg, the FA would now spend double that sum to send a squad to the other side of the world for another knock-out competition that could again only involve one game. The team had gone full circle, back to 1920, when only Englishmen represented Britain. More teams had entered the Olympic football competition in 1920; only 11 teams went to Melbourne, and GB, if they could negotiate their way past Thailand, would face Bulgaria again in the next round. "Poetic justice," said Sir Stanley.

"When we were accepted back in, all the players were delighted. What other chance would ordinary guys like us get to go to the Olympics? No one in the party objected to us going back in," says Mike Pinner. Not everyone agreed. Derek Lewin says: "It was a farce as far as we were concerned because it was just the England team wearing the GB badge."

With the Olympics due in November, there was plenty of time for Creek to produce a more coherent side than in Helsinki. Prospective players were sent to train with their local professional side. Derek Lewin found himself training every week with the Busby Babes at Old Trafford and ended up playing for Manchester United's reserves.

Fifa wrote to the SFA in early 1956 asking the Scots to reconsider, but their position had not changed since Harrogate. In June, newspaper reports continued to suggest that Northern Irish and Welsh players might still take part, but because only England were taking part, the Home Nations Olympic Committee was not involved. Selection for Melbourne was at the behest of the FA's international (amateur) committee.

This committee was chaired not by a gentleman but a player. John "Jack" Bowers was a small, dapper former full England player, who lived in a flat in

Wanstead and was assistant manager at his old club, Derby. Bowers chaired the committee in a jolly fashion but no one from the other Home Nations gained the nod. The squad was announced in dribs and drabs during a programme of pre-Olympic friendlies. Players were reliant on newspapers to find out if they had been called up. Having won the last two Amateur Cups, Bishop Auckland's players should have been expected to dominate. Instead, top Bishop players like defender Dave Marshall mysteriously dropped by the wayside during the selection process. For some in the northern amateur fraternity, this was yet more evidence of southern bias but not in favour of the traditional amateurs.

From the Football League came Terry "Tiger" Robinson, a tall, lean defender from North West England. Robinson had played for Blackpool in the reserves while studying at Loughborough but his ambitions were on working in the teaching system. He explains:

> "I could have gone pro at Blackpool but there was a stigma. I always wanted to be a [physical education] advisor for a local authority and there was a feeling that to be a pro wasn't quite the thing if you wanted to follow a career. If you were up for an interview and said you were a pro footballer, it might not go down well. But I always wanted to play with the professionals as I knew it was a higher level. When I got my first job in Ealing [west London], I was recommended to go to Brentford."

The winged horse was wounded by the row with Corinthian-Casuals over player eligibility. David Miller, an alumnus of Wreford-Brown at Charterhouse, missed the cut and only Mike Pinner would represent the Pegasus traditionalists in Melbourne.

Before the first names were unveiled, the team travelled to Iceland for a brief tour and a game classed as an England amateur international against the Icelandic national side. That game was edged 3-2 but another fixture on the way back in Copenhagen against a team of top Danish players was lost 5-1. Fortunately, the Danes would not be in Melbourne either.

The tourists were described as the GB side for that match, which started the real Olympic preparations. A programme of friendlies followed but a vast disparity in standard between the side's opponents – from a Combined Isthmian & Athenian XI and Newcastle United – prevented Creek's team from gaining any momentum. In one match, GB took on a touring Ugandan national side, who played mainly barefoot apart from their keeper, the Assistant District Commander, A.E. Peagram. Jim Lewis scored after a minute but GB went down 2-1. "It was most awkward tackling," recalls Terry Robinson. "We had to be very careful as we had those boots with big hard toes and could have broken their feet."

GB's final game, a 3-2 defeat to Arsenal, augured slightly better, but given the sum they needed to raise, the FA's committeemen were, understandably, primarily focused on the money. With no help from the other Home Nations, the FA estimated that at least £10,000 was needed to send a side to Melbourne. This figure was later revised to a more realistic £15,000. At a meeting that July in Blackpool's Imperial Hotel, the FA's committeemen pledged to provide no more than £3,000 themselves. Walter Winterbottom was in the room that day and could have provided guidance on what value the FA might get for their money at the Olympics. The FA later agreed to up its donation to £4,000 and launched a general appeal to the county associations and member clubs. This provided a mere £1,420. Some counties and clubs did not see the value in the Olympics but the tournament certainly mattered to a young Rob Hardisty. He recalls sitting in front of a grainy black and white television, beaming with pride, as his father was confirmed as the team's captain on the BBC's *Six O'Clock News*.

As the FA battled to come up with the necessary funds, players like Bob Hardisty still faced the thorny issue of broken time. The FA would pay trainer Jack Jennings a £6 match fee but the players, as the ideals of the movement and the gentlemen at the FA decreed, would get nothing. Six weeks was a long time to go on unpaid leave. The gas board would pay Stan Prince but Southport Town Council convened a full meeting to discuss whether their schoolteacher Jack Laybourne merited the same treatment. A Councillor Brooks proposed that Laybourne's leave of absence must be unpaid. He found a seconder but no other support. The Southport forward travelled safe in the knowledge he was still being paid.

Given the cost, the FA took a smaller squad than in Helsinki, but money or a smaller squad did not prevent Mickey Stewart from going to the Olympics. Once again, that ethereal question of amateurism reared up.

Stewart was a gentleman with Corinthian-Casuals and a player for Surrey County Cricket Club, where his skills as a batsman had earned him a call-up to the England team. Stewart explains:

> "I'd been chosen for the Olympic football squad and even measured up for a blazer. That summer, I was in Hastings playing for Surrey against Sussex and got a message to call Sir Stanley Rous. When I called, he said that the IOC had called him and said that I couldn't play because I played cricket professionally. The Olympic Games could not include players that played any sport for money."

Stewart recalled receiving up to 20 offers to play as a shamateur, usually for about £10 a week. "The best offer was worth £2,000 and that included not only money for playing but a job with a good salary that they offered to find me," he said in 1971. For Stewart, there was never any question of fudging the divide between amateur and professional. "My dad was a bookmaker and professional gambler and said he would support me as a professional [in football] but if I took a penny as an amateur he would kick me out of the house," says Stewart, who – no longer a gentleman in the eyes of the people running the sport – signed a professional contract for Charlton paying £15 a week. His Olympic place went to Jimmy Coates, a petty officer in the Royal Navy and inside-forward at Kingstonian.

Led by Jack Bowers, the squad set off on 16 November for Australia with little confidence among the media. The *Guardian* wrote: "It is difficult to imagine the side enjoying any great success." Trips to Australia via plane were a luxury in the 1950s. Travelling with a British referee, R.H. Mann from Worcestershire, the team's trip by air took three days with stops in Karachi, Calcutta, Bangkok, Singapore, Perth and Sydney. Eventually arriving in Melbourne, the exhausted team were split between three flats. Each group of players were kept under the beady eye of an FA official, whose number included AFA secretary Leonard Kingston. Norman Creek wasted no time. On the team's first day, he held an hour and a half training session at Scotch College. For the next ten days, Creek's amateurs trained three times a day, but Terry Robinson, who knew the fitness levels needed to play against full-timers, was not impressed. He says: "Norman Creek was a very nice chap, too nice by today's standards, but I was devoted to training and the training was woeful. As far as tactics or knowledge of the other team was concerned, no one had any idea."

For all the regular training sessions, Creek found his squad blighted by injury. A friendly was scheduled with the hosts in Moreland. The Australian side included Bill Harburn, who had played for Bishop Auckland in the late 1940s before emigrating. GB won 3-1 but there was little reason for optimism. A few days earlier the Australians had been trounced 15-1 by Russia in another warm-up.

During the Australia game, Dexter Adams, a buyer of television time from Hendon, tore his cartilage. "I missed the opening ceremony because I was in St Vincent's Hospital," recalls Adams. "It was a complete waste of time." Four days after the squad arrived in Australia, Adams got on a plane and set off on another torturous journey home. Next out was keeper Mike Pinner. "I split my finger in training and played with two central fingers bound together with sticks," he recalls. "They filled me full of penicillin and strapped me up but I only had woolen gloves." With four stitches in his hand, Pinner could not possibly play.

The team's goalkeeping options were reduced to Bishop Auckland's Harry Sharratt, one of the craziest keepers the game has ever seen. A relative giant at just under six foot, Sharratt was once booked during a Boxing Day match for building a snowman on his goal-line and often organised snowball fights during matches with the fans. If bored during one-sided matches, he would read a newspaper and often read the half-time scores out to the crowd. Dave Marshall, Bishop's right-back during the club's fabled 1950s period, recalls Sharratt cadging sweets or cigarettes off the crowd during matches. During one FA Cup tie when Bishop were trailing Scunthorpe 1-0, Sharratt insisted on taking throw-ins inside his opponents' half. When Scunthorpe scored a second, Sharratt, with a twinkle in his eye, said: "I blame Derek Lewin, he took his eye off the ball."

He stayed on the pitch after home matches to let the children in the crowd take penalties at him and was hugely popular with fans and his team-mates alike – "He was just a nut, a total idiot," Derek Lewin fondly recalls. The schoolteacher Harry Sharratt was probably the best keeper in the amateur game. But with only solitary Football League appearances for

British amateur side Upton Park take on the French representatives, the USFSA in the 1900 Olympic final. Photo: IOC.

The team and officials that won the 1908 Olympic gold medal. Photo: The Football Association.

Nils Middelboe of Denmark (centre) attacks England during the final of the
1912 Olympic football tournament in Stockholm. Photo: IOC.

R. Sloley, past-president and life
member of the Ealing Association
Football Club, who has been
appointed secretary of University
College Hospital.

Top: The England team that won gold in 1912.
Bottom: English players converge on the
Finnish goal in the 1912 semi-final.
Right: A caricature of 1920 Olympian, Dick Sloley.

Norway repulse a rare English attack in the first round
of the 1920 Olympics in Antwerp. Photo: Scanpix.

Dick Sloley mulls over plans for the Argonauts, his proposal for
a team of amateurs to play in the Football League at Wembley.

Left: The programme for the 1936 Olympics.

Right: Polish inside-left Gad climbs above Bernard Joy to head Poland's second goal in a 5-4 win over GB in the quarter-finals in Berlin.

The GB team that beat China 2-0 in the first round of the 1936 Olympics in Berlin. Sir Daniel Pettit is back row far left, Bernard Joy to his right. Centre rear is Mac Dodds to the left of goalkeeper Haydn Hill. Photo: The Football Association.

Bob Hardisty in action during GB's 1-0 win over France in the quarter-finals of the 1948 Olympics at Craven Cottage. Photo: © The Journal.

Top and Bottom: Queen's Park and Scotland goalkeeper Ronnie Simpson
in action for GB against the Netherlands at Highbury in 1948.
Photos: *Sportweekblad De Sportwereld*.

Action from GB's first round game with the Netherlands in 1948.
Photo: *Sportweekblad De Sportwereld*.

The 1948 GB squad. Top row (left to right): Davie Letham, Jack Rawlings, Jack Neale, Julian Smith, Angus Carmichael, Harry McIlvenny, Andy Aitken, Jim McColl. Middle row: Ron Phipps, Gwyn Manning, Tommy Hopper, Tom Curry (trainer), Matt Busby (manager), Bob Hardisty, capt, Eric Lee, Dougie McBain. Front row: Denis Kelleher, Bill Amor, Frank Donovan, Eric Fright, Peter Kippax, Alan Boyd, Ronnie Simpson. For some reason, Irish goalkeeper Kevin McAlinden is missing.

Left: 1948 Olympians (left to right) Harry McIlvenny, Bob Hardisty, Jack Neale, Tommy Hopper, Julian Smith, Denis Kelleher, Eric Fright and Eric Lee at the Grove Hall Hotel.

Right: Gwyn Manning (left) and Frank Donovan (right) both of Wales in their 1948 Olympic blazers.

GB striker Harry McIlvenny and Denmark's
K.B. Overgaard battle for the ball.

McIlvenny is beaten to the ball by Danish keeper Neilson
during GB's 5-3 defeat to Denmark. Photos PA Pictures.

Lahure foils Alf Noble during GB's shock first round defeat to Luxembourg at the
1952 Olympics. Photo: Archives, Département ministériel des Sports, Luxembourg

The 1952 Olympic squad that stayed behind about to leave on
a brief tour of Scandinavia after their surprise elimination.

Bob Hardisty (front) and Mike Pinner lead out the GB team in Sofia.

The GB XI lines up alongside Bulgaria for the away leg
of their qualifier in Sofia for the 1956 Olympics.

Above: Action from GB's 9-0 mauling of Thailand in Melbourne in 1956.
Below: Action from GB's 6-1 defeat to Bulgaria in the next round. Photos: NLA

The 1960 GB squad at training camp at Bisham Abbey. Photo: The Football Association.

Bobby Brown challenges Salvadore of Italy during GB's highly-charged group match in Rome in 1960. Photo: Ullstein Bild.

GB goalkeeper John Kennedy clears under pressure
from Greece in Athens in 1964. Photo: Topfoto.

Striker Tommy Lawrence heads the ball during GB's 2-1 win
over Greece at Stamford Bridge in 1963. Photo: Topfoto.

The GB squad at the Parthenon.

Above: Charles Hughes demonstrates tactics to the GB squad during a training session in Athens in 1964.

Right: GB players at the Parthenon (left to right) John Martin, John Ashworth, Hugh Lindsay, unknown.

The GB squad line-up before their qualifier
against Greece in Athens in 1964.

Olympians past and present: (left to right) Norman Creek, John Swannell,
Tommy Lawrence and Bernard Joy in the mid 1960s.

his native Wigan in 1952 and for Oldham in 1955, he could not match Pinner's league experience.

26 November 1956
Melbourne. GB vs Thailand

Harry Sharratt must have longed for a newspaper or a colder, snowy day to provide some diversions during his side's first-round match against Thailand – or Siam, as many newspapers still referred to the Asian kingdom. The Thais started brightly but were soon overwhelmed. With GB 4-0 up at half-time, the result was never in doubt. Jack Laybourne bagged a hat-trick and George Bromilow a brace. The Thais could not cope with Charlie Twissell's trademark hard shooting and he also scored twice as Creek's team waltzed home 9-0 in front of a sparse crowd.

The Olympic team were involved in many mismatches over the years and this was another. With his characteristic tactfulness, Bernard Joy described the game as "11 Snow Whites against 11 dwarfs." In addition to providing little preparation of any value for the next game against Bulgaria, another player was injured. The team's figurehead Bob Hardisty went down with a groin strain. Even if his team could beat Bulgaria, Hardisty would not play again in Melbourne and his place went to Derek Lewin.

30 November 1956
Melbourne. GB vs Bulgaria

The Bulgarians did not have any match practice, having received a bye in the first round, but had the measure of Creek's team. His side were 3-1 down by half-time despite tireless running by Jim Lewis, who got on the scoresheet. Creek's players did not let him down, battling manfully against superior opponents.

The crowd was marginally better than the previous game and boosted by a group of 80 or so British naval ratings from HMS *Newcastle*, which was docked in Melbourne. Unimpressed by the first-half display, at half-time the sailors vaulted the fence surrounding the pitch en masse. The police initially stood with mouths agape as the sailors – carrying three giant Union flags, ratchet rattles, a calico sign reading "Up the Lions", and an umbrella with England's colours – marched ominously towards the British players. The ratings planned to inspire Creek's team but the police intervened, escorting the sailors from the ground.

In the second half, Stoker, Topp and Prince continued to play well. Lewis remained a handful but Bulgaria romped home 6-1 due, in part, to poor goalkeeping from Harry Sharratt.

The score was not a fair reflection of the gap between the teams but Bulgaria were too good for the British amateurs with better tactics. "Norman Creek would just say go out and do this or that," recalls Jimmy Coates. Bulgaria's subsequent semi-final with Russia was considered by many watchers to be the real final. Russia needed extra time to edge out Bulgaria 2-1. The Bulgarians had to make do with the bronze medal after a 3-0 win over India.

After being eliminated four of Creek's players, including Lewin and Laybourne, were invited to dine with the Duke of Edinburgh. The squad kept up their training regime as, once again, the FA needed to raise money to compensate for another loss-making Olympic failure. Sir Stanley had organised matches in Singapore, Malaya and Burma on the squad's way home. The entire trip was way over budget, costing the FA £13,770. The sale of TV rights had raised £2,500 and the three tour matches would add another £1,432 to the pot.

For Charlie Twissell, the stop-off in Singapore was a real treat. His father had been in the prison service in Singapore and Twissell lived there until he was seven, departing from the British colony when WWII broke out. Jimmy Coates had been in Singapore before too, during his time as a boy sailor in WWII. For the game against Norman Creek's tourists, a crowd of 6,500, including some of Twissell's relatives, turned up. Creek was finally able to put out his first choice XI. Pinner took the gloves and Bob Hardisty was among the scorers in a 4-0 win, along with a brace from Jim Lewis and a single strike from Derek Lewin. After the game, Twissell took some of the players, including Lewin, to meet the family. "Charlie was a lot of fun back then, particularly when he met up with his relatives," recalls Derek Lewin.

Moving on to Kuala Lumpur, the team were entertained rather more formally by Brigadier Green at the Selangor Golf Club in the morning. After lunch, Creek's team ran out in stifling 90-degree heat and 97 per cent humidity to take on the Malayan national side in front of 9,000 people. Terry Robinson had been denied a game in Melbourne despite the injuries but came in for the Malaya game. "The heat was unbelievable," he recalls. "It shouldn't have been played really."

A hat-trick from Jimmy Coates plus a brace from Hardisty and a George Bromilow strike secured a 6-2 win. Treated like celebrities, the squad flew on to Burma and another reception, this time at the British embassy in Rangoon. The heat was once more suffocating, but Coates again and George Bromilow tied up a 2-0 win. Yet again, a post-Olympic tour produced better results than the actual Games.

After six weeks away, the already fatigued tourists endured a seemingly endless trek home. The flight from Rangoon went via Calcutta, Karachi, Bahrain, Baghdad, Istanbul, Rome and Frankfurt and took as long as the way out – three days. On entering English airspace, the dog-tired players were dismayed to find that their mother country was shrouded in fog. Their flight was diverted to Prestwick and the players were forced to spend a night cooped up in a freezing railway carriage before finally steaming into Glasgow and the train to Euston. Jim Lewis had to wear two jumpers plus his Olympic football shirt and was still cold. "It was the worst part of the journey," said Charlie Twissell. "We had nothing to eat and the carriage was not heated. We were not prepared for the cold and several of us had to wear our tracksuits to keep warm." The team's train finally chugged into Euston at 7.30am on 20 December. Arriving home from their marathon journey, the Olympic gentlemen were immediately met with a simple question from their clubs: "When can you play?"

The team's critics were no more sympathetic. Busby described the win over Thailand as a "result, which, with all due respect, could hardly have been avoided." Writing a year later in 1957, the Manchester United manager described the GB Olympic performance since 1948 as "depressing".

Bernard Joy at least had a solution. He wrote:

> "Once more the British Olympic soccer team were beaten for skill, tactical ideas and stamina. It was only in courage that we matched the opposition. Ever since we re-entered the Olympic Games in 1936 it has been evident that the handicaps are too great. We cannot hold our own with nations who are prepared to evade the definition of amateur in order to parade their best performers. To compete on equal terms we should have to register our full international side as amateurs, persuade

a firm or government department to put them nominally on the staff, pay higher wages than they earn now and have no restrictions on their playing and training.

"Alternatively, we must educate some of our rivals to respect the Olympic oath, which says 'we swear that we will take part in the Olympic Games in loyal competition, respecting the regulations which govern them, and desirous of participating in them in the true spirit of sportsmanship, for the honour of our country and for the glory of sport'. It seems that some nations regard the 'honour of our country' as the most important purpose of the Olympic Games."

The mischievous Norman Ackland's response was to suggest a game between the 1956 Olympians and those Englishmen left behind before selecting the England side to take on Scotland in the annual amateur battle.

Various other suggestions were floated before Bowers and Rous put forward a set of reasonable solutions on behalf of the FA to Fifa and the IOC. The tournament should comprise 16 teams in four groups providing at least three matches. Prompted by the traditionalist element within the FA, the duo also advocated that Fifa hold a periodic eight-team World Amateur championship to stop the Olympics being football's "Cinderella" tournament.

"It is felt that only in this way would members of the IOC realise that Fifa represents untold numbers of amateur players and is not an organisation solely interested in professionals," said Jolly Jack Bowers. The four Home Nations met in Paris in February 1957 and universally agreed with Bowers's proposals, but enthusiasm for the tournament was waning. Writing in *World Sports*, the influential Austrian-born writer Willy Meisl spelt out what so many others thought. Meisl worked with the British Olympic party's press office in Berlin in 1936, where his brother Hugo coached the Austrian football team, then moved into journalism. He had watched the tournament deteriorate. To Meisl, Olympic football was a "sham".

For the players, the great attraction was the Olympics, not the football. Derek Lewin says:

"The greatest thing from my angle was being able to be there and watch all the events as a spectator. You didn't just turn up for your race and go. We went jogging round the track one time and [legendary Czechslovakian runner] Emil Zapotek came and ran round with us. It was like being in the directors' box and such a privilege. Those are the sort of memories I'll always recall."

Lewin was offered a contract to play in New Zealand but returned home. He made a solitary league appearance for Accrington in 1957 and the next year took over the family firm, Heywood & Sons, after his father passed away. He stayed with Bishop Auckland and played and won three Amateur Cups in a row from 1955 to 1957. In 1958, Manchester United's plane crashed in Munich, killing 23 people, including Tom Curry, who a decade earlier had been Busby's coach at the Olympics, and Derek Lewin found himself back at Old Trafford again having trained there before the Olympics.

Busby's squad was decimated. Players were promoted to the first team but he needed to find a new reserve side and turned to his old friend, Bob Hardisty, who had finally decided to quit after the 1957 Amateur Cup win. Hardisty was 37 but when his friend Busby called, he pulled his boots out of the cupboard and took Derek Lewin and Warren Bradley with him. Lewin and Hardisty played for the reserves as amateurs but Bradley, a teacher, made the first team and turned semi-pro. United found Bradley a teaching job and in May 1959 he made his full England debut against Italy, scoring in a 2-2 draw with Bobby Charlton getting the other goal.

The madcap Harry Sharratt stayed with Bishops until 1964 but later in life tired of football after a rule was introduced prohibiting the charging of keepers. For a man who would throw balls to the opposition on occasion simply to liven matches up, that restriction made the game too boring. The Clown Prince of amateur football passed away in 2002, aged 71.

Bob Hardisty later managed the Bishops briefly, but for a man whose longevity on the football field surpassed so many of his peers, he did not look after himself. Plagued by diabetes and circulatory problems, he suffered the cruel ignominy of having a leg amputated in 1984. Less than two years later, his remaining leg was also removed but pneumonia set in. Three days later on October 31st 1986, one of England's greatest amateurs and finest

Olympians, passed away at just 65 – eight years before his great friend Busby. Rob Hardisty adds:

> "In the early '60s, we used to go and watch Man Utd at Roker Park each season and for a few years we would go back to their team hotel in Durham where Dad would chat with Matt Busby. After one such meeting, Matt told Dad he never thought his career would have lasted so long or else he would have asked him to go to Old Trafford before."

After the Melbourne Olympics the world of the British amateurs continued to change. The good quality players who declined to go professional after losing the early part of their career to the war were retiring. The amateur code was under threat in its British heartland. In Wales, there were so few players of amateur international standard that the FAW asked Norman Ackland to appeal, asking for amateurs in English football to come for trials on his page in *Charles Buchan's Football Monthly*.

In Scotland, the SFA's decision to put Queen's Park before Great Britain paid off for the Spiders. In the 1955/56 season Queen's Park had returned to the top flight of Scottish football by winning the second division championship. That stay was to prove short-lived and the club went back down two years later, but the Spiders' brief tenure in the top flight may have been even briefer had their best players been in Melbourne for the first part of the 1956/57 season.

In Northern Ireland, Cliftonville stayed with the amateur doctrine but the code's strength remained in England, where the traditionalists' intransigence was doing little to combat shamateurism in a realistic sense. Instead, the southern gentlemen turned on themselves. A year after Leonard Kingston returned from Melbourne, he lost his position as the AFA's representative on the FA Council. Kingston, who once played a record 50 consecutive first-team matches for Casuals and was one of the first England amateur selectors, travelled to England amateur internationals in France, Germany and Switzerland in 1957 at his own expense. He was widely expected to become chairman of the FA Amateur Selection Committee during a forthcoming election but the conscientious Oxford graduate was a modernist; and the AFA was still no place for modernism. Kingston felt that looking for international amateur players in the AFA leagues was hopeless. He preferred to scour the Athenian, Isthmian and Corinthian leagues. For this seemingly unconscionable sin, a bloc of AFA traditionalists within the FA took umbrage. Kingston lost the vote as shamateurism became more rife than ever.

The previous year, an investigation into shamateurism in all sport for the *Observer* by Chris Brasher, gold medallist in the 3000m steeplechase at Melbourne, found that league clubs often paid up to £5 a week simply to retain some amateurs for their reserve sides. Brasher also claimed that some amateurs even asked league clubs for a £500 signing-on fee. Although the likes of Corinthian-Casuals, Dulwich Hamlet and Pegasus had a reputation as being more "amateur" than most, question marks hung over many of the most prominent players and clubs. Few outside of the amateur clubs' accountants knew the truth.

In 1958, when a manual worker was taking home £7 15s a week, according to government statistics, the PFA managed to drive the maximum wage up to £20 a week in the winter and £17 a week in the summer, but this was for those at the very top of the game. "When I was at Chelsea, the maximum anyone was earning was £25 a week and an awful lot of people were on far less," says Jim Lewis.

Lewis played for London in the 1958 Inter Cities Fairs Cup, a competition played between European cities that staged trade fairs with one city fielding a single team of players from leading professional clubs. The competition eventually evolved into the Uefa Cup, forerunner of the Europa League. In 1958, Lewis left Chelsea after scoring 40 goals in 95 appearances. When he left Chelsea, there was no big money transfer. Jim Lewis simply returned to the non-league ranks and his old club, Walthamstow Avenue.

Terry Robinson left Brentford for Walsall but, unable to keep to his own high standards of fitness, the PE advisor quit league football and took up basketball, where the demands were less strenuous. Gentlemen playing regularly in the Football League were nearly extinct. Charlie Twissell at Plymouth Argyle notched up three more caps for England's amateur team, then went pro with Plymouth Argyle in 1957 before moving on to York, where he achieved a rare feat in any form of football. During one of his 53 games at York, the famously hard-shooting Twissell miscued a shot with such venom that he achieved the difficult feat of shattering a floodlight. He left York in 1961.

The teetotal Jimmy Coates had chances to join the players too. "I turned down many pro contracts, including first division clubs, because I enjoyed playing rather than making money," says Coates, who returned to Melbourne again during his time in the Navy. He played on for Kingstonian until 1965, where he reached the 1961 Amateur Cup final but lost out to a Hendon side including a 37-year-old Laurie Topp. After winning the Cup, Topp finally retired, aged 38.

Only Mike Pinner and Jim Lewis would return for another Olympics, when Norman Creek would face another set of qualifiers. This time it would be with players from across the Home Nations, as the old Corinthians produced a grand last stand for the vulnerable amateur ideal on the Olympic stage.

CHAPTER TEN: ROME 1960
AND A VERY BRITISH FAILURE

"Norman Creek started having a go at me and saying we can't take players like you to the Olympics."

Alf D'Arcy, 1960 GB Olympic player

WHEN TEENAGE STRIKER BOBBY BROWN RETURNED home to Streatham, south London one Saturday night during 1958 to tell his Dad that he had scored six goals that afternoon, little did he know his life was about to change. In the space of a year, Brown would go from the parks of south London to Wembley, the Olympic Games and very nearly a career in Serie A.

Brown's father was a big supporter of the lower echelons of the Football League and amateur game. Along with his son, Bobby, he regularly returned to Barnet, where he grew up, and the terraces at the club's Underhill stadium. "Dad had watched Barnet for 40 years and knew people on the gate," recalls Bobby Brown. "I'd been playing for my school Old Boys' team and Dad said, 'You're finding this a bit easy, shall I ask Barnet for a trial?'"

Through his Dad's contacts, a trial was arranged and by the age of 17 he had broken into a young Barnet first team featuring well-known names in the amateur game like Bobby Cantwell (no relation of Noel) and the D'Arcy brothers, Alf and Denis. After contact with Queens Park Rangers led to nothing, Brown had been playing for his Old Boys' team at Barnet Grammar

School, while working as a clerk at a shipping firm. All he really wanted to do was play football and Barnet, who had reached the Amateur Cup semi-finals in the previous 1957/58 season, was a big deal. The next season, with Brown one of a number of teenagers in the side, along with the likes of Roy Sleap, Barnet reached the same stage of the Amateur Cup. Walthamstow Avenue and Jim Lewis lay in wait. The game at Highbury was goalless but in the replay at White Hart Lane, Barnet won 2-0 to secure a final with Northern league champions Crook Town, whose side featured another well-known former Chelsea and Olympic player, Seamus O'Connell.

Brown, who played with a hankerchief in his football shorts during matches, missed both semi-finals with an injury but was one of six teenagers in the Barnet side for the final at Wembley in front of 60,000 people. Inspired by the experienced O'Connell, Crook won 3-2, but Brown scored two of the most spectacular goals ever seen in an Amateur Cup final. Watching from the stands in his own quiet fashion was Norman Creek. At the age of just 17, the Streatham teenager was called up for a brief England tour of Western Europe. Brown had just turned 18 when he made his debut in a 3-1 win over the Dutch in The Hague. Typically, Brown scored two goals as the dream start to his footballing career continued.

Bobby Brown dared not dream about the next stop on this whistle-stop start to his football career. After the dismal showing in Melbourne, the big question was would there even be a GB Olympic football team in Rome? After the London Games in 1948, the collapse in the fortunes of GB's footballers was striking and depressing for supporters of the amateur game, gentlemen or shamateurs. Against all the odds, Busby's truly British side narrowly missed out on a medal in London, but that brave performance was followed by a team featuring ten Englishmen being abjectly thrashed by Luxembourg. For Melbourne, the FA's decision to take Poland's place after being eliminated remained divisive. The absence of any Scots, Welsh and Northern Irish in the squad that travelled to Australia further undermined the concept of a GB team. Further embarrassment in Rome – or in trying to get there – would be a deadly blow for an amateur international team rapidly being left behind as football galloped into the brave new world.

In 1958, Fifa staged a sixth World Cup. All four Home Nations travelled to Sweden. Uniquely, Wales and Northern Ireland succeeded in reaching the quarter-finals – unlike England and Scotland. This came as the handicaps faced by a GB Olympic team grew by the year. In the communist Eastern Bloc, there were no gentlemen and professionals, only players, who were usually in the armed forces or some Kafkaesque government department, but who spent most of their time playing football to the highest standard possible.

Interpretations of amateurism differed across Western Europe too. The Dutch threw off the shackles of shamateurism in 1954, mirroring the Home Nations with separate amateur and professional sides. In Italy, players could not turn professional until the age of 21. Italian logic insisted that anyone under 21, whether they were playing in Serie A or not, was amateur. All the teams that entered the qualifiers for the Rome Games played to the same rules on the pitch, but off the field, there was very little consistency at all.

The changing world of football swirled around England amateur team boss Norman Creek, whose memories of the dying days of the then independent Corinthians seemed set in another century altogether. Seemingly unaware of the shamateurism that was eating away at the ideals he treasured, the doctrine of the GB team manager did not change. Under-the-table payments were rife. One leading amateur of the time was considering offers from pro clubs until his amateur side put a deposit down on a house for him. As a result, that player stayed in the amateur ranks and would play a role in the forthcoming qualifiers. Did Norman Creek harbour suspicions that his players were taking money? Brian Wakefield, now keeping goal at Corinthian-Casuals, thinks not. "I don't think that Norman Creek would have known," says Wakefield. "He was so very honest and thought everyone was the same. It would never have occurred to him that anyone was getting paid."

The GB manager was either naive or content to ignore the elephant in the midst of British amateur football as the FA began making preparations for Rome, but money stuffed in their boots was not the only reason that some of Creek's players did not want to go professional. The Olympics still held an attraction for many amateurs, providing an opportunity to see a whole new world for players like Alf D'Arcy and his brother Dennis, who came from a very different background to Norman Creek MBE.

Stalwarts of the amateur game, the two brothers came from near City Road in London but were evacuated during the war to Barnet. As a boy, Alf D'Arcy was a regular at Barnet matches and his hero was none other than Denis Kelleher, Matt Busby's Northern Irish centre forward from 1948. D'Arcy's dream was to emulate his boyhood idol.

Turning down a £14-a-week contract with Bristol City, D'Arcy joined Barnet in 1951 and worked first as a plumber and then a factory engineer. On the football field he became, in his own words, "a bigger fish in a smaller pool"; one with his heart set on appearing in the Olympics. "In 1956, I was 21 and really determined to get on the Olympic team but I didn't realise how the system worked and how archaic it was," he says. By the late 1950s, Alf and his brother Dennis, an inside-right and printer by trade, had both broken into the England amateur team and the D'Arcys had an Olympic appearance in their sights.

With Jim Lewis back at Walthamstow, amateurs playing consistently with big Football League clubs were rarer than ever. Amateurs were often playing reserve football for professional clubs but few crossed the divide to give up their status as gentlemen.

Mike Pinner was one of the most well-known amateurs in the professional game, as since Melbourne, he continued to mix playing for Pegasus with ad hoc appearances for the likes of Aston Villa and Sheffield Wednesday. After winning his fifth Blue for Cambridge University and then graduating, Pinner played more regularly for third division Queens Park Rangers in the run-up to the 1960 Olympics. But this ambitious grammar school boy's chief concern was qualifying as a solicitor, not becoming a professional footballer.

With Bob Hardisty retired, Lewis and Pinner would form the backbone of the GB team but Norman Creek had to find fresh faces. This time, he would not be restricted to English players. The prospect of a trip to Rome at the start of their season was more affordable and agreeable to the other three Home Nations, who returned to the Olympic project, which had been almost forgotten since Melbourne due to the four-year cycle of the Games.

In 1957, the British Olympic Association (BOA) had agreed to pay the British Hockey Board the sum of £6 per match for the services of their trainer John Jennings. An ebullient, popular figure with the players, Jennings worked as a trainer in a number of different sports. Over the years, he would have spells at Northampton Town Football Club and Northamptonshire County Cricket Club, and he would retain his role with the GB footballers until the end of the team.

The same year the Jennings fee was agreed, an FA party attended the annual BOA fund-raising dinner at Grosvenor House on 11 July. Sir Stanley Rous was among the 14-man delegation. No players attended.

Preparations for Rome only got under way in early 1959, when the four Home Nations met up at the St George's Hotel in Llandudno, Wales to discuss Rome. The Home Nations had asked the BOA about entering four teams but this had been rejected out of hand. The Scots, Welsh and Northern Irish were initially reluctant to commit completely to a GB team as a debate raged over who would foot the £3,700 bill to send a team to Rome. Tacitly, the other Home Nations agreed to nominate players and let the FA and Norman Creek choose a GB side.

A series of five matches was arranged across February 1959 for amateur players aged 23 or under on 1 September that year. Selection was confined to Englishmen and the fixtures spread across England's regions. Olympic possibles from the Midlands took on Coventry City, while the best young amateurs from the North played Stockport County and Middlesbrough. Results were mixed. Few of these supposedly promising youngsters would make the final cut. The best young amateurs from eastern England were dispatched 3-1 by non-league Cambridge City but their western rivals beat the professionals of Bristol City by the same score. The numbers were thinned down to a Probables vs Possibles game at Villa Park in Birmingham on 22 April 1959. The keeper for the Possibles was a young Chesterfield schoolboy called Bob Wilson. An England schoolboy international, Wilson had caught the eye with a courageous performance for Loughborough in a match against Pegasus, who were surprisingly beaten 3-1. *The Times,* reporting on Wilson's performance in this match, noted: "The Chesterfield Grammar School keeper was fearless to the point of self-destruction."

Wilson's heroics saw him carried off with 12 minutes to go with a leg injury but the Possibles won 2-1. Of the Probables, only two players – both established England amateur internationals – would play roles in the final GB squad: the young Barnet draughtsman, Roy Sleap, who had signed amateur forms with Spurs, and Laurie Brown, a muscular County Durham joiner playing at Bishop Auckland. The only Possible to stay with the side was Tommy Thomson, a Durham factory worker and left-back at Stockton FC.

Players like Pinner and Lewis were certainties and were allowed to miss these matches. Bob Wilson also remained in the frame after his father rejected an offer from Busby to sign schoolboy forms and insisted that he get an education first. When Creek took a squad of 30 players to Bisham Abbey, Wilson was one of three keepers to attend along with Tony Waiters and Malcolm Shaw. Wilson's Olympic dream ended when he broke three ribs and punctured a lung playing for his school team. "Norman Creek eventually went on record stating I was too fearless and injury prone," writes Wilson in his autobiography *Behind the Network*, "[but] I think he simply read that match report in *The Times*."

The GB team had been placed in a qualifying group with the Republic of Ireland and the Netherlands, whose clear division between amateurs and professionals was a boost to Creek's hope that a GB team could qualify by results for the Olympics for the first time.

The FA's decision to go to Australia had created resentment among the other Home Nations but the Scots had played in the last two World Cup finals. The SFA were confident enough of their own identity to embrace the GB team and put six Scotsmen forward for consideration in August 1959. The following month, the dates of the qualifiers were confirmed and Creek interviewed the SFA, the Scottish Amateur FA and Scotland's leading amateur club, Queen's Park, regarding players. Creek was also told that Welsh and Northern Irish players were available for selection. The GB team was back – for now.

The Scotsmen initially put forward three from Queen's Park and a trio of amateurs playing elsewhere, including Dougal Grant, the captain of Highland League side Elgin City. An Olympic call-up did not tempt Grant. "I'd got my first cap for the Highland League and was asked to go to training with the Olympic team in London but I'd just started a new job and decided I couldn't afford a plane and train down there," says Grant, who went on to win 28 caps for Scotland's amateur team.

The other two non-Queen's Park players were Ronnie McKinven, a centre-half who had been with the Spiders but was playing as an amateur in the Scottish second division for St Johnstone, and William "Billy" Neil, a full-back and centre-half at Airdrieonians in the Scottish first division. Unlike Grant, both went to the trial and would play a big part in the team.

Billy Neil's grandfather played in every round on Airdrieonians' way to their sole Scottish Cup win in 1924. Billy Neil treasured his grandfather's medal and joined the same club on leaving school in 1956 at the same time as taking a job with the Commercial Bank. Neil recalls:

> "I asked the bank if I could go part-time as I wanted a
> career in banking. They said 'no' but to take as much time

off as possible to play football. When I was at Airdrie, Jock Stein was at Dunfermline and was interested in me. So were Rangers but it never came to anything and I made a decision to stay amateur. The bank was very good to me and I never regretted not going pro."

The first test for Creek's team came against a touring Caribbean side at the end of a long 13-match tour that had not been particularly successful. Drawn from across the West Indies, the Caribbean side won just four matches against amateur sides Barking, Ely, Newmarket and Spalding.

For Hugh Forde, a half-back from Glenavon, who had been called up to the GB squad after a man-of-the-match performance for Northern Ireland in a recent amateur international against England, the game, played at Portman Road, was an eye-opener.

"'Well played son, good effort, keep chasing,'" Forde recalls the crowd in Ipswich shouting at him. "This contrasted with the comments I received weekly from spectators in Northern Ireland like 'go home Popehead; get stuck into that Fenian b...' and the spittle that was aimed at me when I went to the sideline to retrieve a ball for a throw. I still feel the warmth, generosity and sense of enjoyment of those Ipswich supporters now."

At Portman Road, Creek's team had been stunned to find themselves immediately on the back foot as the Jamaican inside-left Sydney Bartlett created some exciting attacks. GB initially struggled to get into the match but Bobby Brown's star was still climbing. By half-time, GB were leading 3-1. Brown had scored all three. The tourists were no match for Alf D'Arcy's rugged defending and the final score of 7-2 included a hat-trick from one of the three Queen's Park players, Peter Kane. He impressed watching officials from Northampton Town so much that on the Scotsman's return home, he asked Queen's Park to cancel his registration and signed pro forms with the English side. Kane had agreed to join the players and could no longer play a part in the amateur Olympic set-up.

Kane was one of a number of changes before the next game. Billy Neil came, as did Hunter Devine, who had not initially been recommended by the SFA. Devine made the Olympic starting line-up against Burnley after impressing at his club, Queen's Park. The son of a licensed grocer from Kirkintilloch, Devine wanted to be a professional footballer and was encouraged by his father, but his mother had other ideas. "There was a stigma to being a professional footballer back then," says Devine. "If I became a pro I couldn't become an actuary as I would not have got enough practical training. Playing for QP as an amateur, you were up against the pro teams every week and could measure yourself." Devine joined Queen's Park while he trained to be an actuary and made his first-team debut at just 18. In 1955/56, Devine was part of the Spiders team that won the second division of the Scottish league, adding to youth international honours.

With Llandudno's Alan McIntosh (a trainee teacher at Birmingham University) starting, a side with players from all four Home Nations took the field in front of 5,935 people at Turf Moor – and were duly thrashed 5-0; hardly cause for optimism with the first qualifier against the Republic of Ireland coming up a month later. Ten days before that qualifier, Norman Creek was one of ten people in an FA party at the annual BOA bash on 11 November 1959. The other three Home Nations' FAs had committed to the venture but, as usual, the English were the only footballing contingent at the BOA dinner. Most thoughts at Grosvenor House were on fund-raising but Norman Creek knew there was no point raising money for a team that did not qualify.

Five days before the first qualifier, Creek's GB side travelled to Stamford Bridge for a match against Chelsea, whose team included a young Jimmy Greaves. Jim Lewis was eager to play against his old club but there was no dream return. Shortly before the match, Creek's Olympic plans were shattered when Jim Lewis, his most experienced outfield player, broke his leg in a league match. Creek's side went down 4-1 with Billy Neil getting a consolation goal. The only positive was that the Chelsea board, aware of a connection with the GB team that stretched from Jim Lewis back to Vivian Woodward, donated half of the £623 gate receipts from the crowd of 5,000 to the BOA fund to send a team to Rome – if they could get that far.

One of the half-time changes in the Chelsea game was to substitute Bobby Brown and bring on Tooting & Mitcham's Paddy Hasty. A livewire amateur international for Northern Ireland, Hasty was born in Belfast but moved to London and signed for Tooting from Salisbury City in 1955. A good header of the ball despite a lack of height, Hasty had a hard shot from either foot. In the early part of his time with Tooting, Hasty was on national service in the Royal Navy but was considered so valuable that the club hired a helicopter to bring him back for big matches!

Hasty entered Norman Creek's thoughts when Tooting reached the FA Cup third round for the first time in 1959 with Hasty among the scorers in their second-round win over league side, Northampton. In the third round, Tooting took on first division side Nottingham Forest. Professionals and amateurs lined up on Tooting's rough, icy Imperial Fields ground in Morden, the income and standard of living of both sets of players little different. Paddy Hasty worked as a telephone engineer and had played a few league games for Leyton Orient but turned down offers from Everton and Spurs to go pro as wages at the Post Office were better. With the rough pitch on their side, Tooting were 2-0 up by half-time. In the second half, reality took hold. A frozen rut deceived the Tooting keeper and a late penalty secured a 2-2 draw for Forest, who won the replay and later the FA Cup. Paddy Hasty's big moment would come later.

After each receiving a call-up letter from Rous confirming their participation, GB the team gathered at Victoria Station for the trip down to Brighton, where the game was to be played. As Hugh Forde arrived, he bumped into two FA officials comparing their ties. "By the way," said one official to the other, "this is Forde: he has come all the way by himself on a Viscount flight from Belfast. Isn't that a wonderful example of true amateurism?"

Hugh Forde knew he was an example to the footballing authorities but not in that sense. Unknown to his GB team-mates or anyone outside the upper echelons of the IFA, the Irishman had been forced into a shameful deal to keep his Olympic dream alive.

By the late 1950s, Sunday football was growing in popularity in Britain, but playing on God's Day in Ulster remained a mortal sin. For the IFA, the Olympic qualifier presented a particular problem – as the game was on a Sunday. A few days before the Brighton match, Forde received a breathy phone call from an almost apologetic IFA official to tell him that no Northern Irishman could be permitted to play on a Sunday. He was to be deregistered on the Friday before the GB qualifier with the Republic. But there was a catch. If Forde promised not to speak to the press, he would be reinstated on the Monday after the qualifier. The young Forde reluctantly kept his promise and took his place among the reserves on Norman Creek's bench in Brighton. But he never felt quite the same about football again.

21 November 1959

Goldstone Ground, Brighton. GB vs the Republic of Ireland

On a Saturday afternoon on the English south coast, Norman Creek began his Roman quest. The qualifiers were a mini-league, with one team going through, and a victory would put GB in a commanding position as the Irish and Dutch had already played and drawn with each other. For GB, Paddy Hasty took Jim Lewis's place up front, playing centre forward with Bobby Brown and Hunter Devine on either wing.

A Welshman also started. Dave Roberts was a well-built but pacey inside-right who had been a junior at Wrexham and played for Coleraine in the Irish League during his national service before returning to London to work in the City and signing for Tooting & Mitcham.

The team was truly British but Billy Neil's goal against Chelsea meant nothing. He was dropped and did not travel south after being unable to get away from his work at a bank in Scotland. With John Harding of Pegasus injured, Alf D'Arcy was made captain.

The Belgian referee, Blavier, caused some consternation by using a Belgian franc for the toss. After some confusion, Alf D'Arcy realised he had won and waved to Hasty to indicate a change in the direction of play. The Northern Irishman misunderstood and immediately kicked off – to the surprise of both his Irish opponents and his own GB team-mates. Bobby Brown centred a ball that the Irish defence missed completely and Devine instinctively swung at the ball, which was crossing the line as Hasty followed up to make sure of the goal: 1-0, without the Irish even touching the ball.

"Before we had time to get into position, all was over," said Willie Browne, Ireland's captain and most experienced player. His team lacked ideas in possession and defensive positioning but forwards Sonny Rice and Sean Coad responded by running at the GB defence. Nothing, however, was beating Alf D'Arcy. Brown and John Ward, an England amateur international playing with Northampton Town, began to put together a few passes. GB reached half-time two goals ahead as Hasty drove a terrific shot into the roof of the Irish net from Brown's centre.

In the second half, GB were untroubled until D'Arcy conceded an uncharacteristic and unnecessary free kick. Irish forward Ahearne headed home from the resulting delivery. A dull, slow game came alive. Ahearne and Rice began to unsettle D'Arcy's defence. When GB right-back Derek

Gardner of Crook Town pushed a sloppy backpass towards an unsuspecting Mike Pinner, Rice nipped in to equalise.

With only ten minutes left and the sun sinking towards the Sussex skyline, GB were about to drop a crucial home point in their opening match. Waved on by D'Arcy, GB surged into attack. Ward sent a pile-driver onto the post and Hasty's closely-cropped head nodded home the winner and seemingly his hat-trick, although later Hasty's first goal was awarded to Devine.

In the *Chronicle*, Norman Ackland rated matches (not individual teams) in terms of sportsmanship, happy to preach a doctrine he supported in his own dissipated fashion. Surprisingly, given the kick off, Ackland gave the match ten out of ten for sportsmanship, more important to some watchers than the result. Creek's side deserved to win but failed to dominate. The watching media were not impressed. "On this display, they should move through to the ties in Rome next August but little success can attend them there," wrote the *Observer*'s correspondent. The *Guardian*'s Pat Ward-Thomas agreed: "Much of the passing was untidy in its direction and timing and rarely was there any expression of unity."

That was harsh as the Irish had fought back well against a more experienced team, whose match preparation – or lack thereof – had simply not been good enough. Creek would not be caught out again. In the New Year, the squad met up regularly on weekends with two days of punishing training, each followed by a friendly match against decent opposition. Against Arsenal, Pinner was unavailable and the selection committee brought in Murray Crook, an acrobatic Welsh keeper from Milford United. Porthmadoc's Glyn Owen started at left half-back but the team shipped four goals without reply. The next month, GB visited Upton Park and Crook was replaced by a keeper after Norman Creek's own heart. From Manchester, Brian Wakefield moved south after being taken on as a management trainee with construction company, Wimpey. Arriving in London, he signed with Corinthian-Casuals for the 1959/60 season. "Orient would have offered me terms but I wasn't interested," recalls Wakefield.

A young prodigy at West Ham called Bobby Moore had just broken into the side but despite facing a strong team, including Moore and John Bond, a rejuvenated GB side were in the game until the very end, when the professionals' fitness told and they won 5-2. Wakefield adds: "I let in five goals but had quite a good game and was in the squad after that but Mike Pinner was always number one." Wakefield and Pinner had been rivals for the keeper's shirt at Pegasus and the England amateur shirt and renewed this long-standing rivalry in the Olympic team.

Bobby Brown's place was strengthened after he scored the GB side's two goals at Upton Park, where 4,800 people turned up to watch. After the match, the GB committee decided to donate their share of the gate receipts of £620 to a team that many years ago provided an Olympic medal winner. With the FA struggling to raise cash to send a side to Rome, the donation was incredibly generous. Fifty-two years had passed since Clapton FC's Clyde Purnell helped GB win the 1908 title, but someone, somewhere still remembered.

On 22 February, a 2-2 draw was secured against Northampton despite Bobby Brown being absent. In this match the much sought-after 15-year-old, Terry Venables, got a game for the Olympic team. Venables signed schoolboy forms with Chelsea, putting off turning pro because, like Alf D'Arcy, he too dreamt of playing in the Games. The future manager of England and Barcelona was subsequently included in a 20-man squad for the return with Ireland.

Of those 20 players, all but three – Billy Neil, Davie Holt and Hugh Forde – were English. There were no Welshmen. The selection committee waited until after an England amateur international on 5 March in Dulwich before choosing Norman Creek's final squad. Among the new faces was winger Arnold Coates, who had won the Northern league and Amateur Cup with Crook in 1959. After national service, Coates played for the reserves at Sunderland, where he was offered a contract, but the professionals were again beaten by the shamateurs. "I went to sign for Sunderland and while I was waiting outside the room I met two committeemen from Crook," recalls Coates. "They said: 'Come and play for us and we'll sort you out with some money'. The season of the Olympics [in 1960] I'd been at Evenwood Town as they paid a bit more and were helping me out with some groceries."

Terry Venables played in England's 1-1 draw with Germany but was surprisingly overlooked for the qualifier against the Irish in favour of the Barnet teenager, Roy Sleap. Bobby Brown had a poor match against the Germans but scored to keep his GB place.

13 March 1960
Dalymount Park, Dublin. Republic of Ireland vs GB

Norman Creek's starting line-up in Dublin was expected to include Hubert Barr, a teacher who played for Ballymena, but the IFA put Northern Ireland before Britain's Olympic ambitions. Barr was picked for Northern Ireland's full B team for a match against France B three days after the Olympic qualifier in Dublin. After the GB squad had been named, the IFA decided that Barr must not travel to Dublin and Barnet's Tony Harding took his place. With Devine out, Scotsman Davie Holt was the only non-Englishman in the side to face the Irish, who were without their forward, Ahearne.

A big crowd of 19,000 turned up on a Sunday afternoon to see if the Irish could gain revenge for their defeat in Brighton. Sitting in the press box was Norman Ackland, who had returned to Ireland, the land of his birth.

Forward Jim Lewis had recovered from his broken leg but Creek's key players in the game proved to be his defenders. Alf D'Arcy was out and Bishop Auckland's Mike Greenwood came in as captain. He and club team-mate Laurie Brown never stopped in breaking up the Irish attacks and GB had only one chance in the entire first half. Goalless at half-time, Bobby Brown and Harding combined to produce a chance for Arnold Coates to open the scoring early in the second half. On 58 minutes, Ireland equalised as McGrath finally beat Pinner, who had punched numerous shots over the bar in the first half. Soon after, Greenwood delivered a pinpoint free kick to Bobby Brown, who on the turn lashed in the ball. The goal subdued the boisterous Irish crowd and when Harding added a third, the last ten minutes were played in virtual silence. "We were lucky," said Creek on the final whistle. "I thought we were going to be well beaten."

In the *Chronicle*, Norman Ackland gave the match eight out of ten for sportsmanship but noted: "There will be a massacre if [GB] win through to Rome and come up against an [Eastern European] team." Ackland felt that a decisive defeat for GB in Dublin would have been a fairer result. Instead, only victory over the Netherlands was between Norman Creek and the first qualification for an Olympic tournament by a GB team. Terry Venables was again among the 20 players in the squad for the first leg in Zwolle. The most significant change to the team was the introduction of inside-right Hugh Lindsay, who was due to play in the Amateur Cup final a few weeks later for Kingstonian. A talented cricketer, who had played for the second XI at Middlesex County Cricket Club, Lindsay spurned the professional game. Lindsay says:

> "It just wasn't worth it to go professional. I was offered terms at Southampton but it was a big problem if you didn't make it as a pro as you couldn't even play on a Sunday back then. All you could do was go into the Southern league with the other old pros. In some ways, the professional game was a bit of a closed shop, them and us between the amateurs and the professionals. If you went in as a mature person, you were looked on as an amateur because most of the lads had been apprentices and cleaned the boots. If you waltzed in at 20 or 21, you weren't always looked on that favourably."

Lindsay was that age when the 1960 Olympics came round and he was finishing university in London with plans to become a teacher. He had made a couple of first-team appearances as an amateur at Southampton and many more for their reserve side, whilst also playing for Kingstonian in the Isthmian League, and soon made the England amateur squad. A diminutive but creative midfield ball-player, Lindsay gave the GB side more options in Zwolle.

2 April 1960
Zwolle. The Netherlands vs GB

The Dutch were coached by Elek Schwartz, a Romanian who had played professionally in France before World War Two and also managed the full Dutch national side. His selection was a mixture of players from minor clubs and amateurs playing at pro clubs like Heerenveen, NAC, Willem II and Vitesse Arnhem.

The Dutch were on top at the start. Then, Jim Lewis, who had been rusty in Dublin and missed one particularly easy chance, showed why he had won the title with Chelsea. On 21 minutes, Lewis put GB ahead following a pinpoint pass from Hugh Barr, restored at inside-left. A single goal separated the sides until a scoring glut started on 75 minutes by Hugh Lindsay, who slotted home on his debut. Dutch outside-right Bart Hainje of Heerenveen pulled a goal back two minutes later after Mike Pinner could only parry a fierce shot.

Bobby Brown had proved increasingly adept at leading the GB line despite his youth and when the Dutch side appealed for a clear offside missed by the French official, the Barnet striker slipped in for a third. Another GB goal followed as Dutch right-back Van Campen saw a clearance deflected into his own net off the shin of Jim Lewis, who scored again a minute later for his hat-trick from a penalty awarded for a trip on Coates. To the disappointment of a predominantly Dutch crowd of 9,000, GB had coasted home 5-1 and secured qualification. Norman Creek could relax in his own quiet, schoolmasterly way. He had achieved his goal with a match to spare.

13 April 1960
White Hart Lane, London. GB vs The Netherlands

The return was staged under floodlights and details of the crowd vary. Dutch records show a respectable 17,000 fans turning up but the FA put the figure at 3,950. Only two non-English players – Holt and Barr – made the starting line-up for a game that was an anti climax. Bobby Brown opened the scoring after five minutes, knocking home a long pass from Alf D'Arcy, back in the team and captain again. Half an hour from the end, GB's best performer, Lindsay, sent a pass through to Bobby Brown, who released Lewis to score. Ten minutes later the Dutch were reduced to ten men when centre-half Meers hobbled off injured. Olympic rules barred the use of substitutes but the watching Sir Stanley Rous – now Fifa president – agreed to waive this rule after a mid-game request by the Dutch management. Restored to 11 players, the Dutch rallied. De Kleermaker of Vitesse nodded a cross past Mike Pinner. Fifteen minutes from the end, Laurie Brown mis-kicked the ball and Paul Bouwman equalised. The Dutch nearly snatched a late and not undeserved winner but GB held on for a draw. A couple of Dutch players tried to keep the match ball but were beaten to it by the proud GB captain Alf D'Arcy, who had realised his dream – or so he thought.

Creek's side still could not impress the media. The football correspondent of *The Times* praised Lindsay, likening him to Newcastle hero Len Shackleton, but was less enamoured with the rest, writing: "Clearly there is some way to go yet if they are to make their way in Rome. There is spirit in the side and determination, a certain amount of proficiency without a great deal of efficiency."

The naysayers gave Creek's side no chance in Rome, where his side were

215

handed a tough draw against the hosts, Brazil and Formosa (Taiwan). "Oh crikey," said Bobby Brown on seeing the draw, but GB would take their place in Rome alongside these genuine powers, and the likes of Hungary and Yugoslavia, on merit. That unlikely combination of London hardman Alf D'Arcy and the Corinthian Norman Creek had succeeded. With Lindsay growing in ability and no more likely to join the professional ranks than Pinner or Lewis, maybe GB just had a chance in Rome.

Between qualifying in April and the tournament, Creek continued his routine of training weekends, but the biggest guide to the team's chances was a game in Brescia on May 14 against Italy's Under-21 side, who would represent the hosts in the Olympics. Most of the players from that final qualifier played, with the exception of Lewis, whose place was certain. Hendon's Terry Howard took his place in Brescia. An outside-left, Howard had scored for Hendon when they overcame Lindsay's Kingstonian in the thrilling 1960 Amateur Cup final. A cashier at Billingsgate fish market, Howard played a few matches for Leyton Orient's first team and then signed amateur forms for Arsenal. The only new face in the 13-man GB squad was another Hendon player, inside-left Jimmy Quail, a London-based Northern Irishman who came in for the injured Bobby Brown.

Played on a hard pitch in stifling heat, the game was a dreadful blow to the GB side's burgeoning confidence. A crowd of 3,000 saw Norman Creek's side hammered 5-1. Hugh Forde recalls spending most of the game trying to get his shirt back from a determined Italian attacker seemingly intent on relieving him of it. Davie Holt was injured and had to be replaced at half-time by Billy Neil. The only positive was a goal on his GB debut for Terry Howard.

In Naples airport, the blazered GB squad found themselves accosted by a Great American Tourist (GAT). "Hi you guys," said one of the GATs then becoming increasingly ubiquitous in Europe. "I heard you were transiting in Naples and I just wanted to meet the Great Britain Olympic squad. It's my first post-war trip to Europe and I will tell all my friends back home that I met you."

The GAT then shot off in search of another experience, leaving a bemused set of British and Irish footballers unsure of just what had happened. Norman Creek was particularly dejected on his return from Italy but another foreign trip would hopefully prove more encouraging.

The previous year's visit to the UK by the Caribbean touring party resulted in an invitation to send a side back. The offer was made to Middlesex

Wanderers, who under Bob Alaway's stewardship grew into an adventurous touring side of some repute. A place on a club tour was solely by invitation and restricted to gentlemen only. Over the years, many Olympians toured with the Wanderers, from Basil Gates to Guy Holmes, who led a tour to Germany only a few months before the Berlin Games, and Lester Finch and Denis Kelleher, the latter being the captain for visits to the Netherlands in 1949 and Iceland two years later.

The ethos of the club remained close to that of the AFA's ideals and, during the 1950s, George Robb, Idwal Robling, George Bromilow, Harry Sharratt, Laurie Topp, Ronnie McInven and the D'Arcy brothers all toured with the Wanderers.

A Wanderers tour usually included many amateur internationals but the FA were understandably concerned about wearing out key players for the Rome Olympics. The FA agreed to the tour on the condition that no one going to Italy that summer would take part, which would have drastically weakened the Wanderers' squad.

The Wanderers' president was usually elected from within the club but an exception had been made in 1960, when Leonard Kingston was invited on board. After some no doubt lively discussions between Kingston and his old cohorts at the FA, a compromise was reached. Most tourists would be gentlemen in with a chance of going to Rome. Norman Creek would accompany the party and have some say in selection. Alf D'Arcy should have known what to expect but would ultimately regret going to the Caribbean that June.

The Wanderers had first been invited to the Caribbean in 1956 but this would have entailed a three-month slog by boat. By 1960, improvements in air travel made the offer more realistic. The Wanderers would play nine matches on a tour starting on 5 June, sponsored by the Trinidad Football Association. Trinidad hosted the first three matches, where the Wanderers played all three games in five days against the national side, winning two and drawing one. The Wanderers then flew to the northern tip of South America and a match against Surinam in Paramaribo, which was won 4-2 but marred by Mike Greenwood accidentally clashing with Devine and splitting the Scotsman's jaw.

The squad travelled on to Fort-de-France in the French colony of Martinique for a match against the islanders on a pitch with no grass and rocks lodged under the mud surface. The conditions proved the undoing of the Wanderers and Alf D'Arcy. Unable to play their Corinthian football on a dreadful pitch, the Wanderers were down 3-0 by half-time. For most of the tourists, this was frustrating. Alf D'Arcy was more frustrated than most and responded the only way he knew how.

"I did start putting in a few hard tackles," admits Alf D'Arcy, mulling over 45 minutes of football which would destroy his childhood dream. Half a century later, many of his team-mates still wince as they recall those tackles and their repercussions. Martinique could not cope with the brutal tackling but the Wanderers still lost 3-0 – their only defeat on the tour. For D'Arcy, there would be a very different result.

He adds: "After the game, Norman Creek started having a go at me and saying, 'we can't take players like you to the Olympics'. I said that if players didn't want to play on a pitch like that they should put their hands up. After that, he didn't have much to do with me for the rest of the tour."

After the Martinique match, the tourists visited Jamaica. In Trinidad, the matches had been played on the Queen's Park Oval test cricket ground, and the Wanderers faced Jamaica's national side at another famous cricket stadium, Sabina Park. Hunter Devine played wearing a jaw strap and both matches were won, 4-0 and 6-1.

The Wanderers went home via Hamilton, where the team beat Bermuda 6-2. Back in Britain, the tourists were on tenterhooks. Everyone knew their chances of going to Rome depended on what Norman Creek thought of them in the Caribbean but the FA had more pressing matters. On 25 June, the FA sat down at Blackpool's Imperial Hotel to discuss money – again. The professional game's enthusiasm for the GB team was clear. An appeal to the 92 Football League clubs for donations towards the £3,700 bill for sending a team to Rome totalled just £209 – a sum dwarfed by Chelsea's donation of half of the gate receipts from their match against the GB side. A club that would become the great arrivistes of the 21st-century game stumped up three times more than the rest of the league put together. As the other Home Nations had deigned to provide players but no money, the financial onus was on the English and the FA stumped up £2,500. But this would have consequences for all of the players that did go to Rome that summer.

When the squad was named, of the 17 players to tour with the Wanderers, nine were included, but Alf D'Arcy was not one of them. D'Arcy had gone from being the man who captained GB to the Olympics and a virtual certainty for Rome to a pariah. "I was gutted," says D'Arcy half a century later, adding:

> "I'd worked so hard to try and get into the 1956 squad but missed out. I didn't fit in to start with and a lot of people kept me at arm's distance as I was a bit aggressive. As I got a bit older, I learnt to be more aggressive at the right time and be more calculating. It was a shame as I missed out on a few things by getting kicked out."

D'Arcy was not only dropped from the GB side but also the England amateur team, where he had been a regular – almost certainly for his actions in Martinique.

When the selection committee named the squad, there was also disappointment in Wales. Llandudno's Alan McIntosh had not impressed on the Wanderers' tour and was omitted. Dave Roberts missed the cut too. "Just before the Olympic team was picked, I was dropped for Wales," explains Roberts. "The Welsh didn't realise that the Olympic team was about to be named." If Roberts had retained his place in the Wales team, he feels he might still have gone to the Olympics. Instead, not a single Welshman would be in Rome.

To the surprise of most commentators, Roy Sleap was preferred ahead of Terry Venables, who then abandoned his status as a gentleman to sign professional forms with Chelsea. Venables had missed the Caribbean tour, unlike Dulwich Hamlet's Les Brown, who was nicknamed "The Major" for his baggy khaki shorts. Dulwich had not supplied an England amateur international for 21 years until Brown was surprisingly called up for the 1959 game against Germany. From then on, like his namesake, Bobby, his stock rose.

Les Brown had played a handful of games at Crystal Palace and Millwall during his national service. On demob he was approached by Wolves and Watford but had a head for business and took a sales manager's job at publishers, IPC. His choice of amateur club was a foregone conclusion: Les Brown's father Harry had been player and treasurer at Dulwich for 30 years. Harry was often a reserve for the England amateur team before World War Two but never dislodged Jim Lewis Senior. Now both their sons would go to the Olympics together.

The purists' favourites, Pegasus, had been thrashed by Norton Woodseats in the second round of that year's Amateur Cup and could barely canter. None of their players made the squad. From Corinthian-Casuals, Pat Neil had been on the Olympic fringes but Terry Howard of Hendon was chosen instead. Goalkeeper Brian Wakefield would be the only player from the club in Rome.

Wakefield was one of nine Wanderers to go to Italy. Hugh Lindsay was on teacher training and missed the Caribbean trip but, like Bobby Brown, Lewis and Pinner, he was a certainty for Rome. Of the Irishmen, Hugh Barr and Hugh Forde made the cut along with Paddy Hasty, but Jimmy Quail missed out. In Rome, there would only be space for one garrulous London-based Northern Irishman and that was Paddy Hasty.

With the Games in sight, the BOA held a fund-raising bash on 13 July 1960. Sydney Lipton and his Ballroom Orchestra entertained as sport's great and good dined. Corporate sponsorship was creeping in. The dinner programme featured ads for the first time and sponsors' gifts ranged from Bovril to Rothmans and the Kenya Coffee Company. London's mayor, Sir Jocelyn Lucas, even donated a mini Sealyham terrier puppy for auction.

No football players attended the bash; the GB team were used to more Spartan affairs. As the Olympics got closer, their schedule of training weekends at RAF Chessington or RAF Uxbridge followed by a Monday night match intensified. This heavy schedule took its toll on players travelling from Scotland or northern England. "We had RAF PTA instructors who really pulverised us," recalls Devine.

An RAF group captain that led the training roared at his charges: "You may not turn out to be the most skilful team at the Games but I guarantee you'll be the fittest."

GB played 19 trial and qualifying games culminating in a final pre-Rome game against Watford in early August. Instead of playing the XI expected to face Brazil on 26 August for a full 90 minutes, seven of the GB side were replaced at half-time, illustrating that wholesale team replacement is no 21st-century fad. Arnold Coates picked up a foot injury that he would long rue. With Lewis on holiday and Hasty having a poor game, Devine took his chance to impress. A goal down, Devine equalised from a Bobby Brown centre and Laurie Brown scored the winner from a penalty. The tourists, who had been sent to Simpsons in Piccadilly to get kitted out in their Olympic gear, would leave for Italy with a victory in their final game.

The entire GB Olympic party flew to Italy in a fleet of British European Airways planes and arrived in the Olympic village in Rome on 23 August. In Melbourne four years previously, there had been a six-foot-high fence separating the male and female athletes. In Rome, the height of the fence was raised to a more problematic eight foot. The footballers were told that the fence was to separate the Russians and Eastern Europeans from the other athletes.

The Cold War split the athletes' accommodation but, for training, everyone mixed. The footballers trained on a field plateaued on the side of a hill at seven o'clock in the morning to avoid the sultry Roman heat. One morning Hugh Forde was jogging round this field, when a small unkempt man wearing a woolen alpine hat – knitted, it later transpired, by his mother – appeared alongside the Ulsterman.

"What is your name please?" the man asked Forde, who told him. "Where you from?" Forde again provided the answer. "Oh you know my friends Roger [Bannister] and Chris [Chataway]?" Forde had to admit he certainly did not know the legendary British runners.

As the pair jogged round the track, Forde asked the little man his name. "Emil," he answered. "Emil Zatopek?" As Forde tried to hide his sense of awe, Zatopek, who was winning gold medals at the Olympics when Matt Busby was in charge of the GB side, added: "Yes, I like meeting famous athletes, are you famous footballer Hugh?'"

Forde, admitting he was not, added: "I have watched you run against your friends Roger and Chris. You seem to run with so little effort, what is your plan when you run?"

Zatopek replied:

> "I have no plan Hugh. I love running with famous athletes. I run with the pack but one by one they seem to drop away and I am left to run on by myself. I am looking forward to running against my English friends because they each go in front of the other for a little time and I have to catch up with the leader. I was disappointed the last time we ran for after a time they too fell away and I had to run to the end by myself …"

Zatopek trailed off as he ran on, leaving Forde in his wake.

The Irishman and the rest of the footballers were jammed seven players into one flat; everyone had to share a room and some even slept in the kitchen but, having finally made it to the Olympics, no one cared. What the team certainly did care about was that their opener with Brazil was in Livorno, not Rome. The footballers had been told they would miss the closing ceremony if they got knocked out but missing the opening to travel to Livorno was a major blow. "It sounds terrible to say it was a disappointment," says Billy Neil, "but I was only 21 years old and not being at the opening or closing ceremonies was disappointing. We weren't even in the village that much at the start and had to watch the opening ceremony on TV."

Austria and Belgium refused to take part due to familiar rows over amateurism. Attempts to remove football from the Olympics failed but football's significance at the Games was weakening, not least due to six increasingly successful World Cups. After the 1958 World Cup in Sweden, Fifa and the IOC reached an agreement that players from that tournament could not play in Rome. This weakened Hungary, who were on the slide after their elimination by Wales in the 1958 World Cup. Yugoslavia had made the quarter-finals in Sweden but strength in depth and a typically communist – and opaque – approach to amateurism made Marshall Tito's representatives the favourites in Rome for many tipsters.

Two days after arriving in Italy, GB decamped to Livorno to face Brazil, who had won their first World Cup in 1958 with a team featuring a young player called Pele. The Brazilian squad in Rome had the same coach, Vicente Feola, but were mostly amateur under-20 players. They were still strong with players like Gerson, who a decade later scored in Brazil's 4-1 World Cup Final win over Italy, and Roberto Dias, a player Pele regarded as one of the few able to mark him. The GB team was chosen by committee but Creek had plenty of input – much to Arnold Coates's chagrin. He was dropped but Creek accommodated Bobby Brown, Lewis, and Hasty in an attacking side aimed at simply taking the game to Brazil. Creek was widely respected – even by Alf D'Arcy languishing in Barnet. On away trips it was GB's manager, not the selection committee, who picked the team, but there were few tactics. "Norman Creek was a very nice person but I don't recall many tactical talks," recalls Jim Lewis. For squad comedian Paddy Hasty, there was only one tactic against Brazil. "Play all 19 of us," Hasty joked to Hunter Devine.

26 August 1960
Stadio Armando Picchi, Livorno. GB vs Brazil

As the Brazilians warmed up, the astonished GB team began to realise the scale of their task. "We watched Brazil train with all their music playing on the loudspeakers; that was their style but we'd never seen anything like that before," says Les Brown.

Within a minute off the kick-off, GB conceded a goal. Roy Sleap fouled winger Waldir and the Brazilian captain da Silva whipped a perfect free kick past Pinner. For the next 30 minutes, Brazil dominated a shocked GB side. Watched by a tiny contingent of British supporters in short-sleeved shirts, GB could only watch as the Brazilians knocked rapid passes about. Holt twice cleared the ball off the line but the punishing RAF fitness sessions paid off. GB's endeavour kept them in the game and on 22 minutes, Bobby Brown nipped between two defenders to score from 18 yards.

The scores remained level at half-time but Jim Lewis added a second two minutes after the kick-off to the astonishment, this time, of the Brazilians. With 30 minutes left, an unlikely qualification was within reach. Then, moments after a GB shot hit the bar that would have added a third goal, disaster struck. Defender Tommy Thompson went into a tackle and was hammered by a shocking Brazilian challenge that broke his leg. "I was on the bench and I could hear Thompson's leg break from 40 yards away," shivers Les Brown.

Thompson would spend four days in hospital and GB, with no substitutes, were immediately on the back foot. Most of the GB side agree the foul was atrocious. Some even feel the challenge might have been a deliberate act to reduce GB to ten men. Pinner, Laurie Brown and Holt were outstanding but could not stave off the talented Brazilians on a hot, dry Italian summer's day. Brazil knocked in two goals to take the lead and though Bobby Brown battled manfully and later scored another, GB went down 4-3, with da Silva credited as scoring two goals by Fifa.

With only the group winners qualifying, GB had to beat Italy in front of their home crowd back in Rome's Stadio Flaminio to stay in the tournament. FA records show that Devine was dropped for Terry Howard. Perhaps Norman Creek was subconsciously hoping the Hendon player would emulate his performance in the last GB match against Italy but the record book is wrong: Devine retained his place. The only change was Billy Neil at right-back for Thompson.

The Italian side comprised under-21 players, but all from Serie A. Many would soon be household names in Italy; players like AC Milan great, Gianni Rivera, Giovanni Trapattoni, Tarcisio Burgnich, who became one of Italy's finest defenders, and forward Giacomo Bulgarelli. The management was top-flight, with Guiseppe Viani from AC Milan in charge, helped by Nereo Rocco. The fixture was a complete mismatch but Norman Creek's side were about to show some of the grit that the GB press felt they lacked.

29 August 1960
Olympic Stadium, Rome. Italy vs GB
The match attracted the biggest crowd of any Olympic event so far with 45,000 rowdy fans turning up. Mike Pinner had played in front of capacity crowds in the first division but put in his best performance in an England amateur game against Scotland at a practically empty Hampden. Not a man prone to nerves, as he marched out to face Italy under floodlights, his stomach began to grip. "It wasn't an occasion when you say to yourself I am just going out to play. It was something different," Pinner told John Moynihan in his book, *The Soccer Syndrome*. "It was a very fast, tremendously physical encounter. I remember the tremendous green of the grass, the greenest I have ever seen, and the floodlights burning down and I felt nervous then."

The noisy home crowd got behind Italy but Hugh Lindsay was not overawed and easily broke up the Italian attacks. GB eventually settled and a fine pass from Jim Lewis put Bobby Brown through for an early chance, but his shot was blocked. Italian defender Salvatore then had to produce a spectacular diving header to cut out a Devine cross. After 11 minutes, Italy took the lead when the 18-year-old Rossano, who had just been signed as an amateur by Juventus for £20,000, scored from an offside position. The referee initially appeared to agree that it was offside, but then, perhaps swayed by the crescendo of home support, waved for the restart. Creek's men did not object.

The Italians began to spray the ball around but Lindsay's hard tackling and another commanding performance by Laurie Brown kept Italy out. As GB regrouped, Billy Neil won the ball and advanced up the field. The Italians stood off the Scotsman and he advanced into their half before passing to Lewis, whose slight deflection put Bobby Brown through on goal. The teenager was instantly tackled but got the ball away to equalise. After that, GB came under heavy pressure and looked unlikely to score again despite some hard running from Bobby Brown and Paddy Hasty.

The two sides went in at half-time with the score even at 1-1. The second half proved a rare treat for British football fans. The BBC took a live feed of the second half of the game via the Eurovision network. Kenneth Wolstenholme commentated. In the typically grainy footage, the colours wash into hues of grey but there is nothing grey about the British performance. Picking up the game a few minutes into the second half, a breathless Wolstenholme lauds a fine performance. Britons, Wolstenholme tells us, are used to seeing their team outplayed by continental European and South American teams. Not here, not now.

Decades later, Lindsay secured a tape of the second half and you can see why he made the effort. Lindsay is everywhere, blocking out the Italians as he covers a GB defence marshalled by a titanic Laurie Brown. The Italians flood forward, Rivera and Trapattoni running at the GB defence, even Burgnich surges forward. Each time they run into the immovable wall that is Laurie Brown as Holt, McInven and Neil mop up around him.

Then, the Belgian referee makes another appalling error by ignoring a clear, brutal foul on Lindsay. With Lindsay on the floor, the GB team pause, anticipating a free kick that the foul merits. This allows Rossano to send a low hard shot past Pinner. Surely despondent, GB do not surround the referee. Norman Creek stays in his dug-out. His team get up. They get on with the game. Had Vivian Woodward lasted another six years, he would have been able to watch the game and could not have been prouder of the men who followed him into the Olympic side. Was Lindsay fouled? Nearly five decades later, his view remains the same. He says: "Yes, it was a foul on me, and I've been complaining ever since."

After the goal, the Italian crowd go crazy and their team pour forward but each time, thump, they run into Laurie Brown. At one point, Wolstenholme describes GB as England and has to apologise, not unreasonably blaming excitement at the tense game he is covering. GB are penned into their own half and then, against the run of play, they manage to force a corner. Devine swings the corner over. Hasty meets the ball inside the six yard box. The cameraman clearly could not read the game as well as the Northern

Irishman, who is barely caught on the footage as he steers the ball through a mass of feet and into the net.

The home crowd are stunned but Italian fury is unleashed. The watching journalist Desmond Hackett wrote:

> "A mob, I refuse to recognise them as fans, screamed and howled with nationalistic fury that could only recall the pagan days. It was easy to appreciate why in Rome they got full houses for the lions versus the Christians. While the British were rebuked and penalised for charges and tackles that are part of a normal league game, the Italians were given the freedom of the pitch by the Belgian referee."

Amidst all this madness, GB did not falter. Knowing a win was needed to stay in the tournament, Creek's team gained momentum and begin to attack. The Italian fans roar in derision. Cushions rain onto the pitch. Sleap goes down under a dreadful tackle. No yellow card. No complaints. Sleap will surely, Kenneth Wolstenholme tells us, continue. So he does. The man that took Terry Venables's place shrugs off the attentions of his team-mates and limps back into position. By the end of the match, the cream of Italian football, all players from Serie A groomed for international stardom, are struggling to hang on against Britain's clerks, students and teachers. On the BBC, Wolstenholme describes the GB performance as those of a "great British side" that "everyone at home can be mightily proud of". Then with no post-match analysis, the coverage stops, a stock shot of the Olympic Stadium appears. The GB team are gone.

Italy beat Formosa 4-1 in their first game and went on to qualify for the semi-finals with a 3-1 win over Brazil. GB faced the plane home. "We could have won if we'd had the breaks," recalls Billy Neil, still aggrieved half a century later. The BOA agreed. In its official report on the football tournament, the Austrian Dr Willy Meisl wrote: "Without the mishap to Thompson and with a bit of luck we might have got into the last four."

Straight after the match, the squad returned to the Olympic village, many of them severely dehydrated. "In those days we were given no advice on diet or fluid intake other than 'don't drink the water' so the only liquid available to us in the Olympic village was from [Olympic sponsors] Coca Cola. You can imagine what we were like the next morning after four to six bottles of Coke," recalls Hunter Devine, who, frazzled with caffeine, barely slept all night.

The Italy result meant that the final game against Formosa was meaningless and this fixture was again to take the GB side out of Rome to Grosseto, where the players' only compensation was a blonde Italian translator, Dora. Creek and his committee made some changes. Terry Howard really did come in for Devine this time, Greenwood replaced Neil, and Glenavon's Hugh Forde came in for Sleap. To the surprise of many of the players, Creek did not give all the squad a run-out. There was to be no Olympic game for Arnold Coates, Brian Wakefield, Les Brown or Hugh Barr. "I was very disappointed not to get a game," sighs Hubert Barr half a century later.

1 September 1960
Grosseto. GB vs Formosa
After the glory of a packed Olympic Stadium, barely 100 fans turned up in Grosseto to see an overconfident GB team labour against a side they were expected to beat easily. "We nearly won the match we were expected to lose and struggled in the one we were expected to win," recalls Lindsay.

Those few spectators in attendance roared with fury when Hugh Forde put in an early strong challenge on a Formosan attacker. Forde got up, bemused at giving away a free kick for a challenge he felt would have passed without mention in the Irish League.

After 35 minutes, who else but Bobby Brown scored the opener from a Lewis cross, with the Formosan keeper waiting for the referee to blow his whistle for offside. GB knocked the ball about well, sending shots and crosses towards their opponents' goal to no avail. GB were 1-0 up at half-time and only added a second on 60 minutes when Terry Howard, virtually standing on the goal-line himself, centred for Bobby Brown to score a second.

Later, Formosa's best player, Mok Chun Wah, was unmarked and beat Pinner from the edge of the penalty box. The marking was lax on both sides as the game progressed. With five minutes left, Hasty scored a third unchallenged before Mok tricked Mike Greenwood and pulled another goal back with two minutes left.

Norman Creek's team had not won the tournament or even qualified for the last four, but as one of only two really amateur teams – along with Denmark according to *World Sports* magazine – neither was expected to emerge victorious. There were no Welshmen, but was that really the fault of the English organisers? Since the Olympic football tournament started, the tournament barely merits a mention in any of the minute books recording FAW meetings. For the 1959/60 season, the FAW records show virtually no mention of the Olympics or any of the Welsh players that were involved in the pre-tournament games.

Dave Roberts, who won 13 Welsh amateur caps but missed out on Rome, says:

> "The selectors wanted to just play the players from their own [Welsh] clubs. If you got picked from outside Wales, you were really lucky. It was really strange when you turned up for a Wales game. There were no training sessions and you were only introduced on the day of the game. I played an England vs Wales game and was on first name terms with all the England team but the only Welsh player I knew was a player from Kingstonian."

Norman Creek's team might not have been truly representative of all four Home Nations, but still produced a typically gallant British failure. "I thought we did well considering most of the other teams were better than us," says Les Brown, who joined the exodus back to Britain after the Formosa game.

The footballers missed out on enjoying being Olympians. Only Hunter Devine stayed on. "We were told in advance if you get knocked out, you either come home or stay at your own expense, which was three guineas a day," he says, adding:

> "It was a bargain. I would never experience that again so I was up for it even though I was only a poor actuarial trainee. Before we left, I went to my boss and asked for three weeks' unpaid leave as I'd used my holiday entitlement. My boss told me he was so proud of me he paid me for all three weeks."

Mike Pinner stayed an extra couple of days before returning to national service with the RAF. After he left, Devine had the team flat in the Olympic village to himself for ten days. He adds: "I could stroll down to the village, get something to eat and then get the coach to the main stadium. I went to the athletics day after day and the football. It was very casual. There was some security but nothing like today."

Devine got to see Yugoslavia beat Denmark 3-1 in the Olympic football final, which was refereed by Englishman R.J. Leafe. Italy had been eliminated by Yugoslavia after a 1-1 draw and drawing of lots. Levine saw many events including Don Thompson's memorable win in the 50-kilometre walk – the only GB athletics gold. During the athletics, a large American sat down by Devine, dwarfing the slim Scotsman. The pair struck up a conversation. The American asked what Devine had been up to and the actuarial student explained he had been eliminated from the football. Devine asked the American what sport he had been playing. An ebullient Cassius Clay explained that he had just won the light heavyweight boxing gold.

Even though Devine paid to stay on in Rome, he still had to fly back to Britain the day before the closing ceremony, the last British footballer at an Olympic football tournament by right. The Scot would never regret his decision to stay on. After the Olympics, Devine moved to London to work and joined George Taylor, a fellow Scot who also went on the Wanderers' Caribbean tour, to play at Hounslow. Devine later joined Hugh Lindsay at Wealdstone and played there for the 1962/63 season, which was badly disrupted by a severe winter. Many games were cancelled but some were played on pitches heavy with frost. During one winter match played in conditions that would not be considered playable today, one of Devine's ligaments went. With that injury, any thoughts that Devine had of returning to the Olympic team went too. He never played again.

"I'm glad it happened when I was 27 not 17 or I'd never have gone to the Olympics," recalls Devine, who became a successful businessman before retiring. He lives in Hampshire and is a regular golfer. His knee no longer causes him any problems and, just like Stan Charlton, the Olympic blazer fits just as well as when he went down to Simpsons in Piccadilly for that first fitting.

Before going to Rome, Bobby Brown had been attracting professional offers – one newspaper valued the former Battersea Grammar School boy at £40,000 – but he went back to work at the shipping company to consider his future. Brown recalls one day at work when his receptionist called him:

> "She whispered, 'There's two men who look like gang-sters in reception to see you'. I went out there and they had hats and leather coats. They said, 'Do you want to play in Italy?' I said 'OK' and they left. Later on, another guy got in touch and I met him in Soho. There was a rumour then that Jimmy Greaves was going to Italy and he mentioned his name."

The men were all envoys of the Milanese and Italian Olympic manager, Viani. The young Brown showed his contract to Greaves and Jimmy Hill at the Professional Footballers' Association and bought a teach-yourself-Italian book. The only hitch was an offer of a place on a prestigious Football Association tour of the Far East and New Zealand led by Tom Finney. The trip featured 13 professionals and five amateurs, including fellow Olympians Greenwood, Lewis, Pinner and Lindsay. "I couldn't say no to the FA," recalls Brown, who roomed with Bobby Moore for much of the lengthy expedition.

Eventually returning home, Brown was heartbroken to discover that Viani had been struck by a heart attack. He was no longer AC Milan's manager. Brown never heard from the Italians again. One of the most sought-after amateurs of the time, he signed for struggling first division side Fulham as an amateur. Brown only played a handful of games but got among the goals, scoring two in a 4-4 draw with Manchester United. Fulham's eventual contract offer was not great and his dream of a football career began to peter out. He signed pro forms with third division Watford before being sold for £15,000 to Cardiff, where he won the Welsh Cup.

Brown played at the start of Cardiff's intrepid journey to the semi-finals of the 1967/68 Cup Winners' Cup – still the best-ever performance by a Welsh side in European competition – but injury struck. He never recovered. Forced to retire from playing, Bobby Brown worked for many years as a coach for the Football Association of Wales and then at Hull City before leaving the game to run a pub that he still owns near Haverfordwest.

Jim Lewis also went on that Far East FA tour with Bobby Brown but the veteran's career ended rather differently. After scoring the winner in the

1961 Amateur Cup final for Walthamstow, he finally retired. He had scored 506 goals in 673 matches, including 39 goals in 49 England amateur games. He once scored seven goals in two consecutive internationals. Lewis played in three Olympics. Including qualifiers, he scored 10 goals in 11 Olympic appearances – a record that is unlikely to ever be broken on either count.

Arnold Coates rejoined Crook Town after the Olympics and won the Amateur Cup again in 1962 before going part-time with Queen of the South in the Scottish league. "The Olympics was disappointing for me as I didn't play but I'd hurt my ankle and wasn't at my best," admits Coates, who worked in factories and then insurance before retiring to live in Nelson.

A handful of Creek's team joined the professionals, including Davie Holt, who signed for Hearts and showed that the 1960 team had international quality by winning five full caps for Scotland. Paddy Hasty joined Aldershot, Tommy Thompson regained fitness to become a player at Blackpool and Hubert Barr signed for Coventry City.

"It was a big change going professional from teaching, where you are working from nine to five every day. When you go to football, you are working two hours a day at most and I found that a bit difficult at first," recalls Barr, who stayed at Coventry for three seasons, then signed for Cambridge United.

Hugh Forde's amateur international career never recovered from his decision to join the GB team in Brighton and go against the IFA by playing on a Sunday. Along with his two brothers, he went to live in Australia, eventually becoming the national marketing manager for Mazda. He feels only sorrow, not hatred, for the society he left behind, but has never forgotten the compromise he made to get his registration back and go to the Games. "Gentle tones may hide the sounds of hypocrisy but they do not remove its stench," he says, recalling the IFA official during that late night phone call when he agreed to toe the line for Olympic glory.

The hero of GB's game against Italy, Laurie Brown, signed professional forms with Northampton Town and switched from defence to centre forward. In his one season with Northampton, he scored 21 goals in 33 matches as the club was promoted. In August 1961 Brown joined Arsenal and went back to defending, making over 100 appearances before becoming one of a handful of players to switch to deadly rivals Spurs. Brown signed for Spurs for £40,000 in 1964, going on to win the FA Cup three years later. After spells at Norwich and Bradford, he retired in 1969. Unable or unwilling to move out of the game, he went into management, first at Altrincham, then King's Lynn and Stockton.

On 31 July 2010, a reunion was held for all the British athletes that went to Rome at Much Wenlock in Shropshire. Many footballers attended, some having not seen each other for half a century, but not Laurie Brown, who passed away in 1998.

The British game changed decisively in the few years after Rome. In England, pressure mounted on the maximum wage and, in the season of the 1960 Olympics, football was screened on a Saturday night for the first time – much to the dismay of the amateur fraternity. "There will be more people in the shops on Saturday afternoons than there are at football games," raged Clapton official C.L. Richards.

Promotion and relegation between the leagues might have helped stir up interest among supporters tired of seeing their team playing the same sides, but tradition-bound competitions like the Athenian and Isthmian Leagues repeatedly rejected such ideas. Only the Amateur Cup would bring together England's disparate gentlemen, but even here crowds were starting to slide. From a full house a decade earlier, Wembley was not even half full for the first post-Rome Amateur Cup final between Walthamstow and West Auckland – a worrying trend that would continue.

Some of the more frustrated southern amateur clubs, such as Wimbledon, would slowly drift out of the amateur leagues, giving up their status as the home of gentlemen for a place in the semi-professional Southern League. After winning a handful of England amateur caps, Les Brown threw off the amateur status that his father had enjoyed and went pro with Wimbledon. The pro game was not for the entrepreneurial Brown. Leaving publishing, he started up a company that produced advertising on the back of parking tickets. He was so successful in this untapped market that he sold up at 60 and retired. He shares his time between the English south coast and Spain, but is not the only Olympian in his family. His daughter Karen played hockey for GB in three consecutive Olympics from 1988 to 1996, winning a bronze medal at Barcelona in 1992. She is the world's most capped player and after retiring went to the next three Olympics as the GB team's coach. Like Hunter Devine, Les Brown still has his blazer.

Brian Wakefield was never likely to go professional but he did leave Corinthian-Casuals for Kingstonian after the Games and also quit Wimpey.

"I didn't enjoy the commercial world," he admits. Brian Wakefield became a teacher, a role that all his team-mates agree he was born to do. A bastion of Middlesex Wanderers, whose first 100 years he documented in a book published in 2005, Wakefield returned to Corinthian-Casuals to run their veterans' team. To the great concern of many of his Olympic team-mates, the effervescent Brian Wakefield was still capably turning out in goal in his sixties.

His rival for the GB keeper's jersey, Mike Pinner, still had a part to play for the GB team, as did three Rome Olympians: Billy Neil, Roy Sleap and Hugh Lindsay. Despite seemingly missing out on his dream, Alf D'Arcy's Olympic goal would also be surprisingly revived, but not under the tutelage of Norman Creek.

CHAPTER ELEVEN: TOKYO 1964 AND GOODBYE NORMAN CREEK, HELLO CHARLES HUGHES

"We could not possibly delay the match because all of our players must be at work on Monday."

Norman Creek, GB Olympic manager

FOR A QUIETLY-SPOKEN, UNASSUMING MAN, NORMAN Creek had a great sense of occasion. He scored Corinth's first ever FA Cup goal against Brighton in 1922/23 and his last match was against Wiltshire in 1936, when he banged in four goals. On the way back from Italy, the diminutive Corinthinan knew that emulating the heroics played out at the last Olympics in Rome was virtually impossible. The world of the English gentlemen was dissolving.

In 1960, a report entitled "Sport and the Community" by the liberal-minded Lord Wolfenden, who three years previously recommended decriminalising homosexuality, advocated abolishing the distinction between amateurs and professionals. One of the Wolfenden Committee's members was Tony Pawson, who drafted some of the chapters. Pawson wrote that "the time had come to abolish the formal distinction between amateur and professional and to allow any participant, i.e. he or she wishes it, to be paid as a player without stigma, reproach or differentiation." Pawson's view was a minority one. Nothing happened. The divide remained but the foundations were crumbling.

The same year, football's exemption from entertainment tax, introduced during World War One, was scrapped. A decade earlier, Norman Ackland had claimed that amateur clubs were struggling to survive. The tax exemption and a share of receipts from booming Amateur Cup final attendances made that claim questionable – for the big clubs at least. With professional football regularly on TV, and attendances falling at club matches and the showpiece Amateur Cup, that claim was now more justifiable.

The nail in the coffin of the amateur game would be the end of the maximum wage. Bobby Brown's Fulham team-mate Jimmy Hill was leading the fight to end a distinction that left players on less than half the income enjoyed by the average manual workers. Football was an industry but years of intransigence and tradition had allowed the bosses to get away with paying the workers a pittance. As Bobby Brown mulled over his future, he was often cited in the media as an example of the harmful effects of the maximum wage. Why would Bobby Brown want to go pro, columnists screamed, for £20 a week and a career that was over at 30? If only Brown's career had lasted that long. When Newcastle's George Eastham quit football rather than play on and players threatened to strike, the end of the maximum wage came in 1961. "That was the death knell for the amateur game," says Brown.

Football had emulated cricket in staging an annual "gentlemen versus players" match, pitting the would-be heirs to Vivian Woodward against mostly working-class professional players. In 1962, this anachronism ended. The fixture was never played again but the advent of the maximum wage did not immediately sweep away the amateur game. The end would be torturous as pay scales did not balloon at the lower end of the professional game. When Fulham put star player Johnny Haynes on £100-a-week, the media were shocked; unlike many in the amateur game. "I was in the car going to a game when I heard about Haynes on the radio and laughed. I was earning nearly £70 a week from working and playing football," says one of the Isthmian League players that would feature in the next Olympic challenge. Not a boast, simply a fact.

Shamateurism was so rife that the idea of not getting some form of recompense was absurd. "Thinking back, we used to take the piss out of Corinthian-Casuals a bit because they were true amateurs and didn't get any money at all," says a sheepish John Ashworth. "I worked in a hat factory in 1963 and got £16 a week and a similar amount playing for Wealdstone."

Ashworth is sheepish because like virtually all the men who played for him, he liked and respected Norman Creek. Ashworth was involved with the Olympic team in the run-up to Rome, when he was with the Royal Navy and based in Glasgow. Most weekends, just as the Royal Navy had done with Paddy Hasty, Kingstonian chartered a helicopter to bring Ashworth home for Isthmian League fixtures. He appeared in the 1960 Amateur Cup final, but shortly before the Rome Olympic squad was announced Ashworth was posted to the Far East. He admits that taking Laurie Brown's position in 1960 was highly unlikely, but in the run-up to the 1964 Olympics in Tokyo his chances were revived. Brown was in the professional game and Ashworth was out of the Navy. Going to the Olympics was again a possibility.

Football would feature at the 1964 Olympics in Tokyo, although in Britain the amateur code was ever more of an outmoded relic. The brief resurgence of the pursist had faded by the early 1960s. The generation of post-war men who had left the military, worked and then gone to Oxford and Cambridge and led Pegasus to glory, had slowly disappeared. There were not sufficient gentlemen to share between Corinthian-Casuals and Pegasus. Scrapping the one-year rule enabled Pegasus to keep players like Mike Pinner and Brian Wakefield, who returned to the side after the Rome Olympics, but this also alienated ambitious undergraduates.

To restore Pegasus to glory, the club's committee took up Dick Sloley's idea and signed a deal to play four matches a season at White City. The ground where the 1920 Olympian Sloley had hoped to bring his Argonauts into the Football League and where Vivian Woodward lifted Olympic gold would again see top amateur football. Support for Pegasus in Cambridge was non-existent but taking games out of Oxford, whose fans so ardently embraced the Oxbridge team, proved a mistake. A mere 500 fans watched the first game at White City, a friendly with old rivals Bishop Auckland.

Over the years, Pegasus had brought top-class managers to the club like Vic Buckingham and Arthur Rowe, who invented the "push and run" style that won Spurs second and first division championships in 1950 and 1951. By 1961, Ken Shearwood, twice an Amateur Cup winner with Pegasus, was asked out of the blue to produce a revival.

If the club could not produce a gallop in the Amateur Cup, their exemption to the first round would be scrapped. Players' commitments to individual universities meant that fielding their XI before Christmas was virtually impossible. With the exemption to the first round this was not a problem, but the end of the exemption threatened the end of Pegasus. With Brian Wakefield in goal, Pegasus reached the second round in 1961 to keep their exemption but the following season were crushed 6-1 by Hendon in a first-round replay. In a bitter irony, Mike Pinner had briefly embraced the Isthmian League and was in the Hendon goal that day. The defeat forced Pegasus into the final round of qualifiers in 1962/63, where the team lost to Windsor & Eton. The gentlemen's dream was over. The club's last match against Marston in the Oxfordshire Senior Cup was on 6 April 1963. Two-times Amateur Cup winner Denis Saunders was still soldiering on, and Pegasus won but never played again. Tommy Thompson put the club in cold storage, never to emerge. Thompson said:

> "The climate of leading amateur football has deterio-rated so much in recent years that it is very doubtful whether at present the club has any useful function. On the other hand, illegal payments are widespread and amateur football is a misnomer. Even undergradu-ates have been attracted by such incentives. The general principles of loyalty which characterised the early spirit of the club are no longer regarded as desirable by some of the young players … An entirely different approach to amateurism is now necessary."

As Pegasus was about to be put down, a fleeting revival for the true amateur set came from another group of students, but not the Oxbridge set. Loughborough College had entered the Amateur Cup with little impact until 1960/61, when the team reached the second round for the first time and met Bishop Auckland. Bob Wilson was at Loughborough and his opposite number that day was Harry Sharratt. A crowd of 2,000 gathered around Loughborough's roped-off pitch to see Bishops outplayed. Loughborough won 3-1 and made the quarter-finals but, dogged by injuries, bowed out. The likes of Norman Ackland speculated that their students really could keep the amateur ideal aloft. Norman Creek knew better.

A keen cricketer, Creek watched as the distinction between gentlemen and players in the summer game was ditched in 1963. County teams traditionally used gentlemen as captains, although they were often employed in other roles, such as club secretary. Now, every cricketer was a player. Creek knew that football must follow sooner or later. When the Home Nations Olympic Committee convened on 1 October 1962 at the Great Western Hotel in Paddington, west London, an agreement was reached to send a team to Tokyo. Costings – later put at £15,000 – would be explored, but Creek knew his time was up.

The success of the World Cup continued to overshadow the Olympics, where football was dogged by the usual rows over amateurism. Despite this, 62 countries entered the race for a place in Tokyo. The allocation of places was far more equal than in the World Cup. In Europe, 22 countries would compete for just five places. Great Britain were one of four countries in a preliminary round along with Albania, Iceland and Bulgaria. Creek breathed a quiet sigh of relief as Bulgaria were avoided. Iceland came out of the hat. If successful, GB would take on Greece in the first round, but Creek would not be there.

He had already made his thoughts known to his employers and the FA went for a new approach. Walter Winterbottom was replaced as England manager by Alf Ramsey in 1963. Winterbottom also relinquished his post as director of coaching to Allen Wade, the mastermind behind Loughborough's Amateur Cup run. To support Wade an assistant director of coaching with additional responsibility for managing the England amateur team and the GB side would be recruited.

The FA lined up a five-man shortlist, which included 1956 Olympian Dexter Adams, who in 1961 had managed Hendon to the Athenian League title. Before the interview stage, Adams withdrew, as did another candidate, the England amateur and Woking forward Charlie Mortimer. "The FA wanted another schoolteacher," says Adams. A further candidate, Pat Welton, was a teacher and juggled this job with managing Walthamstow and the England youth team. Welton was overlooked, along with Clive Bond, whose footballing experience was mainly overseas.

The job went to an ambitious young former Loughborough student teaching at Leigh Grammar School. Charles Hughes is a divisive figure in the history of English football, an easy but often unwarranted receptacle for many of those looking for someone to blame for the failures of English football during the 1970s and 1980s. In the early 1960s he was an enthusiastic young teacher with ambitions to be a coach. Hughes was as disappointed as the rest of England over the national team's low standing on the world stage. He was fascinated by theories developed during the 1950s by Charles Reep, an accountant and ex-RAF wing commander, whose exhaustive study of a host of big matches showed that most goals came from less than three passes. Reep developed a theory known as the Position of Maximum Opportunity (POMO), which he expounded in the pages of *Match Analysis* magazine. Stan Cullis employed the theories with Bill Slater's Wolves to great success, but most clubs ignored Reep. Hughes was a keen reader of *Match Analysis*. He brought Reep's theories and his own ambition to FA coaching weekends, where he gained his coaching badges and made contacts.

"I met all sorts of interesting people like Jackie Milburn, who was on my course," recalls Hughes. "I passed, which was quite surprising, and Jackie Milburn didn't. I kept saying to him, 'I wish I could play like you' and he said 'I wish I could coach like you'. It was all flannel."

Hughes pauses before continuing: "I was doing some FA coaching during my holidays in Easter 1963 and getting to know some of the top coaches. Norman Creek eventually said to me, 'I'm going to retire soon. Would you be interested in my job?' I said I certainly would." As Hughes readily admits, "there was a strong ethic in the FA that the Corinthian spirit prevailed". Hughes was no Corinthian or member of the Oxbridge set, where POMO found little favour, but he brought to the FA a more pragmatic, professional approach, which was ironic as his initial role was with the amateurs.

Hughes did not want to leave his headmaster in the lurch, so he gave a term's notice. He would not start his new role as FA assistant director of coaching and manager of the England amateur and GB XIs until the New Year. That meant that Norman Creek would take charge of the first set of qualifiers and the old Corinthian ran the rule over potentials in a handful of friendlies, before selecting a squad who spent seven weekends holed up in Chelsea Barracks. England had beaten Iceland 1-0 in an amateur international in 1961 and the selection for the first Olympic qualifier heavily favoured English players. With the FA again controlling the finances, once more the other Home Nations conceded selection to the English. Billy Neil and Peter Buchanan, a combustible forward also at Queen's Park, were the only non-Englishmen chosen to travel to Reykjavik.

7 September 1963
Reykjavik. Iceland vs GB

Today, Reykjavik is a popular weekend destination. In 1963, getting to the capital of Iceland, then a poor European backwater, was far harder. Before departing, the squad were not sure if the match would be on grass or a lava pitch, which would have entailed both sets of players wearing gloves and bandages on their arms and legs.

Before the GB squad left, preparations were thrown into turmoil when the prolific Buchanan was injured, forcing Creek to abandon his proposed 4-2-4 formation. On boarding the plane, Creek's valedictory trip started to get even worse. The plane was delayed and the team arrived early Saturday morning for a game that afternoon. Players like Wealdstone's Charlie Townsend wanted to sleep, not play a game of football. The Icelanders suggested putting the game back a day. "We could not possibly delay the match because all of our players must be at work on Monday," replied Creek, who had travelled out with Harold Thompson and Jack Bowers.

Fortunately for the GB team, the weather was dreadful. GB won the toss. Kicking off with a gale blowing behind them, a GB side featuring ten Englishmen cruised into a 2-0 lead after just six minutes, courtesy of Walthamstow's Brian Harvey and Brian Martin of Wimbledon. Deflated, the Icelanders proved no match for Hugh Lindsay, now at Wealdstone, who grabbed two more goals. Three minutes after the restart, Candey made the score 5-0 and then ran through the Icelandic defence to set up Martin for his second.

For the return in south London a week later, Buchanan was still out. The only non-Englishmen were Billy Neil and Jimmy Quail, who played at Hendon having left Ulster aged three. The dominant Northern league side were 1962 Amateur Cup winners Crook, but in Reykjavik, the northern gentlemen's only representative was a squad player from Bishop Auckland. For the return, the entire Northern League was snubbed.

With an unassailable lead, Creek could have experimented, but in the last months of his reign the GB team contracted into an Isthmian League XI with the odd guest. Within this side, Jimmy Quail encountered what Alf D'Arcy had four years before – further divides. "For people like Alf and myself, it was probably the first time we'd ever been away for the night [but] there were these perceived rules and regulations and if you got on the wrong side, you were told – but only afterwards," says Quail, who worked in the print industry, adding:

> "People don't realise what a big class divide there was then; not as big as cricket, but it was there. Norman Creek was very upmarket. The feeling I got was that if there is someone who had to be left out it would be the raggedy-arsed bloke from down the road rather than a university graduate. There was nothing wrong with being a toff or coming from a normal working-class background but it always felt they were favoured. The northern sides were definitely not university graduates and were physically stronger because they were manual workers. Sometimes, they looked like they'd just come out of the mines."

Quail encountered these divides not just in England, and his appearance in the Northern Ireland amateur team proved brief. After just a couple of caps he was dropped, never to return, as the IFA's focus stayed on players from their Irish League.

Staging the return Olympic leg was a reward for Wimbledon winning the Amateur Cup in 1963. With three Wimbledon players in the starting XI, the match deserved more support than the 3,500 who turned up, but this was indicative of the GB team's standing. Few gentlemen graced the Football League anymore and a chasm was opening up between the two codes, which players like Charlie Townsend felt was no longer worth trying to cross.

Townsend was offered a pro contract by Watford after leaving school but wanted to complete his training as a carpenter first. "I was in Bill Nicholson's office once. He asked me to come and play for the reserves at Spurs, but what with working, England amateurs and the GB team, there wasn't time and I said no," says Townsend. For players mulling over a brief, still poorly paid career in the lower reaches of the Football League, the amateur game provided attractions like trips to exotic locales like Reykjavik and – presuming there was no incredible upset in the return – the Greek capital of Athens.

14 September 1963
Plough Lane, London. GB vs Iceland

If GB had any sort of target to aim for, the crowd at Wimbledon might have been better, but the Icelanders had already been humiliated once. The visitors did set one world record in Wimbledon as Gunnar, Hordur and Bjarni Felixson became the first set of three brothers to start an international football match together, but the Icelanders were no world beaters on the pitch. "The whole affair was so overwhelmingly lopsided that one thought idly of escape to the Church Hall next door, where giant marrows in a garden produce show might have been more competitive," wrote one watching journalist.

GB scored early with a header from Enfield's powerful striker Tommy Lawrence. When Brian Martin broke his leg after ten minutes and John Ashworth badly gashed his head shortly afterwards, Iceland seemingly had a chance to reclaim some pride. With no substitutes permitted, GB would play the rest of the match with nine men. But Hugh Lindsay was far too skilful for the Icelandic midfield, while Charlie Townsend remorselessly broke up the visitors' attacks with rapid interceptions and swift passes.

The Icelanders were 2-0 down before half-time, Lawrence scoring a second. Ashworth returned at half-time but had to go off again after 20 minutes. Lawrence got his hat-trick with a penalty before Brian Harvey rounded off an easy 4-0 win 10-0 on aggregate. The next round would not be so easy, but Norman Creek had done his bit.

The Iceland match also saw the end of Mike Pinner's Olympic career. After combining Pegasus games with ad hoc Football League matches at the likes of Arsenal, Aston Villa, Manchester United, Sheffield Wednesday and QPR, he finally joined the players. The preceding season, Stan Charlton had captained Leyton Orient into the first division for the first time and Pinner joined the 1952 Olympian, signing part-time professional forms. Pinner says:

> "When you are training as an articled clerk, you get al-
> most no money and I needed the money by this time.
> Orient were only 20 minutes away from where I lived.
> The internationals were good fun but I'd played in 50 or

so [for England and Great Britain] by then and didn't think there seemed to be any prospect of further Olympics as it had been difficult enough to qualify and was getting worse."

Having been a reserve to Pinner in an England amateur international, Bob Wilson harboured thoughts of making up for his disappointment in 1960 and making the Olympic set-up. Wilson's expected graduation into the professional game was well known. The only unknown was the club. Wolves were tipped but Wilson went to Arsenal, initially as a gentleman. Arsenal made clear to Wilson that he would go professional the next year, which was the FA's justification for overlooking him. The selectors turned to a Belfast teacher called John Kennedy, who caught the selectors' eyes after Distillery – one of Belfast's smaller clubs – won the Northern Irish league in 1962/63. That win took Kennedy into the European Cup and a first-round clash with Portuguese legends Benfica. On a cold wet night in Belfast, a side led by Eusebio were surprisingly held to a 3-3 draw.

With Hughes at the helm, the GB squad went back to regular training weekends followed by a Monday night fixture against leading professional opposition. Norman Creek, who still took the odd training session, had only chosen the GB team on away matches, letting the selectors have their say at home. Charles Hughes typically developed his own approach that would in time not find favour with the other Home Nations.

"There was a selection committee but in the end they left it to me," he says. "Wales and Northern Ireland were never going to turn up many of the players of the right quality and that's the same today. It was harder for the Welsh players but some of them were in the Isthmian League like Terry Casey."

After an English-dominated preliminary, the squad became more representative of Great Britain with Casey and John Evans, both team-mates of Wilson at Loughborough, entering the frame. Cardiff Corinthians supplied players to the Welsh amateur XI but were short of Isthmian League standard, says Casey, who had marked his Welsh amateur debut with a spectacular goal in a 3-3 draw with England watched by Hughes. "There were not really amateur clubs in Wales, more semi-pro clubs like Llandudno and Colwyn Bay. Cardiff Corries were not the same standard as Barnet," says Casey, identifying the lack of Welsh players in the set-up.

After leaving Loughborough, Casey took a teaching job in Hertfordshire and joined Alf D'Arcy at Barnet, his expenses from football equalling his take-home pay from teaching. From Llanroost, Casey could see the same rifts that dogged the English amateur game in his homeland. A player that had tried to play professionally but not lasted the distance could get reinstated as an amateur, but not everyone succeeded. The unwritten criteria in England and Wales seemed, to some players at least, to be based on class. "If they were professional people, they would probably get reinstated," says Casey. "There was a bit of a divide."

Two more Ulster-based Northern Irish players took part in the friendlies, providing a squad that was more representative of Great Britain and Northern Ireland for the Greek games. Hughes is keen to stress that the squad for the qualifiers was Creek's but the incoming manager made one significant change: a recall for the outcast, Alf D'Arcy. "The FA put their hands up and said they didn't want me but Charlie was a tremendous politician and manipulated the system," says D'Arcy, who tragically lost his brother Dennis in a car accident in the run-up to the Tokyo Olympics. "Charlie would let the FA have their picks in the squad and he'd have his picks, then when it came down to the match he'd put in his players."

Hughes initially trod carefully but the previous approach meant little. Of the Olympic qualifiers, Hughes says, "The philosophy the players had was to win at home and draw away but I couldn't see the sense in that. Surely you should try and win them all. Winning's important – you enjoy it more when you win."

The difference in management was immediately obvious to amateurs who played under both Creek and Hughes, then in his early thirties and barely older than many of his squad. "Norman Creek was a real gentleman. Charlie Hughes was more of a schoolmaster. You didn't want to cross him," recalls Wimbledon's John Martin. Derek Gamblin says: "It all changed when Norman went and it became professional."

In the land of Hughes's first-round opponents, the game was in turmoil. Shamateurism ruled until 1963, when the Greek Olympic Committee recommended to the Greek FA that professionalism be introduced. This would comprise five year contracts, a maximum of 18 pros per club in the top two leagues with first division players on £75 a month and £50 for those in the second division. A codicil was added that these professionals must also have a job outside of the game. Amidst this chaotic new dawn, the Greeks found a team of players still classed as amateurs to travel to London. Although Evans missed out on a place in the squad, Terry Casey was on the bench. With the Welsh Casey in the squad, players from all four Home Nations would take part.

12 February 1964
Stamford Bridge, London. GB vs Greece
GB started brightly but, after 20 minutes, their momentum began to ebb. Only hard tackling typically led by the recalled D'Arcy kept the home side in the game. The skilful Greeks whizzed the ball about but, prompted by Jimmy Quail, GB fought their way back. The Northern Irishman created chances for Tommy Lawrence and Billy Campbell, another Distillery player, who was included up front, but the Greeks held firm. Then on 30 minutes, Quail chipped the Greek defence and Lawrence ran onto the ball to power a hard shot home. Shortly after, Quail again ran past a trio of Greek players, refusing to buckle underneath two crude challenges, before centering for Buchanan to score.

The scoreline at half-time was encouraging but, after the break, Papaioannou, a Greek Under-23 international, dribbled through four home players to score a sensational goal. Townsend then tested the agile Greek keeper Paschalis. Martin hit the post from a free kick, again delivered by Quail, but GB could not add to their scoreline despite Buchanan challenging Paschalis at every attempt. With ten minutes to go, Zaderglou tried to prevent a Buchanan header on goal and was left with a broken collarbone. The Greeks would not forget. The visitors forced two good chances and nearly equalised but GB finished on top, with Harvey, Townsend and Buchanan going close without scoring.

The night of the game, GB's half a dozen non-English players returned to their hotel to find the Greeks also staying there. In the bar, a confrontation blew up between the Greeks and the Brits over Buchanan's challenge. "There was a bit of a contretemps and I didn't have much back up because the other English lads had gone home," says Buchanan with relish. The feisty game at Stamford Bridge would produce an interesting encounter in Athens.

After the first leg, friendlies continued against first division sides. Most of GB's Football League opponents fielded reserves, reflecting the low standing of Hughes's team. Just 1,151 people turned up for a game with Chelsea, producing gate receipts of a paltry £120. At Old Trafford the gate was mildly more encouraging, but 6,000 people made little impact in such a grand amphitheatre. Hughes used these fixtures to try out a new tactic. He had identified one Greek midfielder from the first leg as their creative hub. In the return, this player would be marked out of the game. Hugh Lindsay, perhaps GB side's most naturally gifted ball-player, was given the task and would rehearse for this role in the friendlies. "I was our playmaker," sighs Lindsay. "The first time we tried that was against Manchester United and Eamon Dunphy ran rings round me." Lindsay realised that to stay in the team he had to keep his own counsel. He adds: "I know of several talented players that disagreed with Charlie and never played again."

One of the final friendlies before the visit to Athens was against Coventry, whose manager, Jimmy Hill, fielded a strong side featuring many first-class players. When George Curtis and Tommy Lawrence accidentally clashed heads, the Enfield striker and British amateur of the year in 1963 was left with a depressed fracture of the skull.

The return was initially scheduled for 11 March, but the death of King Paul of Greece saw this fixture cancelled. Greece asked for a new date of 26 March but GB could not make that. Fifa were asked to extend the deadline for completion of the first round of Olympic qualifiers to 8 April.

8 April 1964
Karaiskaki Stadium, Athens. Greece vs GB

The GB squad flew out accompanied by Mike "Tagge" Webster, a former player with Corinthian-Casuals and the Oxbridge universities representative at the FA – the purists again keeping a close eye on the Olympic project. When Hughes's team arrived, the GB players found there was considerably more interest in their team in Athens with 20,000 raucous fans in the ground. Neil and D'Arcy missed out due to injury but the bulk of the GB side remained the same. Casey travelled as a reserve along with a last-minute addition, a young southerner called Derek Gamblin.

At Stamford Bridge, Lindsay had been dropped in favour of his old schoolfriend Quail. For the return, Quail would sit out the game as Lindsay took on his new task. To the frustration of Hughes and Lindsay, the Greek player earmarked for man-marking was missing; so were many of his team-mates from Stamford Bridge; a very different looking Greek side turned up. Hughes's tactics suffered another setback. John Kennedy explains: "Before the game, the FA secretary Denis Follows came in and said there was to be no charging of the goalkeeper in this game. That was the way we were going to beat them. It wasn't often we were told that."

The Greeks scored after just three minutes when Mavrides beat Kennedy from 35 yards. An onslaught threatened. "As soon as we started, we knew we were in trouble," recalls Ashworth. "They just tore us to pieces. We kept looking at each other and couldn't understand what was going on."

The Greek players Mavridis and Pomonis were in charge, only to see their forwards waste chance after chance. Dogged British defending kept the scoreline to 1-0 at half-time, with Skevofyian even missing a penalty. British attacks were rare but, on 74 minutes, Buchanan netted a shock equaliser. The Greeks charged into attack on the restart and Papaioannou, one of the few players left from the first leg, quickly reclaimed the lead.

The Britons suffered with the heat and hard pitch. Ten minutes before the end, with substitutes now permitted, the injured John Martin was replaced by Gamblin. With eight minutes left, the aggregate scores were, surprisingly level, only for Greece to be awarded a penalty. Papazoglou rammed the ball home. When Papaioannou added his second two minutes later, the result was confirmed: A convincing home win and elimination for GB.

"We fell apart but it was because they were full-time and their fitness told," says Kennedy. With the Greek game in upheaval during the transition from shamateurism to professionalism, the home side had not even bothered with the pretence of fielding supposed amateurs. Greece had simply fielded a team of professionals.

This revelation surfaced two days after the game. The Greek Olympic Committee immediately withdrew their football team in shame and disassociated themselves with their country's footballers. "Inconceivable, unbelievable, tragically wrong," roared the Greek press in protest over the decision to withdraw. For the British, a glimpse of a return opened. Norman Creek had travelled to Paris on Hughes's behalf to watch France be eliminated by Czechoslovakia, who lay in wait. The Italian FA invited the GB team to an amateur tournament in Liguria in May 1964, which would be a useful rehearsal, but the British had reached the end of this Olympic road.

At the 1964 BOA annual dinner on 4 July 1964, Gerry and the Pacemakers entertained and the Peter Stuyvesant girls distributed free cigarettes after dinner, but there would be no British footballers at the Olympics that summer. The FA refused to re-enter, ignoring the vociferous protests of the players. The reason was pragmatic. "The FA didn't want to pursue it as the next team to play were Czechoslovakia and they were European champions," explains Kennedy.

The veterans Lindsay and Neil would get another chance, but Peter Buchanan's Olympic dream was over. He explains: "In a game at Chelsea, I scored in the first half and [Charles Hughes] subbed me at half-time because we all had to play in these little boxes. I was in the wrong box but I still scored. After the match I gave him a mouthful." Buchanan played on until 1969 and was top scorer for the Spiders in every season. He has never seen Charles Hughes since returning from Athens.

Czechoslovakia travelled to Tokyo without even playing a qualifier. They were one of Europe's five finalists, all from Eastern Europe. Italy's under-21 team prevailed against Poland in the qualifiers but made the mistake of flaunting their status as supposed amateurs. The Italians Mazzola and Facchetti had won the World Club championship with Inter and pocketed a bonus rumoured to be £1,800. Most of the Italians were earning close to £15,000 a year but were deemed amateur due to their FA's crazy ruling that anyone under 21 was not professional. Eventually, the Italian Olympic Committee intervened. Italy's footballers withdrew, reducing the tournament to a 15-team event. Hungary, Czechoslovakia and East Germany won gold, silver and bronze respectively.

GB missed the finals of an Olympic football tournament for the first time since Amsterdam in 1928. The GB side had been undermined and eliminated by opponents who had not played by the rules – a frustrating sign of what was to come. Charles Hughes had a four-year wait for another attempt at qualification, during which time the old concept of a traditional amateur virtually disappeared. Some clubs like Terry Casey's Barnet simply turned professional and joined the Southern league. "Rather than pay people and get caught, they just went pro," says Casey, who signed semi-professional forms with Barnet and later travelled the world working for Fifa. Charlie Townsend would return to the Olympic fray, as would Roy Sleap, who was on the fringes in 1964. But that year's failure would see many other players in that squad drift out of contention for the next Olympic challenge.

Distillery's Billy Campbell later went professional, playing for Sunderland, Dundee and Motherwell and winning six full caps for Northern Ireland. After the Greece game, John Kennedy was also called up for the full Northern Ireland team as a reserve goalkeeper to Pat Jennings for an away World Cup qualifier in Lausanne against Switzerland. A young 18-year-old called George Best was in the squad. Kennedy was charged with seeing the prodigy safely back home after the squad landed in Belfast. The Manchester United youngster and the rest of the side received a £60 match fee. As an amateur, Kennedy got nothing. "The IFA had a meeting in Switzerland to see if they could give me extra expenses but decided that they couldn't break their own rules, so all the players had a whip round to pay for my fee," says Kennedy. "It was very kind of them but terribly embarrassing."

Kennedy later signed for Celtic, where he stayed for a number of years, but was mostly third choice behind one of his Olympic predecessors, Ronnie Simpson. Leaving for Lincoln, he combined teaching with football, and nearly forgot his brief sojourn with the Olympic team until he retired from teaching in 1995. Kennedy adds:

> "Each time I was away [with the Olympic team], I got a letter saying I wouldn't be paid as an amateur and was being taken out of service. Back then, I didn't know what it meant and didn't really care but, when I retired, I found out the education authority in Northern Ireland had deducted 16 days from my pension. Looking back now, I think that's a bit mean spirited."

CHAPTER TWELVE: MEXICO 1968 AND A FRAGILE ALLIANCE SHATTERS

"I feel that a player, when he accepts the honour to play for Great Britain, must accept responsibilities. He must subordinate other loyalties. He must put his priorities in the right order. If eight or ten players put their clubs first, it could make the whole policy of the Olympic team impossible. My position would become untenable."

GB manager, Charles Hughes

BY THE LATE 1960S THE AMATEUR GAME HAD CHANGED beyond recognition. Amateurs bulked out Football League clubs' reserve sides but the gentlemen were rarer than ever in the first XIs of the professional game. Amateurs might play a handful of league games with the pros but often only as a preamble before signing professional forms. The maximum wage had not unleashed a tsunami-like boom in earnings and footballers with a decent education or a well-paid trade still often saw little point in joining the professionals.

The easy-going former Hendon striker Roddy Haider recalls:

"I remember playing for Charlton one rainy night in November in a reserve game at QPR. I'd been offered a contract by Charlton but I was also on the verge of the England amateur team. There were three or four amateurs playing in that match and the only ones trying – apart from Keith Peacock – were the amateurs. The professionals were just strolling about, not really trying. It brought it home to me that to them it was a job but to me it was a release.

"Manchester United had just got into Europe but none of the other pro clubs had, it was really just the amateur clubs [that travelled]. I worked for an insurance company, who encouraged me. I got eight to ten weeks a year paid leave to travel round the world playing football."

Haider is convinced that most of the players in the 1968 GB team could have at least played in today's version of the Championship, where a good wage back then might have been £50 or £60 a week at best. In contrast, the amateur game offered experiences that were rare even at the top of the professional English game: a chance to travel in style paid for by the FA and to be an international, albeit within the limitations of the gentlemen's game. For players with a decent education, a well-paid job or a good trade, the professional game was simply not that attractive to the likes of Roddy Haider. Some players considered turning pro but had bad experiences like Jimmy Quail, who was at Crystal Palace under Arthur Rowe but found his successor Dick Graham so difficult that the Irishman vowed to stay amateur.

John Swannell played briefly for Corinthian-Casuals, who were forced back into the Amateur Cup qualifying rounds again in 1967. Another would-be 1968 Olympian, John Robertson of Tooting & Mitcham, also turned out for the club but, even with the attraction of playing at The Oval, holding onto players remained difficult and a divide remained. After Swannell left for Hendon, a Corinthian-Casuals official sent the young keeper a letter, criticising him for leaving. "My mum was very upset when she saw the letter," says Swannell. While at Manchester University, Swannell signed as an amateur for Stockport County but, like his future club and international team-mate Haider, he too was not impressed. "I didn't like the attitude of some of the players – do as little as possible at training, and then go to a greyhound meeting in the afternoon," says Swannell. "That didn't appeal to me."

Derek Gamblin had not been impressed by the pros either. He signed as an amateur at Portsmouth and made his first XI debut on the final day of the 1965/66 season. After the game, Pompey manager George Smith offered Gamblin a chance to join the pros. Suspecting this was going to happen, Gamblin had asked Charles Hughes for advice. Hughes suggested asking for a £5,000 signing on fee. Smith refused and Gamblin objected, citing a far greater sum paid to a professional, who was released 12 months later. "I can see we're not going to get on," said Smith before telling Gamblin to get out of his office and the club. Gamblin never looked back, embracing the dying days of the amateur game. "We had new suits and new bags [from the FA], all the lads had half-decent jobs and were seeing the world for nothing," says Gamblin.

The top of the amateur game had changed from one with at least a nod to the old ideals into a scene far more recognisable now. "It was already like non-league is today," says Gamblin's Sutton team-mate Dario Gradi, who had played in Loughborough's Amateur Cup run before moving into teaching.

His ambitions already lay in coaching but Gradi played in a number of the GB side's warm-up games for 1968 until unwittingly becoming tied up in the new FA rules aimed at combating shamateurism. "I was working as a regional coach for the FA and they decided that because of that I was a professional," explains Gradi. "It was all a bit of politics and that was their answer but I accepted it as I was on my way to working as a coach at Chelsea then."

The FA had not targeted Gradi but were bound by their own strictures aimed at hunting out the shamateur. These included classing illegal payments as misconduct and demanding signed declarations from clubs entering the Amateur Cup that players were not being paid. Any player or club who refused to sign would immediately be under suspicion, complained the Isthmian League, who insisted that the proposals did nothing to stop professional clubs making secret payments to amateurs to play in their reserve teams.

"It seems that the FA, once more are merely fulfilling their historic role of compromise while those who remember true-blue amateurism as it once was are making their last, fighting stand before realism and the hard economic facts of the new age finally overtake them," wrote the football correspondent of *The Times* about the new rules.

253

Behind this last-ditch attempt was Harold Thompson, by this time on the FA Council committee, where he was trying to combat the perfidy of the shamateurs. Amidst Thompson's crusade and the turmoil this created in the amateur game, Charles Hughes set about trying to modernise the game.

Unlike his friend Alf Ramsey, there was no World Cup for Hughes to aim for. Olympic football was the chalice of the amateur game until 1967, when in belated recognition of the FA's post-Melbourne recommendations, Uefa set up an international tournament. In 1964 the IOC had demanded that Fifa set up an amateur section or football would be withdrawn from the Olympics. But to Hughes's embarrassment, England's debut in the inaugural European amateur championships was dismal. Like Alf Ramsey, Hughes eschewed flair players, preferring to stifle the opposition and prevent them playing, but his side were eliminated in the qualifiers by Austria. A Scottish side featuring mainly Queen's Park players qualified for the finals in Spain and reached the final, narrowly losing to an Austrian team inspired by future World Cup star Josef Hickersberger.

Buoyed by the success of their amateur XI, the SFA finally agreed to help bankroll the cost of attempting to qualify for Mexico. A Scotsman, Tom Patterson, was provided as a selector. The Northern Irish and the Welsh remained lukewarm at best to the Olympic project and declined to contribute financially. With the FA putting up most of the funds, the other three men on the selection committee aimed at finding players for Charles Hughes were English.

For all Thompson's railing, in 1968 the amateur game still had an important function for the FA, who staged a game at Enfield between Hughes's team and Alf Ramsey's world cup winners. "They told us not to put in any crunching tackles," recalls Roddy Haider. The GB team had a more important role to play than providing tame friendly opposition for Ramsey's squad – but only if they could reach the Mexico Olympics.

A total of 81 countries entered the race for a place in the Mexico Olympics, which would be staged at high altitude conditions that many athletes and footballers had never been subject to. Two years later, Ramsey would take his World Cup winners to Mexico to defend their trophy. If GB could qualify, their experiences playing in Mexico would be vital to Ramsey. For the GB players, the reward for Olympic qualification was greater than ever – the trip of a lifetime. Haider adds: "The FA arranged for us to go to Mexico for eight weeks if we qualified. They wanted to do tests on us to check how the altitude would affect us and use them for the full England side."

Hughes was doing everything possible to make the GB set-up more professional within the wearisome constraints placed on him by the "amateur" ethos. To try and give his players an edge in the often unequal contests they faced, Hughes floated the idea of his England amateur XI entering the Isthmian League or even all join one club. Enfield was mooted but nothing materialised. Hughes's focus on organisation and efficiency helped his players compensate against better teams from countries with a looser approach to amateurism. But a greater onus on this more muscular approach and the accompanying tactics made the game harder for ball-players, particularly shorter ones like Hugh Lindsay.

Lindsay says: "The game was condensed to ten yards either side of the halfway line. I found myself getting bypassed as everyone played with a big number nine and the ball was whacked up to him, but I was looking to put my foot on the ball." The rugged defender Alf D'Arcy was still playing. Having won the 1967 Amateur Cup with Enfield, he had not quite given up on an Olympic quest that began back in 1956.

Hughes was able to choose his own side with a little input from the selectors, but the notion of a GB team, like amateurism itself, was dying. A "British Amateur Select" took on Queen's Park at Hampden in early August 1967 to celebrate the centenary of the famous Scottish gentlemen's club. Glenavon's Dennis Guy played up front and another Irishman, Jackie Patterson of Crusaders, was in defence. Gilbert Lloyd of Llanelli, who would go on to win more amateur caps (33) than any other Welshman, was also among the subs but this was not the GB Olympic team.

The IFA not only declined to make any financial contributions but also to nominate any players. "The Irish FA opted out of the 1968 Olympic qualifiers because they contended there were no candidates from here," says Irish football historian Malcolm Brodie. No players from the Irish League would get a chance, nor would Jimmy Quail but the London-based Irishman knew that he was being left behind in every sense. Quail recalls:

> "[Before Charles Hughes], no tactics were even talked about. It sorted out the men from the boys, those that could play and those that couldn't. I don't even recall

any free kick training but England won the World Cup paying 4-3-3, which cut space down in the middle of the park. After Ramsey and '66, you had to conform, do things a certain way and I was an awkward bugger and liked to do things my own way."

Amateurs from Wales were considered but failed to make an impression on the GB selectors for the 1968 qualifiers. "I think part of the problem with the Welsh and Irish," offers Derek Gamblin, "was because they couldn't get together as often as the English players did."

A few days after the Queen's Park centenary game, Hughes's initial GB squad set off on a brief tour to Dublin, Iceland and Sweden. The trip was originally an England amateur affair but when some invited players dropped out through injuries and work commitments, the FA agreed to use the programme as a pre-Olympic tour. Four Queen's Park players and George Cumming from Partick Thistle joined the trip. All three tour matches were won but GB needed two own goals to make headway in Reykjavik before Roddy Haider sealed a 3-0 win over Iceland. The tour barely attracted the attention of the SFA but afterwards Hughes took time to write individually to all his players – English and Scots – thanking them for their contribution to the "excellent" team spirit. George Cumming's "thoughtfulness" and "unselfish efforts" were noted by Hughes in his letter to the Partick Thistle player.

Back home, the friendlies with league clubs continued, including a memorable game with a strong, motivated Chelsea side at Stamford Bridge. To ensure decent opposition the Chelsea team were put on a win bonus, but the Olympians triumphed, prompting a mini-riot among the handful of fans at Stamford Bridge. Disgusted with the Chelsea performance, the crossbar was pulled down.

The Isthmian League clubs were supportive of releasing players for Hughes's training get-togethers at Bisham Abbey ahead of the first qualifying match away in West Germany. For these clubs, the success of the England amateur and GB teams helped justify the continuation of the amateur classification. Queen's Park had no such needs. When Hughes asked the Spiders' players he had selected for the first leg – Niall Hopper, Millar Hay and Billy Neil – to miss a league game, the fragile Olympic coalition fell apart.

Hughes's sometimes abrupt manner did not help but the SFA's concern was ensuring that Queen's Park put out a full-strength side for a fixture with Arbroath. This took priority over the Olympic side. The losers were the players. Billy Neil says:

> "The club demanded I played for them and was told if I didn't play, then I would be banned sine die [for life]. I went back to the GB committee and said I had to play for the club. It all went on for a while and eventually I said I wouldn't play. That was the end of it for me."

Hughes eventually relented and agreed to let the three Scotsmen come down, but there was no repairing the rift. No Scotsmen would travel to Augsburg, much to Hughes's disgust. In 1967, he said: "I feel that a player, when he accepts the honour to play for Great Britain, must accept responsibilities. He must subordinate other loyalties. He must put his priorities in the right order. If eight or ten players put their clubs first, it could make the whole policy of the Olympic team impossible. My position would become untenable."

Hughes planned to take 16 men to Augsburg and named a squad of 20 players well before the row erupted. The loss of Neil, Hay and Hopper, coupled with other drop-outs through injury, was a crippling blow. Hughes says:

> "The Scots wanted to have a little protest of their own; not the players, who wanted to play. We should have taken 16 players to Germany but we'd named our squad and couldn't change it so we went out with 12 fit players. The twelfth player was Peter Deadman, who was on the bench with an ankle injury. In the circumstances, the result was quite outstanding."

GB's opponents in the qualifiers faced even worse internal wrangles. West Germany had been recognised by the IOC in 1951 and East Germany provisionally four years later. One condition of East Germany's recognition by the IOC was that an all-German football team was put together before any Olympic qualifiers started. In protest, West Germany withdrew from the Melbourne Olympics.

For the 1960 Games, the East Germans proposed a play-off to settle which side would enter the qualifiers. West Germany surprisingly beat East Germany's professional amateurs 4-1 over two highly secretive legs played behind closed doors, but failed to qualify for Rome. Four years later the Berlin Wall was up and East Germany triumphed 3-0 in front of 50,000 fans in Karl-Marx-Stadt (now Chemnitz). West Germany won the return in Hanover 2-1 but the East Germans went through and claimed bronze.

In 1965 East Germany was fully recognised by the IOC and both sides entered separate teams, but the indignity of the Tokyo qualifiers had stung the West Germans. For the Mexico qualifiers, 21 leading West German amateurs pledged not to join the professionals until their side were eliminated from the Olympics, whether in Mexico or earlier. The West German squad even held a ceremony in Frankfurt to cement this pledge, although their approach to amateurism would not have sat easily with any true British gentlemen. "In the German team there were also players which were paid," explains West Germany's star player, Rainer Zobel, who later won three Bundesliga titles with Bayern Munich in the 1970s and a hat-trick of European Cup wins from 1974 to 1976.

"Some of these players played in the first Bundesliga [in West Germany] like Helmut Bergfelder and Paul Alger [FC Koln] and Gunter Keifler [Eintracht Frankfurt]. Payment was legal but limited. I earned in those years 1,200 German Marks [about £550 a year], which I think was the highest."

The West Germany Olympic squad also had half a dozen players playing in the second tier of the Bundesliga like Egon Schmidt of Kickers Offenbach, who were ultimately facing an Isthmian League XI. Udo Lattek was in charge but the only manager to win the European Cup, Cup Winners' Cup and Uefa Cup with different teams would find himself outmanoeuvred by Charles Hughes.

25 October 1967
Rosenau Stadium, Augsburg. West Germany vs GB

Peter Deadman took his seat in the away dugout at the Rosenau Stadium in his full kit. GB's only spare player – apart from back-up keeper John Shippey of Oxford United – grimaced in pain as he pulled socks over a severely swollen ankle in the changing rooms. Fortunately for his team-mates, none of the German contingent noticed him bravely hobbling into the dug-out, clearly in no state to replace anyone if an on-field substitute were needed.

Autumn hung in the Augsburg air as the GB team filed out. Hughes's squad had returned to an England amateur side but his team of players would be a great advert for the Isthmian League. The Germans only left their training camp in Munich hours before kick-off. After a bright opening ten minutes the hosts, playing to a 1-4-3-2 formation, looked lost against a determined GB side. A crowd of 8,000 saw Hendon's David Hogwood open the scoring on 21 minutes and GB overpowered the hosts in every sense.

Keifler, Ahmann and Thelen all had to leave the pitch for treatment in the first half. Just before half-time, Zobel replaced Bauerkamper only for Bergfelder to suffer concussion moments later and go off for good. With only one substitute then allowed, West Germany were down to ten men. By the 63rd minute, Faltermeier was so badly injured that he could only limp around the pitch, but he refused to come off and leave the hosts with only nine players.

GB won a penalty on 72 minutes; German keeper Schuilte parried Andrews's spot-kick but Sutton United's Larry Pritchard sealed a deserved 2-0 win three minutes later.

For the teenage Gunter Keifler, the visitors had gone too far. "If we fought with such roughness as that in the Bundesliga, then I'd hang up my football boots," he reflected after the match, but the British press were less sympathetic. "The prima donna antics of the Germans were, to be blunt, laughable," wrote one watching British journalist.

Lattek accepted the defeat, saying: "The guests were better, but they took their physicality too far." For Charles Hughes this did not matter. He had emulated his mentor Ramsey in securing a memorable – and in the amateur's case totally unexpected – victory over West Germany.

8 November 1967
Claremont Road, Hendon. GB vs West Germany

Hendon had won the Amateur Cup in 1965, reached the final again a year later and supplied four starters for the GB team in the return, including 1960 veteran Roy Sleap. Having trounced the Germans away, Hughes had hoped for a better crowd than the 4,000 fans who turned up at Hendon, but internecine rivalry and lack of enthusiasm among the other Home Nations had reduced the GB side to a team of Englishmen. Charles Hughes would rely on the players he knew and trusted from the Isthmian League.

The visiting Gerhard Faltermeier, who had recovered from the injuries he suffered in the first leg, recalled enjoying a far better atmosphere at a first division match between Arsenal and West Ham that he attended the night before the Olympic qualifier.

Helmut Schoen, manager of the full West Germany team, had been in Augsburg and travelled to Hendon, where he saw Germany's players overwhelm the home side, many of whose players were complacent and had a poor game. Leytonstone's Ken Gray forced a fine early save out of the German keeper Schulte but, five minutes later, Germany scored. The otherwise excellent Swannell slipped on the wet turf, conceding an unnecessary corner. FC Bamberg's Dieter Zettelmaier swung the ball over and Keifler scored with a fine volley.

GB played to a 4-4-2 formation and Gray and Horseman tried running at the Germans, often dribbling round two or three players, but three chances came and went before half-time. This time, Peter Deadman was fit to come on. He went close twice in the second half but Germany had more possession. Twice in the last ten minutes, the ball ran across Swannell's goalmouth with no Germans in sight. Haider had a late chance but GB finished the game clinging onto the lead as the Germans desperately tried to force extra time, the veteran Zettelmaier missing a fine late chance for the Germans with ten minutes left. But GB held on. "Tonight it was we who played like amateurs instead of professionals," admitted Hughes after the game. "I was most disappointed and the players know it."

Months would pass before GB's next game but confidence grew that Hughes's team, having avoided an Eastern European side and been matched with Spain, could qualify. ITV asked the FA if a match could be staged later that year to help fund sending a squad to Mexico. Lancaster Gate said no, citing fixture congestion. The FA also rejected an invite from the Libyan FA to send the Olympic team to Tripoli. Italy's Olympic team actually visited England as preparation for their own qualifiers, but the FA did not bother to arrange a game for Hughes's side. Instead, the Italian Olympic XI took on Millwall, who won 1-0. Hughes persisted with the regime of training weekends and Monday night friendlies ahead of the first leg in Spain.

Billy Neil and Niall Hopper refused to rejoin to the squad because of the row between Charles Hughes, the SFA and Queen's Park. Then at Clyde as an amateur, Millar Hay was training to be a teacher and wanted to be part of the Olympic experience, something he would not find elsewhere. "It was my first experience of a professional way of running a team. The preparation was very professional, the meals and training, then a sleep in the afternoon, then training again," recalls Hay, who would later manage Scotland's women's side. Hay adds:

> "People do this all the time now but then it was very innovative. What Charlie was trying to do, even with the ruckus we had then, is just what we've got now and not playing on the Saturday before the game. It definitely wasn't an amateur set-up and that's why I went back. Charlie was a difficult man, I only argued with him once, he took no dissent, but when I went down he put me up and he and his wife were great. There's nothing like being able to play for your country; well, the whole of Britain."

Hay might have been enthused but the SFA's ardour was lost. In February 1968, the SFA quit. Their players could still participate but their selector was withdrawn and there would be no more contribution to expenses. SFA secretary Willie Allan said: "It is felt that the present set-up has not worked out too well. Neither Ireland nor Wales has a man on the committee. We do not think anything will be gained by Scotland continuing to have a representative."

Players from Northern Ireland and Wales were sidelined – "Charlie was not impressed with the Welsh or Northern Irish," recalls Hay – and the press routinely called Hughes's GB side an Isthmian League representative side. But Millar Hay was welcomed back, not in any supine response to media pressure, but on footballing grounds. Hughes put aside petty British rivalry and wanted the Scotsman because he had been in the Scotland side that had beaten GB's next opponents Spain 3-1 in the semi-finals of the 1967 Uefa amateur championships.

Hughes found little support at Queen's Park but Hay would not be the only Scotsman. Loughborough's day had passed in the Amateur Cup but good quality players could still be occasionally found in the university system. George Cumming was at Strathclyde University and played as an amateur at Partick Thistle. A Scottish amateur international, he was readily embraced into the GB set-up. "There was a really good atmosphere down at Bisham Abbey," says Cumming. "There were no problems at all, it was very much a British team but very much English based and organised. All the communication came from their FA."

Another university student who joined the set-up was Alan Gowling, an economics student at Manchester University playing reserve team football at Manchester United, once scoring seven goals in one match.

27 March 1968
Nova Creu Alta Stadium, Sabadell. Spain vs GB

The GB team's stock was low back home but the team found themselves the subject of media attention on arriving in the Catalonian city of Sabadell. Spectators would attend training sessions. So would the press, who recorded the GB team's training moves in the local papers. Charles Hughes would come to regret this.

To Hughes's embarrassment, Spain used the same free kick routine that GB had been trialling in their open practice sessions to take the lead, Ortega rising above the visitors' defence to head home after just seven minutes. GB fought back; Dagenham forward Peter Greene − scorer of seven goals in four trial matches − hit a post, but on 25 minutes GB were lucky not to concede a penalty after a defender appeared to handle in the box. To the frustration of the home side and the 20,000 fans in the stadium, Spain were awarded a corner instead.

The robust approach that Hughes drilled into his team won little sympathy from the fans or the referee. Ten minutes from the end, Millar Hay was scythed down in a challenge that merited a yellow card. "I got booked for trying to retaliate," recalls Hay. "Then George [Cumming] got sent off for kicking their player."

The GB side tried to chase the game but, with a man down, the task was too great. Gowling strived up front but a strong Spanish side were mostly untroubled. There was to be no repeat of their Augsburg heroics. If the GB players wanted that trip of a lifetime, they would need to win the return by two clear goals.

Disappointed by England's tame exit from the Uefa amateur championship, Hughes made no excuses for the tactics adopted by GB in Germany and Spain. He said:

> "It is difficult for amateur players to play away from home. Their away matches in the Isthmian League are more often than not just a few miles away. Playing abroad is so different. We were not good competitors abroad. I had to introduce not only a more competitive spirit but also make more use of it in matches away from home."

To try and inspire his players, Hughes asked the FA's amateur international committee, which now included Harold Thompson, to take the return game to Wembley. "It would have been helpful to play the Spain game at Wembley," he says. "We wouldn't have drummed up much of a crowd but it would have meant a lot to the players, while White City didn't mean much to them at all. There was a real will among the players; they did everything they could, including getting time off work to play games at Celtic or Manchester United on a Monday night."

That will was not reciprocated by the fans. In March, GB played a rare friendly international against a Republic of Ireland side featuring eight debutants. GB romped home 6-0, Larry Pritchard scoring a hat-trick and a rejuvenated Roy Sleap also among the scorers. The crowd at Watford's Vicarage Road was just 1,564. Thompson and Bowers went against Hughes and his players. The game would go to the *de facto* home of the English amateur, White City.

10 April 1968
White City, London. GB vs Spain

A better than expected crowd turned up on a cold night to see if a return to the Olympics after an eight-year absence was possible. Hughes was hindered in Spain by the loss through injury of Larry Pritchard, who returned for the second leg. Greene and Gowling started up front, the Manchester University student having played for United's first team in their previous two league games.

GB needed to win but fielded a side of defensive players, whilst trying to attack on the break. That was a tactic the Spanish knew and played far better. After just ten minutes, right-winger Otuno forced a good save from Swannell with a header. The defenders Moxon, Reid and Robertson showed admirable skill but Pritchard was clearly still injured and GB could not press home their advantage in possession. Millar Hay says: "We had numerous chances. The ball kept crossing the box but we couldn't get it in. The clock was running down and the Spanish were diving everywhere. It was the most frustrating game I ever played as a player."

In the second half, 26 minutes passed with just one shot on goal, which came from Rayo Vallecano's Ortuno. Roy Sleap tried a long-range shot to no avail. Roddy Haider came on along with Ken Gray, who quickly earned a yellow card for bundling Spanish defender Mora off the field as he tried to reach a corner. In the game's dying moments, Haider missed a chance that he has been ruing for the past four decades. "I was clean through," he says. "But I put it over the bar. We'd have been level and would have gone on to win as Spain were struggling." Instead, Spain were through. GB were out, Hughes foiled again – the trip of a lifetime gone.

GB had fallen at the last in another tournament marred by withdrawals. Denmark had been behind the introduction of the rule barring players that had played in World Cup finals tournaments from participating in the Olympics, but the heirs to Nils Middelboe did not even take part in 1968. The previous year a war had broken out between Israel and the surrounding Arab nations and when Morocco were paired with the Israelis in a qualifier, the Moroccans pulled out. Elsewhere, Surinam were disqualified after fielding a professional in their win over Trinidad & Tobago. In Mexico's high altitude conditions, Hungary surprisingly took the gold medal, beating Bulgaria in the final, but the tournament was again troubled by politics and that age-old divide between amateurs and professionals.

Spain reached the quarter-finals, putting GB's elimination in a better light. The GB players were left wondering what they might have achieved in Mexico with the FA's proper backing. Three weeks after being eliminated, Millar Hay went to the doctors about the injury he had suffered in Sabadell. The diminutive Scotsman found he had played through not one but two qualifiers with a hairline fracture in his leg. Hay recovered, later turning professional with Clyde. Fellow Scotsman George Cumming went professional too, playing in the Scottish first division for St Mirren and

Hamilton Academical before becoming a first-class referee. Probably the only man to play against Celtic and Rangers, and then referee an Old Firm derby, Cumming later joined Fifa, becoming head of refereeing in 2000 and taking charge of the referees for that year's Olympic tournament and the 2002 World Cup.

The team's other student, Alan Gowling, signed professional forms for Manchester United and played 87 games without ever becoming a regular first choice. He was later sold to Huddersfield Town before moving to Newcastle United, where he partnered Malcolm Macdonald up front. The other older, more established GB players, found too many diversions in the English amateur game to consider joining Hay, Cumming and Gowling in the professional game. Players like Derek Gamblin, Roddy Haider and redoubtable centre-half Ted Powell would return for another challenge at the Olympics.

Effervescent keeper John Swannell would also return but his deputy, John Shippey, dropped out, partly due to the new FA rules aimed at combating shamateurism. Shippey left Oxford in 1969 and wanted to sign for Slough, whose new manager Tommy Lawrence would lead the team to the 1973 Amateur Cup final. Shippey found himself barred from signing for Slough because he fell foul of a new rule that banned amateurs playing for clubs further than 50 miles away from their homes. Stumped, Shippey had to settle for Western League Andover, an outpost that attracted few selectors for the England amateur or Olympic teams.

These restrictions were doing little for football or hardly upholding the great amateur ideal, which received another setback in 1968 when segregation in tennis finally ended at that year's British Hard Court Championships in Bournemouth. A first-round loser in that year's open at the West Hants Club could expect to receive £20.

By way of comparison, around the same time leading players at a big amateur football club commanded a £1,000 signing-on fee – that they personally pocketed. These secret payments would have to stop, fulminated Sir Harold Thompson, who could no longer "maintain respect for hypocrites and humbugs". The founder of Pegasus was undergoing a dramatic conversion. The purists had established the sectarian division between amateurs and professionals and, fittingly, one of their own would exterminate the shamateur. But not before one last glorious but much neglected attempt to reach the Games.

CHAPTER THIRTEEN: MUNICH 1972
AND THE LAST SCOTSMAN IN BRITAIN

"Sir Harold Thompson had got it into his head that the downfall of Pegasus was shamateurism and that it had to be done away with."

Charles Hughes, GB Olympic manager

AS THE 1970S DAWNED, AMATEURISM WAS VIRTUALLY obsolete. Traditionalists like Avery Brundage, the ageing president of the IOC, referred to professional sportsmen as "performing monkeys", but his views were an outmoded throwback, particularly in football. Driven by venal self-interest at a handful of bigger, mostly southern clubs, shamateurism was rampant.

"I was at Crystal Palace when I was at school and played for the reserves, then went to Loughborough. When I left, Arthur Rowe said, 'Do you want some money?' and I said I wasn't averse to it," says Andy Williams, the new GB back-up keeper. "[Rowe] suggested I went to Wealdstone instead of Corinthian-Casuals, who were OK for a season as they would help with accommodation. It was pretty much accepted [at that time] that there was money there."

Peter Hardcastle would join Williams for the final Olympic push. After qualifying as a teacher, Hardcastle signed for ambitious Northern League side Skelmersdale. "I was getting more playing football than I was teaching," reflects Hardcastle.

Clearly out of control, most amateur players knew that the game was up and what the cost would be. "We knew that was the end of it then," says the GB side's striker, Roddy Haider. "The BOA had to say all the players were amateur and it was getting increasingly difficult to do that as the players were then looking to get paid."

The 1972 Olympics would be in Munich. Charles Hughes too knew that this would be his last chance to emulate his predecessor, Norman Creek, and take a team to the Olympic Games. Hughes also knew that his chances of doing that were rendered virtually impossible by the Iron Curtain countries' stance on amateurism.

Football in the Olympics was on the verge of being forgotten in Britain and the English amateur game was not attracting much more support either. With no promotion or relegation between leagues, regular fixtures often drew paltry crowds. Only the Amateur Cup had meaning. To secure success in the competition, clubs paid increasingly bigger bonuses to players. This rise in expenditure, coupled with a slump in attendances, was killing clubs. The government's Chester Report into football in 1968 failed to come up with any meaningful solutions for the amateur game or combating the problem of the shamateurs.

In the North, once proud Bishop Auckland were unlikely to add to their 18 Amateur Cup performances. The FA's 50-mile limit made recruiting players harder than ever. Dismal performances on the field led to disinterest off it; in 1971, Bishops did not draw a single crowd of more than 1,000 people. Down south, Tooting & Mitcham had managed to rack up a £10,000 overdraft by 1971. When Enfield won the Amateur Cup and Isthmian League double in 1970, the club made a profit of just £1,000. The 33,000 attendance at that season's Amateur Cup final – staged, unhelpfully, on the same day as the Boat Race and Grand National – was the lowest since 1949.

Some progressive clubs in the South built social clubs and stoked takings with bar money, but in the North a social club was competition for working men's clubs. Amateur clubs survived not on gates but through fund-raising or betting totes. Clyde Purnell's staunchly amateur Clapton scrapped their third team and no longer even paid legitimate expenses. "If the tote collapsed we'd be in dire trouble," said Clapton secretary Jack Haynes. "The gate money is only worth a few bob. There have been so many ideas over the years to stop shamateurism. The only way is for club officials to say 'stop'."

Killing off the amateur code would have once been anathema to Harold Thompson but the Pegasus founder had been converted. "Many reply that if the formal distinction between amateurs and professionals were removed, there would be too many complications and repercussions," he said. "What they say would happen to the Amateur Cup and what about the Olympic Games? Would amateur standards really fall? Better that than remain a sham."

Yet there was little impetus to stop from the top of the game. Shamateurism suited the Football League. Instead of building up a big squad of players on increasingly expensive contracts, amateurs could be paid on a match-by-match basis to fill spaces in their reserve XIs. Shamateurism was so rife that players openly spoke out.

"The top amateurs are real professionals now," said Welsh former GB Olympic player Dave Roberts in the early 1970s, when he had moved to the purists of Dulwich Hamlet. "The contact is usually made by phone to your home and the offer made outright. But with no personal contact and nothing in writing, everything can be denied later. Everybody acknowledges that payments are made so why continue covering up?"

Another former would-be Olympian, Tommy Lawrence, was typically forthright. Speaking to *World Sports* magazine in 1971, he said: "Amateur soccer today is a farce." Lawrence managed just one match after the Greece qualifier before being forced to quit by the FA for his own health. He added:

> "For a start, we must call everyone players, do away with this amateur business, it doesn't mean a thing. I would wipe out every senior amateur league in the country and make it all one big league – the FA National League. Then you could split into divisions decided in geographical locations. The former amateur clubs would all be mixed in with the present non-league clubs, with a place in the Football League as the ultimate target for every club."

As interest in watching football waned and big amateur clubs struggled to stay afloat, Sunday football took off. No one was paid. Instead, players themselves paid to play. And competitions were flourishing. The Sussex Sunday league was founded in the early 1960s. By 1971, the competition had sufficient cash to spend £20,000 on converting Brighton's drill hall into a sports centre, loan the county FA another £3,000 and still have £14,000 left in the bank.

Against this background of turmoil, the FA tried hard to find a solution. With Stanley Rous ensconced at Fifa, Denis Follows had been FA secretary for nearly a decade and he was despatched on a fact-finding mission to Belgium, the Netherlands and Switzerland in 1971 to see how the Europeans coped. Unable to control the purse strings of the rogue clubs, the FA took out their frustrations on the players, not all of whom were getting paid anyway. "The FA were evil with money," says John Delaney, then a centre-half at Wycombe Wanderers. "All the old farts in the FA would be getting pissed and we'd get nothing. I worked as a chairmaker and didn't get any paid time off. I spent four days away [for an Olympic qualifier] and all I got was the price of the bus fare back from Heathrow."

For the Olympics, the other Home Nations were as disinterested as ever. The FA were left to organise and fund the venture. An effort was made to bring into the Olympic squad some non-English players, but with their own FAs not willing to contribute financially, those players had to abide by the same rules as the Englishmen.

"If a bus fare was 98p, say, and we rounded it up by a couple of pence to a pound before submitting our expenses, we'd get an individual letter from the FA telling us not to round anything up," says Scotsman Bill Currie, who went to the same Govan school as Alex Ferguson but was less keen on embracing the professional game. In the early 1970s, Currie was playing for Rutherglen Glencairn FC in the Scottish junior leagues, when a tussle erupted over his signature. Currie explains:

> "I'd had trials at Queen of the South and they offered me a contract but I was working at a bank, the same one as Billy Neil, and they said you can't do that. Then the Albion Rovers blazer Tom Fagin rang up Rutherglen and offered them a free strip if they persuaded me to go with them. I didn't really want to go to Dumfries so I joined Albion Rovers. I thought about going pro but if I'd gone pro I would have had to give up banking and the money [in football] wasn't great. It wasn't like it

was Celtic and Rangers, it was Queen of the South and Albion Rovers."

Outside of Queen's Park, amateurs playing regularly in the Scottish League were rare. Currie was soon called up to the Scottish amateur team. A recommendation to Charles Hughes that the imposing centre-half join his Olympic squad soon followed. Having turned down the pros, Currie would get a chance – albeit an outside one – of going to the Olympics.

Amateurism was not the only outmoded ideal in British football. So was the idea of a united British side. The full Wales XI took on a team of full internationals from the rest of the UK in 1969 in a fund-raiser for the Aberfan disaster, but the concept of a GB side was virtually extinct. Only in the Olympics was the notion alive and that anomaly – like amateurism – was clearly on borrowed time.

The Scots, despite their withdrawal in the 1968 qualifiers, were persuaded to give the GB Olympic team fresh thought ahead of the 1972 Olympics by a government quango, the newly-formed Sports Council. The SFA agreed to return but only to a reconstituted Olympic Committee with one vote per association. The Sports Council convened a meeting with the FA and the other recalcitrant Home Nations. In early 1969 everyone agreed that this was the way forward. In October that year, all four Home Nations met again in London. A committee would be formed with two members per association with the FA providing a secretary in Denis Follows. As the Sports Council had propagated the idea, all four FAs agreed to ask the government for financial help.

In the interim, Charles Hughes had been looking to grow his power base. The GB manager alone chose the side and wanted the same freedom with the England amateur XI. He wrote a letter to the FA proposing this. At a meeting of the international amateur committee, Harold Thompson and Denis Follows discussed Hughes's missive. A vote was taken but Hughes was stymied, his proposal voted down 5-3.

That was the end of 1970. In April the next year, Hughes and Follows convened a meeting with the Welsh and Northern Irish representatives in London's Dominion Hotel to discuss the Olympics. This time, no one from the SFA even bothered to turn up. Scotsmen could play in the Olympics but the SFA were out. Despite the best efforts of the FA, the committee had already been neutered.

By this time, Hughes had welded his England team into one of the best prepared amateur sides seen in Britain. That set-up would form the bedrock of his GB squad. Many players from four years before were still in the frame but Derek Gamblin would have missed out had Charles Hughes not intervened. Gamblin lived on the south coast but played in the Isthmian League, whose clubs were scattered across London. By 1971 the travelling had got too much for Gamblin but the England and GB manager did not want to lose one of his more valued players and intervened personally. "I signed for Winchester but Charlie came up and asked me to sign for Wycombe and get back into the Isthmian League if I wanted to play for the England team," says Gamblin, who took Hughes's advice and was back on the Olympic trail.

Now into his late thirties – almost unheard of for a top-level amateur then – Alf D'Arcy won the 1970 Amateur Cup with Enfield. D'Arcy's rugged defending had a place in the game's new tactics but there was nowhere for older, more creative midfield players. Hugh Lindsay was only in his early thirties but one of the most talented post-war English players never to go professional was left behind. He says: "No one played at that age because of the work-rate and long balls that had come into the game. As someone who would put his foot on the ball, I usually ended up in a heap."

Breaking into the Isthmian League-controlled southern-based cartel of the England amateur and GB squads was difficult. Skelmersdale were the strongest Northern League side, having reached the 1967 Amateur Cup final, when 75,000 fans saw the team lose to Enfield. In 1971 Skelmersdale returned to the Amateur Cup final and captured the trophy, beating Dagenham in front of an improved crowd of 42,000. Skelmersdale had decided to go professional in the following 1971/72 season, but had yet to ditch their amateur status and would be the only northern club to provide Hughes with players for this Olympic squad – selected from their amateurs.

"We'd been beating all these Isthmian League sides and half a dozen of us went down but I was not expecting to play," says Peter Hardcastle. His expectations lowered further after nearly falling foul of the GB team's strict disciplinarian manager. Hardcastle explains:

> "I was a bit uppity as you are at that age and was set up by
> the other players to argue back with Charles Hughes. He
> had this way of cutting you dead and when I approached

him, he said, 'Who's behind you Peter?' and when I looked round, the entire squad had backed off ten yards. After that, it was all 'Yes Charles, no Charles'. He didn't have much choice really as he wasn't that much older than some players, but he was the best coach I've ever had."

A Welsh accountant called Allan Phillips, who played as a defender in the Isthmian League for Tooting & Mitcham, was involved from the outset. At the squad's first get-together, the 1968 bust-up with Queen's Park was still clearly on Hughes's mind. He told the assembled players: "Put Britain before England and England before the club."

Hughes's GB XI won their first four warm-up matches before a 3-3 draw with an IFA side in Belfast, which helped bring in Northern Ireland's sole representative, Distillery forward Jim Savage. A sixth friendly with Preston – a 0-0 draw – saw Bill Currie make his debut. Currie and another Scotsman, Queen's Park's Ian Robertson, both made the squad.

The friendlies finished with a 4-0 thrashing of a Southampton side featuring half a dozen first-team regulars. In seven games, Hughes's team had not lost. Even with this run in, their opponents made the qualifier a monumental mismatch: the Bulgarians were back.

In 1968 Bulgaria won the silver medal at the Mexico Olympics and held the full England team to a 1-1 draw at Wembley. In 1970, Bulgaria qualified for their third consecutive World Cup finals and returned to Mexico. The rule barring players who had played in a World Cup from featuring in an Olympics lapsed. Some Iron Curtain sides ran separate teams, often fielding a B team for the Olympics, but the Bulgarians had a more interchangeable squad.

Nine players who travelled to Wembley for the 1971 Olympic qualifier had been in Bulgaria's 1970 World Cup squad. The star was CSKA Sofia's Dimitar Yakimov, an army officer who played in the 1962 and 1966 World Cups and was the Bulgarian first division's top scorer. Hristo Bonev also went to Mexico, where keeper Stoyan Jordanov, left-back Milko Gaydarski, midfielder Asparush Nikodimov and striker Dimitar Maradjiev all started. All would play against GB's schoolteachers and market gardeners at Wembley.

On arrival, some Bulgarian officials did not seem to realise that the Great Britain team was not the same as the English one to compete in Mexico but the players did. Stoyan Jordanov recalls: "We knew that our team would play the British amateur team at Wembley [and] not the England players who have taken part in World Cup finals in Mexico."

A sign of the FA's expectations was that no one had been asked to explore the cost of sending a side to Munich. Hughes was more confident but dogged by the ague gripping the amateur game. When the FA confirmed that the qualifier would be at Wembley, Hughes was initially elated, saying: "The decision to play at Wembley is already having a tremendous psychological effect on the squad. With the right kind of support we can go into the second leg in the lead if every man plays to the peak of his ability." Closer to the game, Hughes admitted that a crowd of less than 10,000 would be a disaster. "There's too much insularity," he reflected.

24 April 1971
Wembley Stadium, London. GB vs Bulgaria

To the joy of Harold Thompson, more than 20,000 fans watched the latest Varsity game at Wembley. The FA hoped some of those same fans would return for the qualifier but the Oxbridge set were divorced from the Olympic football project. Expectations were so low that no one appears to have brought a camera to the game. That was for the best. A mere 2,000 fans, including two representatives apiece from each of the four Home Nations, rattled around Wembley on a dismal rainy April night.

In the dug-out, Charles Hughes sat with the GB team's longstanding trainer, Jack Jennings, who wore a baseball hat on his head and tied his glasses behind his head with string. Well-liked by the players, Jennings was an accidental comedian, often spraying water in his face instead of on the limbs of injured players because he had the nozzle back to front.

With Allan Phillips out, the GB team was virtually an Isthmian League XI with two exceptions: Peter Hardcastle and Bill Currie. The solitary Scotsman and GB's skipper Ted Powell would play one of the greatest games of their lives. The Bulgarians expected a bigger crowd but GB were not deterred by the paucity of support. Hughes's team sprang into attack. After 15 minutes Slough Town's Roger Day latched onto a rebound from a Peter Hardcastle cross and drilled the ball past a stunned Jordanov.

The Bulgarians initially sat back, allowing GB to force more attacks, but the visitors soon began to press harder. Hughes's tactics tasked Enfield's John Payne, a tough-tackling midfielder, with winning the ball and immediately passing it off to the nearest GB player. With Yakimov outstanding, the sterling Payne was bypassed.

The Bulgarians swamped the midfield but Hughes's tactics caught them out. The visitors' wingers were forced into the centre of the British defence, where Ted Powell was virtually unbeatable. Currie and the other defenders never gave up, their confidence boosted by the presence of the livewire Swannell behind them. Somehow, GB held out for an astonishing 1-0 win. "It was like Crawley Town beating Germany," says David Barber, the FA historian, then helping out Hughes. "They all played with such courage."

To the Bulgarians, a 1-0 defeat in the home of the World Cup winners was, somehow, seemingly an acceptable result. Stoyan Jordanov adds: "We lost the match but our head coach [Hristo Mladenov] said 'That is a good result for us, boys'."

Incredibly, GB would take a win and a clean sheet to Sofia. Bulgaria were surely a stronger test than Turkey, Spain or Greece, who lay in wait for the winners along with the more intimidating Poles. GB returned to their friendlies but with less success as the squad changed. Micky Mellows was a rare amateur playing regularly in the Football League at Reading and came in. Andy Williams was injured so a replacement back-up goalkeeper was needed.

Hughes called up Grenville Millington, a teenage keeper from Queensferry in North Wales. Millington, who later had a long career as a professional at Chester, caught Hughes's eye after his part in the FA Cup exploits of Rhyl, who reached the fifth round that season. That run was ended by Swansea, whose keeper Tony Millington was a full Welsh international and the brother of Grenville, who says: "They must have had me watched and caught me on a good day. It was a great honour to be called up for the Wales amateur team. I never even thought I'd make the Olympic team."

Bill Currie certainly expected to go to Bulgaria. He was asked by the FA to bring his passport down for the final training session before departing for Sofia. When he turned up at the session in Hendon and spotted John Delaney, Ted Powell's usual defensive partner in the England amateur team, Currie felt uneasy. Shortly after, Hughes told Currie that he would not be going to Sofia after all. "I don't know if Delaney had been injured for the first game," says Currie. "What surprised me was that I'd brought my passport down and they'd got me a visa but never gave me any reason why I wasn't going." Despite his unexplained rejection, Hughes promised Currie that he was guaranteed a place on a tour that the confident GB manager was planning for that summer after his GB side had eliminated Bulgaria.

Few players managed a full-blown row with the GB team's martinet manager and played again. John Delaney was one. He explains:

> "I had a row with Charlie after an England amateur international in Brest, when I'd played like a right wally and he'd had a right go at me. He could make grown men cry and I told him to stuff it. Then after we got back, someone had a word with me and I spoke to him. Charles had a lot of confidence in my scoring from corners."

Hughes had sufficient bravado and belief in his players to believe they could go to Sofia and repeat one of the greatest upsets in Olympic football. With Bill Currie dropped, Grenville Millington was the only non-Englishman in the squad for Sofia. "I remember there was a squad of 16 players and everyone was English apart from me but they treated me like one of them," says Millington. Barring an injury to Swannell, Millington had no chance of starting. The GB side were back to their beginnings; disinterest and dispute had reduced the starting XI to a side of Englishmen.

5 May 1971
Vasil Levsky Stadium, Sofia. Bulgaria vs GB

Prior to the game, Hughes's squad had been guests of honour at the British embassy in Sofia and, while the attendance for the return in the Levksy Stadium did not match the huge throng that had turned up for the GB side's last visit in 1955, a decent 30,000 crowd still turned up. "Bulgaria was the best team I ever played against. There was a red wall coming at us in Sofia. I'm sure they could have done the same at Wembley," says John Swannell.

The hosts cruised to a 4-0 lead by half-time with Asparuh Nikodimov to the fore. During one Bulgarian attack, Delaney shouted across to Gamblin to bring the GB team out of defence. "What's the point?" replied an exhausted Gamblin. "They'll be back in a minute."

The onslaught never let up. Gamblin adds: "Charles said, 'You'll have to get tight with this chap', and after Wembley said 'Well done'. In Sofia, he said, 'You'll have to get more lively with them and get up close and give this guy a bump'. The situation arrived and the guy went off at half-time but got replaced by someone else who was even more lively."

For Roddy Haider, there were no chances during a lonely game. "I was marking some guy who was a major but I doubt he'd ever been in a barracks in his entire life," says Haider. In a rare GB corner, John Delaney recalled Hughes's advice to target Jordanov. He says: "Charles told me their keeper was a coward so I went up with him for this corner but he hit me so hard that he sent me and the ball back up to the halfway line."

The GB side were tough, the Bulgarians tougher. Peter Hardcastle, who turned pro on returning home, signing (along with fellow Olympian Paul Fuschillo) for Blackpool, says: "We only had two or three attacks and it could have been 20-0. They were taking pot-shots from everywhere. I've never played against players like that. It was the sheer size of them that struck me."

Jordanov adds: "I saved a lot of shots during the game at Wembley but in Sofia in the second match I did not have one on the goal." A hat-trick from Lokomotiv Sofia's Atanas Michaylov plus strikes from Petar Jekov of CSKA Sofia and Slavia Sofia's Yancho Dimitrov secured a comfortable 5-0 win. GB were out 5-1 on aggregate. The final score was testament to the brilliance of Swannell, formidable defending and Bulgaria, aware that the game was won, easing off. With the final whistle in that game in Sofia, the GB side were gone.

After the game, the shocked GB squad returned to the British embassy for another reception, but the glamour had gone. "When we went to the embassy the first time we were feted but afterwards they didn't treat us the same," recalls Paul Fuschillo.

A pallor hung over the squad as the players returned to the land of the soon-to-be extinct shamateur. Millington adds: "It wasn't a happy journey back as some of the players had been together a long time and it was a sad end." Bill Currie never went on the Olympic tour of Scandinavia that summer. Many of his Olympic team-mates did but only those from England, whose amateur side took over the programme of fixtures.

Bulgaria were ultimately knocked out of the Olympic qualifiers by Poland, who won gold by beating Hungary in the final in Munich – a precursor for a run of success for Polish football over the next decade. But there would be no more Olympics for the United Kingdom of Great Britain and Northern Ireland.

In May 1974, the FA Council with Harold Thompson to the fore finally recommended abolishing amateurism. This was approved in September. The purists had created the amateur distinction to reinforce their long-since passé Corinthian ideals. Fittingly, one of their own, the man who inherited Wreford-Brown's mantle, put the ideal to sleep.

From 1974 onwards, everyone was to be a player. The distinction, the social status, the credo of the amateur was consigned to history. The game played outside of the Football League gained a new catch-all name – non-league. Collateral damage included the scrapping of the Amateur Cup. Bishops Stortford won the last final. The trophy remains in the FA foyer at Wembley. The cup was replaced by the FA Trophy for larger clubs and the FA Vase for smaller sides.

England did take part in the 1974 Uefa amateur championships but lost out to West Germany in the qualifiers. With interest dwindling, the tournament was only staged once more, in 1978, without England. By then, a role in active team management had gone for Charles Hughes. Both his teams were sacrificed like neglected pawns in a great game of footballing chess. Though sanguine about the inevitable, he knows the culprit. "[The FA] knew they couldn't clean up amateurism," says Hughes, adding:

> "Harold Thompson had got it into his head that the downfall of Pegasus was shamateurism and that had to be done away with. The powers that be were not so keen and worried about moves within Fifa. There were countries within Fifa that didn't want England, Scotland, Northern Ireland and Wales playing independently as there were all sorts of vacancies on committees and the powers that be did not want to lose their power base."

The same year that amateurism was killed off, Harold Thompson was voted onto Uefa's executive committee. Two years later, Thompson took over as FA chairman and – to the eternal frustration of 1952 Olympian Bill Holmes – later turned down Brian Clough's application to become England manager. Clough once remarked that Thompson knew as much about football as the ebullient Nottingham Forest manager and two-time European Cup winner knew about chemistry – nothing.

That year of 1974 saw a flurry of changes in English football as another former GB Olympic manager lost his job. Sir Stanley Rous was deposed as head of Fifa by the machinations of the Brazilian Joao Havelange, who immediately placated the Home Nations by promising that there would be no merger, nor a joint team. A GB team was seemingly confirmed dead. That same year, Alf Ramsey was sacked as England manager. Charles Hughes's stock was sufficiently high in some sections of the FA for him to be touted as a possible replacement. He had managed the GB team for eight competitive matches, winning three, drawing one and losing four. They never qualified for an Olympics. His England amateurs played 77 matches, winning 48 and losing a dozen. "He could have become the next England manager as he was very close to Ramsey," says Derek Gamblin. "What stopped him was that pros wouldn't have taken a blind bit of notice as he was a manager of amateurs." Instead, the England post went to Don Revie.

Hughes's managerial roles gone, he took a different path – not unlike the old gentlemen amateurs who settled for the halls of administration after losing their power on the pitch. Charles Hughes would now attempt to influence the entire English game as he became the FA's national director of coaching.

As kick and run began to rule, the more extreme acolytes of the church of POMO spread far and wide. Managers like Allan Batsford, who led Walton & Hersham to Amateur Cup success in 1973, a victory that denied the veteran Alf D'Arcy – then at Slough – a last glory day. In Batsford's team was Dave Bassett, later another POMO acolyte at Wimbledon. The POMO style helped Wimbledon win the FA Cup and reach the highest levels of the professional game. Graham Taylor – a team-mate of John Kennedy at Lincoln – adapted the style during his tenure as England manager.

Hughes stayed with the FA for 33 years, even voting in the Premier League. In retirement, the last manager of the GB Olympic team feels traduced by the blame laid at his door:

> "It's grossly unfair [says Hughes]. We played some long balls but not all the time. It's about finding the right time. For England and GB, we always went out to win the game. I always said we should support the player with the ball. If he isn't in a position to pass it forward, be in a position to take the ball back.

"I wrote 31 books and made three films and if there's something in those people don't agree with, come and see me and we'll talk about it. But they never came to see me because they never read those books or saw those films. Very few people would find it easy to write 31 books and make three films just on long-ball play."

Hughes had brought a new level of professionalism and expectation to an amateur game that was anything but, certainly in terms of payment. Hugh Lindsay explains: "Charles expected us to be more professional in our attitude to the game. I was very lucky that my job [as a teacher] enabled this to be possible. Others were not so fortunate and suffered as a result. It meant that there was always some ill-feeling within the squad, which resulted in us 'under-achieving' to a certain extent."

For all his critics, Hughes has plenty of supporters too. He might have been a tyrant on the training ground at times but players travelling long distances, like the Scots or Peter Hardcastle, were often put up and made very welcome at his Buckinghamshire home. Hughes regularly advised players about their careers and, if they were turning pro, the size of signing-on fees. He also inspired successful coaches whose teams played cultured football, such as Dario Gradi. The former Sutton player went on to become one of the longest-serving managers in the Football League at Crewe Alexandra, famous for their progressive football. Gradi says:

"Charles needed a press officer. He did and still does get an awful press. If people read his books or watched those films they would think differently. Charles took Reep's ideas on board but his aides took it too literally. That wasn't what Charles was about. He taught me the art of preparation to defend. With amateur teams then, that was really important as most of your opponents were better, and he left the attacking to two-touch football."

Roddy Haider, who became the most capped England amateur player of all time with 65 appearances, four more than John Swannell, says: "To be fair to Charles, most of my goals were scored from four or five touches.

What he said was that the only way to keep managers in a job was to play effective, winning football."

Hughes was forced to take on teams, particularly in the Olympics, in an increasingly unequal battle. With their opponents exploiting the rules off the field, an uncompromising approach on the field was the only solution. John Delaney says: "We were limited being amateurs and [Charles] knew that was the only way we could get at teams. He was one of the best men I met."

Shortly before the divide between amateurs and professionals vanished, John Delaney turned professional with Bournemouth at the then ripe old age – for a footballer – of 31.

In 1964, 30-year-old Tony Book had been signed by Malcolm Allison for Plymouth Argyle. Book had most recently been with Bath City and Toronto in Canada and the future Manchester City star had yet to make his Football League debut. When Delaney signed for Bournemouth, he took Book's record but the ex-Wycombe player was not enamoured by life with the professionals.

"The *Guinness Book of Records* phoned me up but I said let Tony Book have the record," says Delaney. "I played 20 games for Bournemouth then went back to Wycombe. I couldn't wait to get back. I had the time of my life then, there was a great camaraderie between the players and I wish I was still in touch with them now."

CHAPTER FOURTEEN: THE END?

"If you're good at something you want to get paid for doing it."

Jimmy Quail, GB Olympic player

WITH THE END OF THE DIVIDE, CLUBS AND PLAYERS began to enjoy a freedom few could have imagined before, tempered by a torrid time for football over the next two decades. The Olympic team was soon forgotten, a barely remembered relic. The ideas championed by Tommy Lawrence took many years to realise but the likes of Barnet and Wimbledon, who had quit the amateur game for the semi-pro Southern league in the 1960s, would ultimately win that prize of Football League status.

Other clubs like Skelmersdale went fully professional but soon after realised that resources were too thin and returned to a more open semi-professional status. Gradually, the non-league game evolved into a system with a national league, where many of the clubs in this top echelon are full-time. That is an almost unimaginable notion anywhere else in the world but the transition to an open game claimed many casualties among the clubs who supplied Olympians.

In 1988, Jim Lewis's Walthamstow Avenue were absorbed by the newly merged Leytonstone-Ilford, then their tenants at Green Pond Road. A year later, the ground was sold to developers. The newly enlarged club changed its name to Redbridge Forest, began ground-sharing with Dagenham and then merged again to create Dagenham & Redbridge, who made the Football League.

Other clubs found their level in the non-league game but with much reduced status. Bishop Auckland lost their famous Kingsway ground and drifted into the game's lower echelons. Harry Stapley's Glossop North End toil in the North West Counties League, Clyde Purnell's Clapton in the Essex Senior League and Yorkshire Amateurs play in the Northern Counties East League.

Other once vital parts of the amateur game vanished altogether, leaving a hollow imprint of their existence in memories, in books and engraved on trophies. In 1985, White City, where Vivian Woodward won Olympic gold, where Dick Sloley initially planned to lead his Argonauts into the Football League, where Pegasus hoped to recuperate, was demolished. Like the amateur distinction, the stadium was obsolete.

The roll call of those lost from the story of amateurism includes not just clubs like Stockton, who folded in 1975, but entire leagues. The Athenian League was one of the first leagues to embrace sponsorship in the late 1970s. Weakened by remorseless expansion of the Isthmian and Southern leagues, the competition closed in 1984. The Isthmian League survives under a sponsor's name but founder members London Caledonians – Amateur Cup winners in 1922/23 – are gone, unable to muster a squad of southern Scotsmen since WWII.

Northern Nomads won the Amateur Cup three years after Caley but lack of a permanent ground – the club were often known as the Roaming Brigade – finished the side off. The team joined the Lancashire Combination but, after ground-sharing with Stalybridge Celtic and Glossop North End, the Nomads folded in 1984.

The idea of a team that does not play in a league was impossible to maintain but some other vestiges of the purists' game still remain. The Arthur Dunn Cup is still contested annually, while the Amateur Football Alliance is going strong with more than 400 affiliated clubs running 1,200 teams. Most of the dozen leagues under the AFA's jurisdiction are expected to provide food and drink after matches for both teams and the referee. "We pride ourselves on the skill and competitiveness of our leagues, and on our traditions of fair play and respect for opponents and match officials," says the league. Three former FA Cup winners – Old Etonians, Clapham Rovers and Wreford-Brown's Old Carthusians, who play on in the Arthurian League premier division, are all members of the AFA.

The Northern Irish gentlemen of Cliftonville embraced the professional game in 1975 after a 21-year run during which the side had to seek re-election in all but one year. For decades, the doctors and lawyers of Cliftonville's only recompense for playing was a free plate of bacon, eggs, sausage and chips at a nearby restaurant. Famously, when one player – weary of the same meal after every game – ordered steak, he was ordered by Cliftonville's secretary to settle the bill himself.

In 1979, a Cliftonville team still including many amateurs but bolstered by semi-professionals on around £10 a week, won the Irish Cup. The success was the club's first senior trophy in 82 years. Bohemians turned professional shortly after Cliftonville but the two clubs continued to play annually for the Pioneer Cup until the 1990s. "It couldn't go on," sighs former Cliftonville chairman and IFA president Jim Boyce. "Cliftonville now is like every other league club. Now they can compete with the other teams."

Queen's Park, Scotland's gentlemen, remain staunch amateurs and labour on in the lower reaches of the Scottish League. Cardiff Corinthians play in the Welsh Football League. Their namesakes, Corinthian-Casuals, hold to the purists' credo in the lower reaches of the enlarged Isthmian League, but Pegasus are a distant remembrance, though their name has been adopted by many other clubs. The former players regularly held reunions until 2008 when, their numbers dwindling, a final get-together was held in Pembroke; another chapter closed on the amateur game's history.

The amateur game's greatest chronicler in print – albeit not a mantle he perhaps sought – was killed off in 1960, when Pangloss said "goodbye" and the *News Chronicle* folded. The idea of rating matches in terms of sportsmanship soon went out of fashion. Norman Ackland wrote on, chiefly for *Charles Buchan's Football Monthly*, but his mandate was gone. In 1974 came a double blow: not just the scrapping of the amateur distinction, but the sudden closure of *Charles Buchan's Football Monthly* after 274 issues. Rising costs of paper, printing and distribution that could only be offset by a substantial price rise, which publishers IPC did not want to inflict on readers, were cited.

Norman Ackland stayed with the Press Club secretary, Jane, but when she died of cancer, the old journalist, now confined to a wheelchair, went to live with his son Joss. Ackland later moved to a nursing home in Cheam, where he died in the 1990s. "I would like to have known my father," says

Joss Ackland in his autobiography. "I wish he had kissed me."

Norman Creek, who retired to Folkestone and later passed away in 1980, was a very different man to Ackland but his obituary suggested a similarity, reading: "He departed as he had lived, peacefully, for he was the kindly gentle soul with a ready laugh who always sought the best in people and things. No player who ever played with or for F.N.S. Creek would disagree."

The concept of fraternity that Norman Ackland, the AFA and the other purists espoused so vigorously had somehow managed to survive and even thrive in the grubby world of shamateurism. "We used to go to matches with all our families, wives and children," says John Swannell, who played on into the brave new world, later reaching the FA Trophy final with Leatherhead. "Everyone from both sides stayed on after the game but that soon stopped."

All that seemingly remains of the Corinthian ideal and amateur code which united with such early great success in the Olympic team, are memories. For many amateurs, those recollections are coloured, "Are you going to write about the money?" being the most frequently asked question by most players interviewed for this book. Shamed by years of disapproval by the establishment, a stigma remains. In his 1975 book on Pegasus, two-times Amateur Cup winner Ken Shearwood pointedly called Walthamstow Avenue "semi-professionals". But were the players the hypocrites? Or was it the people who archly called them shamateurs, people who were mostly paid to work in football as administrators, to write about the game for newspapers, or so well-off that they need not work? "People forget," says Jimmy Quail, "when I started playing football in the 1950s, times were hard. If someone offered you a couple of pounds a week to play football you weren't going to say no. If you're good at something you want to get paid for doing it."

For these players, money was not brandished as a sign of social status. Usually, payments were quietly removed from boots and pocketed. Sometimes, even the players' own families did not know. "Did Dad take money? I honestly don't know," says Rob Hardisty candidly. "He told me he didn't because he didn't want to damage his chances with the England amateur team and for the Olympics. Money didn't mean much to Dad and didn't seem to be such an issue."

Amateurism was a dirty word by 1974. As the decades have passed the ideal of the amateur in football has been lost. Bob Hardisty was proud to be considered an amateur, to enjoy the status that conveyed, but today to be an amateur is an insult, a rank amateur the worst of all. A representative team for the English non-league scene exists, drawing players together from outside the Football League and playing against the other Home Nations in a British championship. The team is known as England C.

Overseas, the rapid acceleration of the game has left the amateur behind. In 2009, the Asian Football Confederation banned all amateur teams from the lucrative Asian Champions League. As a result, only 10 of the AFC's 46 members were guaranteed inclusion. Links between the grass roots of the game and the professional game are being severed around the world, yet far more people play football for nothing than receive a reward.

In England, home to five divisions of virtually fully professional football and a vast network of semi-professional clubs, only 6,100 players play for money. By comparison, 656,000 people in England over the age of 18 play as "gentlemen", as amateurs. In Scotland, the ratio is closer – 4,100 players and 39,000 amateurs – but in Wales just 550 people get paid for playing football against 36,000 amateurs. In Northern Ireland, there are 23,000 amateurs and a mere 220 people getting money for playing football.

The amount of people playing 11-a-side football in leagues is dropping but the game remains the most popular to watch and play in the United Kingdom. As money from sponsors and television floods into the professional game, the vast majority of people involved in football today pay out for the privilege: either in the form of subs to play, match day tickets and merchandising, or through subscriptions to satellite television.

That situation was almost unimaginable when Great Britain first hosted the Olympic Games in 1908. Four decades later, thrift ruled the Austerity Games, but 2012 will be a very different Olympics. Football today is incomparable with those last London Games in 1948, but the world's richest team sport has retained its place in the world's biggest sporting event with the onus on younger players. Football in the Olympics today specifies an 18-man squad with all but three players to be under 23 years of age.

So in 2012, a team of footballers representing the United Kingdom of Great Britain and Northern Ireland will once again take the field. Like so many of their antecedents, the team will probably all be English. They will again play for no money and, as the original Olympic credo says, those players will be expected to fight well. This time, they will also be expected to win.

GB OLYMPIC RECORDS

This section details involvement by teams representing the United Kingdom only since 1908, when football was first officially recognised as an Olympic Games sport. Information here is mostly taken from the minute books of the Football Association. Some missing details have been added from newspaper reports or – in the case of attendance figures – Colin Jose's book, *The Complete Results & Line-ups of the Olympic Football Tournaments 1900-2004* (2004, Soccer Books Limited) and the Sports Library of Finland.

Biggest win .... 12-1 vs Sweden, London 1908
Biggest defeat .... 1-6 vs Bulgaria, Melbourne 1956
Most goals .... 9 .... Harry Walden (1912)
.... 9 .... Jim Lewis (1952, 1956 & 1960)
Most goals in a match .... 6 ..... Harry Walden (vs Hungary, 1912)
Most Olympic finals .... 3 .... Bob Hardisty (1948-56)
.... 3 .... Jim Lewis (1952-60)
Most matches in Olympic finals.... 6 .... Bob Hardisty (1948-56)
.... 6 .... Jim Lewis (1952-60)
Most competitive appearances..... 11 .... Jim Lewis
.... 11 .... Mike Pinner

COMPETITIVE PLAYING RECORD
Olympic finals

P	W	D	L	F	A	+/-
18	11	1	6	68	35	+33

Qualifying matches

P	W	D	L	F	A	+/-
16	8	3	5	29	20	+9

Total record

P	W	D	L	F	A	+/-
34	19	4	11	97	55	+42

OLYMPIC SQUADS

Only includes squads travelling to the finals of the Olympic Games from 1908 to 1960. All players in the squads for the 1908, 1912, 1920 and 1956 Olympics were English. First/common names are used where known.

LONDON 1908 – Manager Alfred Davis

Goal
Horace Bailey (Leicester Fosse)
Ron Brebner (Northern Nomads)

Backs
Walter Corbett (Birmingham)
Herbert Smith (Oxford City)
A.H. Bell (Woking)
Albert Scothern (Oxford City)

Half-Backs
Frederick Chapman (South Nottinghamshire)
Reverend Kenneth Hunt (Wolverhampton Wanderers)
Bob Hawkes (Luton Town)
Corporal W Daffern (Royal Engineers)

Forwards
Harry Stapley (Glossop)
Clyde Purnell (Clapton)
Harold Hardman (Northern Nomads)
Vivian Woodward (Tottenham Hotspur)
Arthur Berry (Oxford University)
Thomas Porter (Northern Nomads)
W. Crabtree (Blackburn Crosshill)
George Barlow (Northern Nomads)

STOCKHOLM 1912 – Manager: Adrian Birch

Goal
Horace Bailey (Leicester Fosse)
Ron Brebner (Northern Nomads)

Backs
Thomas Burn (London Caledonians)
Arthur Egerton Knight (Portsmouth)
William Martin (Ilford)

Half-Backs
Joe Dines (Ilford)
Ted Hanney (Reading)
Henry Littlewort (Glossop)
Douglas McWhirter (Bromley)
Harold Stamper (Stockton)

Forwards
Walter Bailey (Reading)
Arthur Berry (Oxford City)
Gordon Hoare (Glossop)
Samuel Sanders (Nunhead)
Ivor Sharpe (Derby County)
Harry Walden (Bradford City)
Vivian Woodward (Tottenham Hotspur)
Ted Wright (Hull City)
Leonard Dawe (Cambridge University & Southampton)

ANTWERP 1920 – Team manager: Colonel R.J. Kentish

Goal
James Mitchell (Manchester University)
G Wiley (Belmont Mines Athletic)

Backs
Basil Gates (London Caledonians)
Arthur "A.E." Knight (Portsmouth)
Humphrey Ward (Oxford University)
Jack Brennan (Manchester City)

Half-Backs
Reverend Kenneth Hunt (Wolverhampton Wanderers)
George Atkinson (Bishop Auckland)
Charlie Harbridge (Reading)
John Payne (Leytonstone)

Forwards
Harold Prince (Royal Army Medical Corps)
Dick Sloley (Corinthians)
Kenneth Hegan (Corinthians)
Wesley Harding (Cambridge University)
Frederick Nicholas (Army & Corinthians)
Harry Buck (Millwall)
H.A. Hambleton (Army & Corinthians)
C.R. Julian (Old Westminsters)
Maurice Bunyan (Chelsea & Racing Club, Belgium)

BERLIN 1936 – Manager: Stanley Rous/Charles Wreford-Brown

Goal
Haydn Hill (Yorkshire Amateurs & England)
Terry Huddle (Casuals & England)

Backs
Guy Holmes (Ilford & England)
George Roylance (Yorkshire Amateurs & England)
Bertie Fulton (Belfast Celtic & Northern Ireland)
Stoker Bill Peart (Gloucester, Royal Navy & Wales)

Half-Backs
Bernard Joy (Casuals & England)
Jackie Gardiner (Queen's Park & Scotland)
Lance Corporal Stan Eastham (Army & England)
Ifor Fielding (Royal Navy & Wales)
John Sutcliffe (Corinthians & England)
Daniel Pettit (Corinthians & England)

Forwards
Mac Dodds (Queen's Park & Scotland)
Bill Clements (Casuals & England)
Fred Riley (Casuals & England)
Lester Finch (Barnet & England)
Maurice Edelston (Wimbledon & England)
Jimmy Gibb (Cliftonville & Northern Ireland)
Joe Kyle (Queen's Park & Scotland)
Donald Shearer (Corinthians & England)
Jimmy Crawford (Queen's Park & Scotland)
A.C.I.C. Coventry Brown (Royal Air Force & Scotland)

LONDON 1948 – Manager: Sir Matt Busby

Goal
Kevin McAlinden (Belfast Celtic & Northern Ireland)
Ronnie Simpson (Queen's Park & Scotland)

Backs
Jack Neale (Walton & Hersham & England)
Gwyn Manning (Troedyrhiw & Wales)
Jim McColl (Queen's Park & Scotland)
Angus Carmichael (Queen's Park & Scotland)

Half-Backs
Eric Lee (Chester & England)
Dougie McBain (Queen's Park & Scotland)
Eric Fright (Bromley & England)
Julian Smith (Barry Town & Wales)
Bob Hardisty (Bishop Auckland & England)
Davie Letham (Queen's Park & Scotland)

Forwards
Tommy Hopper (Bromley & England)
Harry McIlvenny (Bradford Park Avenue & England)
Peter Kippax (Burnley & England)
Denis Kelleher (Barnet & Northern Ireland)
Frank Donovan (Pembroke Borough & Wales)
Jack Rawlings (Enfield & England)
Andy Aitken (Queen's Park & Scotland)
Ron Phipps (Barnet & England)
Bill Amor (Reading & England)
Alan Boyd (Queen's Park & Scotland)

HELSINKI 1952 – Manager: Walter Winterbottom

Goal
Ted Bennett (Southall & England)
Ben Brown (Pegasus & England)

Backs
Bombardier Stan Charlton (Bromley & England)
Tommy Stewart (Queen's Park & Scotland)
Laurie Stratton (Walthamstow Avenue & England)
Ken Yenson (Leyton & England)

Half-Backs
Laurie Topp (Hendon & England)
Bill Hastie (Queen's Park & Scotland)
Charlie Fuller (Bromley & England)
Derek Saunders (Walthamstow Avenue & England)
Idwal Robling (Lovell's Athletic & Wales)

Forwards
Kevin McGarry (Cliftonville & Northern Ireland)
Alf Noble (Leytonstone & England)
Jim Lewis (Walthamstow Avenue & England)
Bill Holmes (Blackburn Rovers & England)
Derek Grierson (Queen's Park & Scotland)
Tony Pawson (Pegasus & England)
George Robb (Finchley & England)
Bill Slater (Brentford & England)
Bob Hardisty (Bishop Auckland & England)

MELBOURNE 1956 – Manager: Norman Creek

Goal
Mike Pinner (Pegasus)
Harry Sharratt (Bishop Auckland)

Backs
Tommy Farrer (Walthamstow Avenue)
Dexter Adams (Hendon)
Terry Robinson (Brentford)

Half-Backs
Laurie Topp (Hendon)
Stan Prince (Walthamstow Avenue)
Don Stoker (Sutton United)
Henry Dodkins (Ilford)

Forwards
Charlie Twissell (Plymouth Argyle)
Bob Hardisty (Bishop Auckland)
Jim Lewis (Chelsea)
George Bromilow (Southport)
Petty Officer Jimmy Coates (Royal Navy & Kingstonian)
Derek Lewin (Bishop Auckland)
Jack Laybourne (Corinthian-Casuals)

ROME 1960 – Manager: Norman Creek

Goal
Mike Pinner (RAF, Queens Park Rangers & England)
Brian Wakefield (Corinthian-Casuals & England)

Backs
Tommy Thompson (Stockton & England)
Bill Neil (Airdrieonians & Scotland)
David Holt (Queen's Park & Scotland)

Half-Backs
Laurie Brown (Bishop Auckland & England)
Ron McKinven (St Johnstone & Scotland)
Hugh Forde (Glenavon & Northern Ireland)
Mike Greenwood (Bishop Auckland & England)

Forwards
Jim Lewis (Walthamstow Avenue & England)
Bobby Brown (Barnet & England)
Les Brown (Dulwich Hamlet & England)
Hugh Lindsay (Kingstonian & England)
Roy Sleap (Barnet & England)
Arnold Coates (Evenwood Town & England)
Hunter Devine (Queen's Park & Scotland)
Paddy Hasty (Tooting & Mitcham & Northern Ireland)
Terry Howard (Hendon & England)
Hubert Barr (Ballymena & Northern Ireland)

COMPETITIVE FIXTURES

London Olympic Games – 1908

First round
20-10-1908 .... Great Britain vs Sweden, White City 12-1
GB team: Bailey (Leicester Fosse), Corbett (Birmingham), Smith (Oxford City); Hunt (Wolverhampton Wanderers), Chapman (South Nottingham), Hawkes (Luton Town), Berry (Oxford University), Woodward (Tottenham Hotspur, captain), Stapley (Glossop), Purnell (Clapton), Hardman (Northern Nomads). Reserves: Daffern (Depot Battalion Royal Engineers), Porter (Northern Nomads). Scorers: Purnell 4, Woodward 2, Hawkes 2, Stapley 2, Berry, Chapman. Attendance: 2,000.

Semi-final
22-10-1908 ....Great Britain vs The Netherlands, White City 4-0
GB team: Bailey (Leicester Fosse), Corbett (Birmingham), Smith (Oxford City), Hunt (Wolverhampton Wanderers), Chapman (South Nottingham), Hawkes (Luton Town), Berry (Oxford University), Woodward (Tottenham Hotspur, captain), Stapley (Glossop), Purnell (Clapton), Hardman (Northern Nomads). Scorers: Stapley 4. Attendance: 3,000.

Final
24-10-1908 ....Great Britain vs Denmark, White City................ 2-0
GB team: Bailey (Leicester Fosse), Corbett (Birmingham), Smith (Oxford City), Hunt (Wolverhampton Wanderers), Chapman (South Nottingham), Hawkes (Luton Town), Berry (Oxford University), Woodward (Tottenham Hotspur, captain), Stapley (Glossop), Purnell (Clapton), Hardman (Northern Nomads). Scorers: Chapman, Woodward. Attendance; 6,000.

Stockholm Olympic Games – 1912

First round
30-06-1912 ....Great Britain vs Hungary, Stockholm 7-0
GB team: Brebner (Northern Nomads), Burn (London Caledonians), Knight (Portsmouth), Littlewort (Glossop), Hanney (Reading), Dines (Ilford), Berry (Oxford City), Woodward (Chelsea), Walden (Bradford City), Hoare (Glossop), Sharpe (Derby County). Scorers: Walden 6, Woodward. Attendance: 8,000.

Semi-final
02-07-1912 .... Great Britain vs Finland, Stockholm 4-0
GB team: Brebner (Northern Nomads), Burn (London Caledonians), Knight (Portsmouth), Littlewort (Glossop), Stamper (Stockton), Dines (Ilford), Wright (Hull City), Woodward (Chelsea), Walden (Bradford City), Hoare (Glossop), Sharpe (Derby County). Scorers: Walden 2, Sharpe, Woodward. Attendance: 4,000.

Final
04-07-1912 .... Great Britain vs Denmark, Stockholm 4-2
GB team: Brebner (Northern Nomads), Burn (London Caledonians), Knight (Portsmouth), McWhirter (Bromley), Littlewort (Glossop), Dines (Ilford), Berry (Oxford City), Woodward (Chelsea), Walden (Bradford City), Hoare (Glossop), Sharpe (Derby County). Scorers: Hoare 2, Walden, Berry. Attendance: 25,000.

Antwerp Olympic Games – 1920

First round
29-08-1920 .... Great Britain vs Norway, Antwerp 0-2
GB team: Mitchell (Manchester University & England), Gates (London Caledonians & England), Knight (Portsmouth & England, captain), Hunt (Corinthians & England), Atkinson (Bishop Auckland & England), Harbridge (Reading & England), Nicholas (Corinthians & Wales), Hardinge (Cambridge University & England), Prince (Royal Army Medical Corps & England), Sloley (Corinthians & England), Hegan (Corinthians & England). Attendance: 5,000.

First round

06-08-1936 .... **Great Britain vs China, Berlin** **2-0**

GB team: Hill (Yorkshire Amateurs & England), Holmes (Ilford & England), Fulton (Belfast Celtic & Northern Ireland), Gardiner (Queen's Park & Scotland), Joy (Casuals & England, captain), Pettit (Corinthians & England), Crawford (Queen's Park & Scotland), Kyle (Queen's Park & Scotland), Dodds (Queen's Park & Scotland), Edelston (Wimbledon & England), Finch (Barnet & England). Scorers: Dodds, Finch. Attendance: 9,000.

Quarter-final

08-08-1936 .... **Poland vs Great Britain, Berlin** **5-4**

GB team: Hill (Yorkshire Amateurs & England), Holmes (Ilford & England), Fulton (Belfast Celtic & Northern Ireland), Gardiner (Queen's Park & Scotland), Joy (Casuals & England, captain), Sutcliffe (Corinthians & England), Crawford (Queen's Park & Scotland), Shearer (Corinthians & England), Clements (Casuals & England), Riley (Casuals & England), Finch (Barnet & England). Scorers: Shearer 2, Clements, Joy. Attendance: 11,000.

London Olympic Games – 1948

First round

31-07-48 .... Great Britain vs The Netherlands, Arsenal ...... 4-3 (aet)
GB team: Simpson (Queen's Park & Scotland), Neale (Walton & Hersham & England), Manning (Troedyrhiw & Wales), McBain (Queen's Park & Scotland), Lee (Chester & England), Fright (Bromley & England), Hopper (Bromley & England), Hardisty (Bishop Auckland & England, captain), McIlvenny (Bradford Park Avenue & England), Kelleher (Barnet & Northern Ireland), Kippax (Burnley & England). Scorers: Hardisty, McBain, Kelleher, McIlvenny. Attendance: 21,000.

Second round

05-08-1948 ....Great Britain vs France, Craven Cottage 1-0
GB team: McAlinden (Belfast Celtic & Northern Ireland), Neale (Walton & Hersham & England), McColl (Queen's Park & Scotland), Lee (Chester & England), Fright (Bromley & England), Donovan (Pembroke Borough & Wales), Hardisty (Bishop Auckland & England, captain), McIlvenny (Bradford Park Avenue & England), Kelleher (Barnet & Northern Ireland), Kippax (Burnley & England). Scorer: Hardisty. Attendance: Not known.

Semi-final

11-08-1948 .... Great Britain vs Yugoslavia, Wembley 1-3
GB team: McAlinden (Belfast Celtic & Northern Ireland), Neale (Walton & Hersham & England), McColl (Queen's Park & Scotland), McBain (Queen's Park & Scotland), Lee (Chester & England), Fright (Bromley & England), Donovan (Pembroke Borough & Wales), Hardisty (Bishop Auckland & England, captain), Kelleher (Barnet & Northern Ireland), Kippax (Burnley & England). Attendance: 40,000. Scorer:Donovan.

Bronze medal play-off

13-08-1948 .... Great Britain vs Denmark, Wembley 3-5
GB team: Simpson (Queen's Park & Scotland), Neale (Walton & Hersham & England), Carmichael (Queen's Park & Scotland), Hardisty (Bishop Auckland & England, captain), Lee (Chester & England), Fright (Bromley & England), Boyd (Queen's Park & Scotland), Aitken (Queen's Park & Scotland), McIlvenny (Bradford Park Avenue & England), Rawlings (Enfield & England), Amor (Reading & England). Scorers: Hardisty, Aitken, Amor. Attendance: 5,000.

Preliminary round

16-07-1952 .... Great Britain vs Luxembourg, Helsinki ....3-5 (aet)
GB team: Bennett (Southall & England), Stewart (Queen's Park & Scotland), Stratton (Walthamstow Avenue & England), Topp (Hendon & England), Fuller (Bromley & England, captain), Saunders (Walthamstow Avenue & England), Hardisty (Bishop Auckland & England), Noble (Leytonstone & England), Lewis (Walthamstow Avenue & England), Slater (Brentford & England), Robb (Finchley & England). Goals: Robb, Slater, Lewis. Attendance: 3,656.

Melbourne Olympic Games – 1956

Qualifying match – first leg

22-10-1955 .... Bulgaria vs Great Britain, Sofia 2-0
GB team: Pinner (Cambridge University), Beardsley (Hendon), Farrer (Walthamstow Avenue), Hardisty (Bishop Auckland, captain), Prince (Walthamstow Avenue), Dodkins (Ilford), Littlejohn (Bournemouth & Boscombe Athletic), Jeffrey (Doncaster Rovers), Lewis (Chelsea), O'Connell (Chelsea), Neil (Portsmouth). Reserves: Sharratt (Bishop Auckland), Cross (Ilford), Stoker (Sutton United), Lewin (Bishop Auckland). Attendance: 45,000.

Qualifying match – second leg

12-05-1956 .... Great Britain vs Bulgaria, Wembley 3-3
GB team: Pinner (Cambridge University), Alexander (Corinthian-Casuals), Farrer (Walthamstow Avenue, captain), Topp (Hendon), Prince (Walthamstow Avenue), Dodkins (Ilford), Lewis (Chelsea), Hardisty (Bishop Auckland), Laybourne (Corinthian-Casuals), Bromilow (Southport), Twissell (Plymouth Argyle). Reserves: Robinson (Brentford), Lewin (Bishop Auckland). Attendance: 28,000. Scorers: Hardisty 2, Lewis. (Bulgaria win 5-3 on aggregate. GB qualify after withdrawals)

First round

26-11-1956 .... Great Britain vs Thailand, Melbourne 9-0
GB team: Sharratt (Bishop Auckland), Stoker (Sutton United), Farrer (Walthamstow Avenue), Topp (Hendon, captain), Prince (Walthamstow Avenue), Dodkins (Ilford), Lewis (Chelsea), Hardisty (Bishop Auckland), Laybourne (Corinthian-Casuals), Bromilow (Southport), Twissell (Plymouth Argyle). Scorers: Laybourne 3, Bromilow 2, Twissell 2, Topp, Lewis. Attendance: Not known.

Second round

30-11-1956 ....Bulgaria vs Great Britain, Melbourne 6-1
GB team: Sharratt (Bishop Auckland), Stoker (Sutton United), Farrer (Walthamstow Avenue), Topp (Hendon, captain), Prince (Walthamstow Avenue), Dodkins (Ilford), Lewis (Chelsea), Lewin (Bishop Auckland), Laybourne (Corinthian-Casuals), Bromilow (Southport), Twissell (Plymouth Argyle). Scorer: Lewis. Attendance: Not known.

Qualifying group

21-11-1959 ... Great Britain vs Republic of Ireland, Brighton.......... 3-2
GB team: Pinner (Queens Park Rangers & England), Gardener (Crook Town & England), Thompson (Stockton & England), Sleap (Barnet & England), D'Arcy (Barnet & England), Greenwood (Bishop Auckland & England, captain), R. Brown (Barnet & England), Ward (Northampton Town & England), Hasty (Tooting & Mitcham & Northern Ireland), Roberts (Tooting & Mitcham & Wales), Devine (Queen's Park & Scotland).Reserves: M. Crook (Milford United & Wales), W Neil (Airdrieonians & Scotland), P. Neil (Corinthian-Casuals & England), Forde (Glenavon & Northern Ireland), Fogg (Southend United & England). Scorers: Hasty 2, Devine. Attendance: 7,800.

13-03-1960 .... Republic of Ireland vs Great Britain, Dublin 1-3
GB team: Pinner (RAF, Queens Park Rangers & England), Holt (Queen's Park & Scotland), Thompson (Stockton & England), Sleap (Barnet & England), L. Brown (Bishop Auckland & England), Greenwood (Bishop Auckland & England, captain), Lewis (Walthamstow Avenue & England), Harding (Barnet & England), R. Brown (Barnet & England), Ward (Northampton Town & England), Coates (Evenwood Town & England). Reserves: Wakefield (Corinthian-Casuals & England), Neil (Airdrieonians & Scotland), Forde (Glenavon & Northern Ireland). Scorers: Coates, R. Brown, Harding. Attendance: 19,000.

02-04-1960 .... The Netherlands vs Great Britain, Zwolle 1-5
GB team: Pinner (RAF, Queens Park Rangers & England), Holt (Queen's Park & Scotland), Thompson (Stockton & England), Sleap (Barnet & England), L. Brown (Bishop Auckland & England), Greenwood (Bishop Auckland & England, captain), Lewis (Walthamstow Avenue & England), Barr (Ballymena & Northern Ireland), R. Brown (Barnet & England), Lindsay (Kingstonian & England), Coates (Evenwood Town & England). Reserves: Wakefield (Corinthian-Casuals & England), Neil (Airdrieonians & Scotland), L Brown (Dulwich Hamlet & England), Devine (Queen's Park & Scotland). Scorers: Lewis 3, R. Brown, Lindsay. Attendance: 9,000.

13-04-1960 .... Great Britain vs The Netherlands, Tottenham 2-2
GB Team: Pinner (RAF, Queens Park Rangers & England), Holt (Queen's Park & Scotland), Thompson (Stockton & England), Sleap (Barnet & England), L. Brown (Bishop Auckland & England), D'Arcy (Barnet & England, captain), Lewis (Walthamstow Avenue & England), Barr (Ballymena & Northern Ireland), R. Brown (Barnet & England), Lindsay (Kingstonian & England), Coates (Evenwood Town & England). Scorers: R. Brown, Lewis. Attendance: 3,950.

Olympic Games finals – Group 2
26-08-1960 .... Great Britain vs Brazil, Leghorn 3-4
GB team: Pinner (RAF, Queens Park Rangers & England), Holt (Queen's Park & Scotland), Thompson (Stockton & England), McKinven (St Johnstone & Scotland), L. Brown (Bishop Auckland & England), Sleap (Barnet & England), Lewis (Walthamstow Avenue & England), Hasty (Tooting & Mitcham & Northern Ireland), R. Brown (Barnet & England), Lindsay (Kingstonian & England), Devine (Queen's Park & Scotland). Scorers: R. Brown 2, Lewis. Attendance: 25,000.

29-08-1960 ....Great Britain vs Italy, Rome 2-2
GB team: Pinner (RAF, Queens Park Rangers & England), Holt (Queen's Park & Scotland), Neil (Airdriconians & Scotland), McKinven (St Johnstone & Scotland), L. Brown (Bishop Auckland & England), Sleap (Barnet & England), Lewis (Walthamstow Avenue & England), Hasty (Tooting & Mitcham & Northern Ireland), R. Brown (Barnet & England), Lindsay (Kingstonian & England), Devine (Queen's Park). Scorers: R. Brown, Hasty. Attendance: 60,000.

01-09-1960 .... Great Britain vs Formosa (Taiwan), Grosseto........... 3-2
GB team: Pinner (RAF, Queens Park Rangers & England), Greenwood (Bishop Auckland & England), Holt (Queen's Park & Scotland), McKinven (St Johnstone & Scotland), L. Brown (Bishop Auckland & England), Forde (Glenavon & Northern Ireland), Lewis (Walthamstow Avenue & England), Hasty (Tooting & Mitcham & Northern Ireland), R. Brown (Barnet & England), Lindsay (Kingstonian & England), Howard (Hendon & England). Scorers: R. Brown 2, Hasty. Attendance: 100.

First qualifying round

09-09-1963 .... Iceland vs Great Britain, Reykjavik 0-6
GB team: Pinner (Leyton Orient & England), J. Martin (Wimbledon & England), Law (Wimbledon & England), Ashworth (Wealdstone & England), Neil (Queen's Park & Scotland), Lindsay (Wealdstone & England), Townsend (Wealdstone & England), Candey (Maidstone & England), B. Martin (Wimbledon & England), Lawrence (Enfield & England), Harvey (Walthamstow Avenue & England). Substitutes: Shaw (Walthamstow Avenue & England), Quail (Hendon & Northern Ireland), Ardrey (Wimbledon & England). Scorers: Martin 2, Lindsay 2, Candey, Harvey. Attendance: 7,500.

14-09-1963 .... Great Britain vs Iceland, Wimbledon 4-0
(Great Britain win 10-0 on aggregate)
GB team: Pinner (Leyton Orient & England), J. Martin (Wimbledon & England, captain), Ashworth (Wealdstone & England), Ardrey (Wimbledon & England), Neil (Queen's Park & Scotland), Lindsay (Wealdstone & England), Townsend (Wealdstone & England), Candey (Maidstone & England), B. Martin (Wimbledon & England), Lawrence (Enfield & England), Harvey (Walthamstow Avenue & England). Reserves: Shaw (Walthamstow Avenue & England), Quail (Hendon & Northern Ireland), King (Hitchin & England). Scorers: Lawrence 3, Harvey. Attendance: 3,500.

Second qualifying round

12-02-1963 .... Great Britain vs Greece, Chelsea 2-1
GB team: Kennedy (Distillery & Northern Ireland), J. Martin (Wimbledon & England, captain), Neil (Queen's Park & Scotland), D'Arcy (Enfield & England), Ashworth (Wealdstone & England), Townsend (Wealdstone & England), Campbell (Distillery & Northern Ireland), Buchanan (Queen's Park & Scotland), Lawrence (Enfield & England), Quail (Hendon & Northern Ireland), Harvey (Walthamstow Avenue & England). Reserves: Griffin (Leytonstone & England), Pollatschek (Queen's Park & Scotland), Casey (Barnet & Wales), Lindsay (Wealdstone & England). Scorers: Lawrence, Buchanan. Attendance: 4,175.

08-04-1964 .... **Greece vs Great Britain, Athens** **4-1**

(Greece win 5-3 on aggregate)

GB team: Kennedy (Distillery & Northern Ireland), J. Martin (Wimbledon & England, captain), Robertson (Tooting & Mitcham & England), Ashworth (Wealdstone & England), Law (Wimbledon), Townsend (Wealdstone & England), Campbell (Distillery & Northern Ireland), Buchanan (Queen's Park & Scotland), Lindsay (Wealdstone & England), Quail (Hendon & Northern Ireland), Harvey (Walthamstow Avenue & England). Substitute: Gamblin (Sutton United & England) for Martin on 80 minutes. Reserves: Griffin (Leytonstone & England), Casey (Barnet & Wales), Johnston (Glenavon & Northern Ireland), Gamblin (Sutton United & England). Scorer: Buchanan. Attendance: 20,000.

First qualifying round
Bye

Second qualifying round
25-10-1967 ...... West Germany vs Great Britain, Augsburg............. 0-2
GB team: Swannell (Hendon & England), Gamblin (Sutton & England), Powell (Sutton & England), Robertson (Tooting & Mitcham & England), Hogwood (Hendon & England), Andrews (Leytonstone & England), Sleap (Hendon & England), Townsend (Wealdstone & England), Haider (Hendon & England), Pritchard (Sutton & England), Gray (Leytonstone & England). Unused subs: Shippey (Oxford City & England), Deadman (Barking & England). Scorers: Hogwood, Pritchard. Attendance: 8,000.

08-11-1967 .... Great Britain vs West Germany, Hendon.............. 0-1
(Great Britain win 2-1 on aggregate)
GB team: Swannell (Hendon & England), Gamblin (Sutton & England), Powell (Sutton & England), Robertson (Tooting & Mitcham & England), Hogwood (Hendon & England), Andrews (Leytonstone & England), Sleap (Hendon & England), Townsend (Wealdstone & England), Haider (Hendon & England), Gray (Leytonstone), Horseman (Wycombe & England). Subs: Deadman (Barking & England) for Horseman. Unused sub: Shippey (Oxford City & England). Attendance: 4,002.

Third qualifying round
27-03-1968 .... Spain vs Great Britain, Sabadell 1-0
GB team: Swannell (Hendon & England), Robertson (Tooting & Mitcham & England), Powell (Sutton & England), Moxon (Enfield & England), Reid (Enfield & England), Sleap (Hendon & England), Pritchard (Sutton & England), Cumming (Partick Thistle & Scotland), Hay (Queen's Park & Scotland), Greene (Dagenham & England), Gowling (Manchester United & England). Unused subs: Shippey (Oxford City & England), Townsend (Wealdstone & England), Haider (Hendon & England), Andrews (Leytonstone & England), Gray (Leytonstone & England). Attendance: 20,000.

10-04-1968 ....Great Britain vs Spain, White City 0-0
(Spain win 1-0 on aggregate)

GB team: Swannell (Hendon & England), Robertson (Tooting & Mitcham & England), Powell (Sutton & England), Moxon (Enfield & England), Reid (Enfield & England), Hay (Queen's Park & Scotland), Sleap (Hendon & England), Cumming (Partick Thistle & Scotland), Greene (Dagenham & England), Gowling (Manchester United & England), Pritchard (Sutton & England). Subs: Haider (Hendon & England) for Greene, Gray (Leytonstone & England) for Pritchard. Attendance: 23,000.

Munich Olympic Games – 1972

First round
24-03-1971 .... Great Britain vs Bulgaria, Wembley 1-0
GB team: Swannell (Hendon & England), Fuschillo (Wycombe & England), Currie (Albion Rovers & Scotland), Powell (Wycombe & England), Gamblin (Leatherhead & England), Payne (Enfield & England), Day (Slough & England), Haider (Hendon & England), Hardcastle (Skelmersdale & England), Gray (Enfield & England), Adams (Slough & England). Substitute: Pritchard (Wycombe & England for Hardcastle). Unused: Williams (Enfield & England), Reid (Slough & England), Deadman (Hendon & England), Savage (Distillery & Northern Ireland). Scorer: Adams. Attendance: 2,200.

05-05-1971 .... Bulgaria vs Great Britain, Sofia 5-0
(Bulgaria win 5-1 on aggregate)
GB team: Swannell (Hendon & England), Fuschillo (Wycombe & England), Delaney (Wycombe & England), Powell (Wycombe & England), Gamblin (Leatherhead & England), Payne (Enfield & England), Day (Slough & England), Haider (Hendon & England), Clements (Skelmersdale & England), Gray (Enfield & England), Adams (Slough & England). Substitutes: Pritchard (Wycombe & England) for Clements, Mellows (Wycombe & England) for Adams. Unused: Millington (Rhyl & Wales), Reid (Slough & England), Deadman (Hendon & England). Attendance: 30,000.

OTHER FIXTURES

Over the years, the teams that represented Great Britain in the Olympics played a large number of non-competitive matches. Statistical records of some games vary as the text makes clear. As a result, some of the results below may not be entirely reliable. NK = Not known.

12 August 1936	vs Germany	Berlin	1-4
28 February 1948	vs Queen's Park	Portsmouth	4-1
20 June 1948	vs The Netherlands	Amsterdam	1-2
10 July 1948	vs Basle XI	Basle	2-3
25 July 1948	vs France	Nantes	3-2
14 May 1952	vs West Germany	Dusseldorf	NK
19 May 1952	vs West Germany	Nuremburg	NK
22 July 1952	vs Kuopio	Kuopio	6-0
25 July 1952	vs Greece Olympic XI	Hämeenlinna	2-4
29 July 1952	vs Norway	Oslo	2-2
1 August 1952	vs Vaasa XI	Vaasa	3-4
13 September 1955	vs Arsenal	Highbury	1-2
26 September 1955	vs West Ham United	Upton Park	1-6
8 October 1955	vs North. & South. Counties	B. Auckland	NK
10 October 1955	vs Queens Park Rangers	Loftus Road	1-2
17 October 1955	vs Luton Town	Luton	1-2
25 August 1956	vs Copenhagen Combination	Copenhagen	1-5
26 September 1956	vs Uganda	Ilford	1-2
8 October 1956	vs Luton Town	Luton	3-2
13 October 1956	vs Isthmian & Athenian Lgs	Wimbledon	3-1
22 October 1956	vs Newcastle United	Newcastle	0-5
27 October 1956	vs Combined Universities	Kingston	4-1
5 November 1956	vs Arsenal	Highbury	2-3
?? November 1956	vs Australia	Melbourne	3-1
10 December 1956	vs Singapore	Singapore	4-0
13 December 1956	vs Malaya	K. Lumpur	6-2
16 December 1956	vs Burma	Rangoon	2-0
10 October 1959	vs Caribbean	Ipswich	7-2

19 October 1959	vs Burnley	Turf Moor	5-1
16 November 1959	vs Chelsea	St Bridge	4-1
25 January 1960	vs Arsenal	Highbury	4-0
8 February 1960	vs West Ham United	Upton Park	5-2
22 February 1960	vs Northampton Town	Timkin Gr	2-2
14 May 1960	vs Italy	Brescia	5-1
13 August 1960	vs Watford	Uxbridge	2-1
17 August 1963	vs Queens Park Rangers	Loftus Road	1-1
16 December 1963	vs Chelsea	Stamford Br	3-3
20 January 1964	vs Chelsea	Stamford Br	1-1
3 February 1964	vs Manchester United	Old Trafford	0-4
24 February 1964	vs Tottenham Hotspur	White Hart La	0-1
27 February 1964	vs Aston Villa	Villa Park	2-2
2 March 1964	vs Coventry City	Highfield Rd	1-0
8 August 1967	vs Sweden U-23	Gothenburg	1-0
11 August 1967	vs Republic of Ireland	Dalymount Pk	2-0
14 August 1967	vs Iceland	Reykjavik	3-0
4 September 1967	vs Chelsea	Stamford Br	1-0
11 September 1967	vs Charlton Athletic	The Valley	1-1
9 October 1967	vs Celtic	Lesser Hamp	0-4
16 October 1967	vs Watford	Vicarage Rd	2-3
29 January 1968	vs Oxford United	Manor Grd	0-1
12 February 1968	vs Watford	Vicarage Rd	1-0
26 February 1968	vs Charlton Athletic	The Valley	2-3
8 March 1968	vs Republic of Ireland	Vicarage Rd	6-0
18 March 1968	vs Arsenal	Highbury	3-2
3 November 1970	vs Watford	Vicarage Rd	4-2
9 November 1970	vs Oxford United	Manor Grd	1-0
14 December 1970	vs Derby County	Baseball Grd	1-0
11 January 1971	vs Reading	Elm Park	2-0
25 January 1971	vs Irish FA	Windsor Pk	3-3
8 February 1971	vs Preston North End	Deepdale	0-0
22 February 1971	vs Southampton	The Dell	4-0
15 March 1971	vs Sheffield Wednesday	Hillsborough	1-3
19 April 1971	vs Sunderland	Roker Park	3-2
26 April 1971	vs Motherwell	Fir Park	1-0

THE LIST OF AMATEUR LASTS

Last amateur to captain England in a full international – Alfred "Baishe" Bower (Corinthians & Chelsea) vs Wales, 1927

Last amateur to play for England in the Home International championship – Stan Earle (West Ham United) vs Northern Ireland, 1927

Last amateur to play for England – Bernard Joy (Arsenal & Casuals) vs Belgium, 1936

Last amateur in an England squad – Peter Kippax (Burnley & Yorkshire Amateurs) vs France, 1947

Last amateur to win the first division title – Jim Lewis & Seamus O'Connell (Chelsea), 1954/55

Last amateur to play in an FA Cup Final – Bill Slater (Blackpool), 1951

Last amateur to play in the English first division – Nigel Clough (Nottingham Forest), 1984

Last amateur to play for Scotland – Jimmy Crawford & Bob Gillespie (both Queen's Park) vs England, 1936

Last amateur to play for Wales – Len Evans (Birmingham C) vs N Ireland, 1933

Last amateur to play for Northern Ireland – Ernie McLeary (Cliftonville) vs Wales, 1955

Last amateur club to win the FA Cup – Old Etonians, 1882

Last amateur club to win the Scottish Cup – Queen's Park, 1893

Last FA Amateur Cup winners – Bishop's Stortford, 1974

REFERENCES/FURTHER READING

This book is not intended to provide a detailed history of individual Olympic tournaments but simply to tell the story of the British footballing efforts. Many excellent books have been written covering individual Olympic Games, particularly on Berlin in 1936 and London in 1948. Suggested titles are included below along with a number of other sources that have been helpful in the writing of this book.

BOOKS

Ackland, Joss 'I Must Be In There Somewhere' (Hodder & Stoughton 1989)

Adamthwaite, Alan – 'Never Again: The Story of Bob Hardisty, England's Greatest Amateur Footballer' (Jacqal Press)

Adamthwaite, Alan - 'Glory Days – The Golden Age of Bishop Auckland' (Parrs Wood Press 2005)

Alaway, RB - 'Football All Round The World' (Newservice 1948)

Baker, Kenneth - 'The 1908 Olympics: The first London Games' (Sports Books 2008)

Ballheimer, David & Lush, Peter - 'Hendon Football Club – The First 100 Years' (London League Publications 2008)

Bonde, Hans - 'Football with The Foe' (University Press of Southern Denmark 2008)

Brodie, Malcolm - '100 years of Irish Football' (Blackstaff 1980)

Buchanan, Ian - 'British Olympians' (Guinness 1992)

Busby, Matt - 'My Story As Told To David R Jack' (Souvenir Press, 1957)

Cavallini, Rob - 'A Casual Affair: a History of the Casuals Football Club' by Rob (Dog'N'Duck 2009)

Cavallini, Rob - 'Around the World in 95 Games: the Amazing Story of the Islington Corinthians 1937/38 World Tour' (Dog'N'Duck Publications 2008)

Cavallini, Rob - 'Play Up Corinth – A History of the Corinthian Football Club' (Stadia 2007)

Collins, Mick – 'All Round Genius: The Unknown Story of Britain's Greatest Sportsman' (Aurum 2006)

Creek, FNS - 'A History of the Corinthian Football Club' (Longmans, Green & Co 1933)

Eisenberg, Christine (ed) et al - 'One Hundred Years of Football – The Fifa Centennial Book' (Weidenfeld & Nicolson 2004)

Fabian, AH (ed) - 'Association Football Volume Four' (Caxton 1960)

Finch, Lester - 'Playing for Fun' (DL Finch 1988)

Glanville, Brian - 'England Managers: the Toughest Job in Football' (Headline 2007)

Golesworthy, Maurice (ed) 'The Encyclopaedia of Association Football' (Richard Hale 1963)

Gowarzewski, Andrzej - 'Encyklopedia pilkarska Fuji, volume 2: "Bialo-czerwoni. Dzieje reprezentacji Polski(1)' (Wydawnictwo GiA: Katowice 1991) Translated by Dariusz Kurowski

Grayson, Edward - 'Corinthians and Cricketers: And Towards a New Sporting Era' (Yore Publications 1996)

Hapgood, Eddie - 'Football Ambassador' (Sporting Handbooks 1945)

Hampton, Janie - 'The Austerity Olympics - When the Games Came To London in 1948' (Aurum 2008)

Hilton, Christopher - 'Hitler's Olympics – the 1936 Berlin Olympic Games (Sutton Publishing 2006)

Hugman, Barry J (ed) - 'Football League Players Records 1946-1992' (TW 1992)

Imlach, Gary - 'My Father & Other Working Class Football Heroes' (Yellow Jersey 2006)

Inglis, Simon - 'League Football and the men who made it' (Willow 1988)

Jacobs, Norman - 'Vivian Woodward: Football's Gentleman' (Tempus 2005)

James, Blair - 'Queen's Park Football Club' (Stadia 2007)

Jose, Colin - 'The Complete Results & Line-ups of the Olympic Football Tournaments 1900-2004' (Soccer Books 2004)

Joyce, Michael - 'Football League players' records 1888-1939' (Soccerdata 2004)

Melekoglou, Mendrinos at al - 'Ethniki Ellados: Poreia Mesa Sto Xrono'. Translation by Spyros Chatzigiannis

Member, Old - 'The Story of the London Caledonians Football Club' Yore Publications

Moynihan, John - 'The Soccer Syndrome – From the Primeval Forties' (Sportspages 1966)

Porter, Dilwyn et al 'Amateurs & Professionals in Postwar British Sport' by (Routledge 2000)

Riddoch, Andrew & Kemp, John - 'When The Whistle Blows: The Story of the Footballers Battalion in the Great War' (JH Haynes 2008)

Rous, Sir Stanley - 'Football Worlds - A lifetime in Sport' (Faber & Faber 1978)

Samuel, Richard - 'The Complete FA Amateur Cup Results Book' (Soccer Books 2003)

Scott, Les - 'End to End Stuff' (Bantam Press 2008)

Sharpe, Ivan - 'Forty years in Football' (Hutchinson's 1952)

Shearwood, Ken - 'Pegasus: The famous Oxford & Cambridge soccer side of the fifties' (Oxford Illustrated Press 1975)

Simpson, Ronnie - 'Sure it's a Grand Old Team' (Souvenir Press 1967)

Taylor, Matthew - 'The Association Football Game: a History of British Football' (Pearson 2008)

Taylor, DJ - 'On the Corinthian Spirit: The Decline of Amateurism in Sport' (Yellow Jersey 2006)

Various - 'Stanley Matthews Football Album 1949' (Marks & Spencer 1949)

Wakefield, Brian - 'Middlesex Wanderers – Sporting Ambassadors for a Hundred years 1905-2005' (Replay Publishing 2005)

Walker, Murray - 'Unless I'm very much mistaken' (HarperCollinsWillow 2002)

Walters, Guy - 'Berlin Games: How Hitler Stole The Olympic Dream' (John Murray 2007)

Walvin, James - 'The People's Game – the Social History of British Football' (Allen Lane 1975)

Wilson, Bob - 'Bob Wilson My Autobiography: Behind the Network' (Hodder & Stoughton 2003)

JOURNALS/NEWSPAPERS

Athletics News

'British Played Excessively Hard' *Hamburger Abendblatt* October 26 1967, translated by Paul Joyce

Charles Buchan's Football Monthly

Chums

County Times

'China's First Olympic Adventure – the Footballers' Story of 1936' by Vincent Heywood. Soccer History Summer 2008, Issue 20

Evening News

Evening Standard

'Revenge of the Crouch End Vampires: The AFA, the FA and English Football's Great Split, 1907-14' by Dilwyn Porter (Sport in History, Vol 26, No 3 December 2006)

'Kicking around – England's amateurs' by Brian Glanville (Sportstar Weekly, Volume 30, Number 41 13-10-2007)

'No trip to Mexico' *Hamburger Abendblatt November 9* 1967, translated by Paul Joyce

'One Hundred Years of Servitude: Contractual Conflict in English Professional Football before Bosman' by David McArdle, LLB, PhD, Research Fellow, Sports Law and Management, De Montfort University (Web Journal of Current Legal Issues 2000)

Suomen Urheilulehti (17 July 1952) and *Hufvudstadsbladet (*17 July 1952) translated by Vesa Tikander of the Sports Library of Finland

Guardian/Observer archive

'The Early Development of Association Football in South Wales, 1890-1906' by Brian Lile & David Farmer (Transactions of the Honourable Society of Cymrudorrion, 1894)

'The New Craze'; Football and Society in North East Wales, c. 1870-90' by Martin Johnes & Ian Garland (The Welsh History Review, Vol 22, No 2, December 2004)

The Non League Paper

The Olympic News (1912, published by Idrottsbladet, Nordiskt Idrottslif and Tidnin for Idrott, translated by Martin Alsiö)

Northern Echo

The Scotsman archive

The Times archive

'The Reverend Kenneth Hunt - Wolves Footballing Parson' by Patrick A. Quirke (Wolverhampton History & Heritage Society)

'The Significance of the Olympic Soccer Tournament from 1908-1928' by Joel Rookwood & Charles Buckley (Journal of Olympic History, Volume 15)

'The World Game Downunder' edited by Bill Murray & Roy Hay (ASSH 2006)

'Walter Watty Corbett: Birmingham's Olympic Gold Medallist' *Soccer History* Summer 2002, Issue 2

'When East met West' by Paul Joyce, *When Saturday Comes* August 2009

World Soccer

World Sports

WEBSITES

11v11.com – The Association of Football Statisticians

BBC

Bygonederbyshire.co.uk

Carthusianfootball.com

Charlesbuchansfootballmonthly.com

Chesterfield-fc.co.uk

Corinthian-Casuals.com

Cricketeurope.com

Cricketeurope4.net

Cwgc.org – Commonwealth War Graves Commission

Englandfootballonline.com

Fchd.btinternet.co.uk – Football Club History Database

Hayesfc.net

Historybarnetfc.co.uk

Iffhs.de - International Football Federation of Football History &
Statistics

Nifootball.blogspot.com

Ozfootball.net

Swanseacity.net

Wfda.co.uk – Welsh Football Data Archive

INTERVIEWS

The following players and their families were interviewed during the course of the research for this book. The Olympic tournaments that they were involved with are in brackets.

The family of Charles Wreford-Brown (1920 & 1936)
The family of Frederick Nicholas (1920)
The family of Dick Sloley (1920)
Sir Daniel & Richard Pettit (1936)
The family of Terry Huddle (1936)
Angus Carmichael (1948)
The family of Bob Hardisty (1948-56)
The family of Dougie McBain (1948)
The family of Gwyn Manning (1948)
The family of Jack Neale (1948)
Jack Rawlings (1948)
Stan Charlton (1952)
Derek Grierson (1952)
Bill Holmes (1952)
Jim Lewis (1952-60)
Maurice Masters (1952)
Bill Slater (1952)
Dexter Adams (1956)
Jimmy Coates (1956)
Tommy Farrer (1956)
Derek Lewin (1956)
Roy Littlejohn (1956)
Pat Neil (1956)
Mike Pinner (1956-64)
The family of Stan Prince (1956)
Terry Robinson (1956)
Micky Stewart (1956)
Roy Hay (Australia, 1956)
Hubert Barr (1960)

Bobby Brown (1960)

Les Brown (1960)

Arnold Coates (1960)

Alf D'Arcy (1968-64)

Hunter Devine (1960)

Hugh Forde (1960)

Dougie Grant (1960)

Mike Greenwood (1960)

Hugh Lindsay (1960)

Bill Neil (1960-68)

Tommy Thompson (1960)

Jimmy Quail (1960-64)

David Roberts (1960)

Brian Wakefield (1960)

John Ashworth (1964)

Peter Buchanan (1964)

Terry Casey (1964)

Derek Gamblin (1964-72)

Dario Gradi (1964)

Charles Hughes (1964-72)

John Kennedy (1964)

Tommy Lawrence (1964)

John Martin (1964)

Charlie & Maggie Townsend (1964-68)

George Cumming (1968)

Rod Haider (1968-72)

Millar Hay (1968)

John Swannell (1968-72)

Andy Williams (1968)

Rainer Zobel (West Germany, 1968)

Bill Currie (1972)

John Delaney (1972)

Paul Fuschillo (1972)

Peter Hardcastle (1972)

Stoyan Jordanov (Bulgaria, 1972)

Grenville Millington (1972)